Fly Fishing Kentucky

Your Guide to Tackle, Techniques and the Best Trout Waters in the State

Written by
J. Thomas Schrodt and Valerie L. Askren

Illustrations by
Christine Schrodt

With detailed recommendations for:

Fly, Tackle and Gear
Basic Casting Skills
Special Fishing Techniques
Reading Water to Find Trout
Matching the Hatch and Fly Selection

Fly Fishing Kentucky
Your Guide to Tackle, Techniques and
the Best Trout Waters in the State

Published by 42nd Parallel, LLC. While not fly fishing, we can be reached at FlyFishingKY@gmail.com. If you need to snail mail us, you can send any correspondence to 233 Kingsway Drive, Lexington, KY 40502.

Printed in the United States of America. First edition.
Lightning Source Inc. (a division of Ingram)
1246 Heil Quaker Blvd.
La Vergne, TN 37086

All photos are by the authors, with the exception of those noted below. Jason Neuswanger, aka The Troutnut, took the insect and larvae pictures. Jason is a phenomenal photographer and entomologist at heart. He also shares our passion for fly fishing and can be reached at Jason@troutnut.com. Kathleen Rose took the front cover photo at Bark Camp Creek and permitted us to use her talents (Thanks Kathy!). We also threw in a few illustrations of various trout species from US Fish and Wildlife that are in the public domain (easily found through Wikimedia Commons.) Tom, Valerie, Jason and Kathy retain all rights to their photos.

The pencil drawingss were created by Christine Schrodt, who retains all rights to her artwork. She also did the two Cumberland River Tailwater maps. Christine, you're awesome!

ISBN 978-0-692-22962-0

Front Cover: Bark Camp Creek. Photo taken by Kathleen Rose.
Back Cover: Cumberland River Tailwater. Photo taken by an author.

Scattered Light

By a boulder
Pool, dark and deep.
They swim about
Out of sight.

Overhead Mayfly spinners
Wings like shattered glass.
One flutters, touches down
Then loses flight.

Surface breaks
Scatters light.
See it now
A rainbow trout.

Contents

PART I Tackle and Techniques

- Fly Rods
- Fly Reels
- Fly and Other Lines

- On-the-Water Toolbox
- Personal Gear

- Rod and Reel Assembly
- Line Assembly
- At the End of the Day

- Basic Casting
- Special Fishing Techniques
- Hooking, Playing, Landing and Releasing Fish

- Trout species
- Stocking

- Life Cycles of Aquatic Insects
- Matching the Hatch: What to Feed the Hungry Trout
- Artificials: Fly Selection for Kentucky Trout
- Dream Box of Flies

PART II The Best Trout Waters in Kentucky

Select Illustrations, Charts and Photographs

Acknowledgments

Two years ago, while trout fishing together, we came to realize that no one had ever published a book completely devoted to fly fishing for trout in Kentucky. That may have been because trout fishing in the state had for so long taken a backseat to fishing for bass, crappie and those monster strippers. We resolved to remedy that and took on the daunting challenge of writing a book, more or less a compendium, covering every aspect of the sport from tackle selection to the best streams, lakes and tailwaters to fish for trout.

It became apparent to us that we needed some help, so we conferred with staff at Kentucky's Department of Fish and Wildlife Resources (KDFWR), talked with current and former fly shop owners, and compared notes with other expert trout anglers and fishing guides. Their reviews, comments and suggestions were invaluable, kept us on the right track throughout the writing process and proved invaluable in preparing the manuscript for publication. If we have failed the writing challenge it is our fault, but we have given it our best effort. Now we wish to acknowledge their help.

Dave Dreves, fisheries research biologist, and Jeff Ross, assistant director of fisheries, at KDFWR adeptly answered our numerous questions regarding the Lake Cumberland tailwater, the new Hatchery Creek and the state's trout stocking program. We are fortunate to have such committed professionals working diligently for the environment and the people of Kentucky, and we kindly thank them for their patience and competence.

We are indebted to both Gene Slusher and Alan Creech, of The Lexington Angler, and Fred Pfister, former owner of The Sporting Tradition, for their insightful reviews and suggestions for those parts of the manuscript that deal with the selection and assembly of tackle, and its use on trout waters. Each of these men are savvy fly anglers and exceedingly generous in sharing their knowledge of the sport.

Our book received several great suggestions and an indispensible review from a good friend and very knowledgeable fishing guide on the Cumberland River tailwater, Hagan Wonn. Hagan knows the river, knows what flies to use, and knows where to use them. But make no mistake—he still has some secrets he is reluctant to share— but we are immensely grateful for his insights.

Our special thanks to Dave Baker, editor of "Kentucky Afield" for writing the prologue and giving a concise history of the state's trout program. Dave worked relentlessly with the historian at the U.S. Fish and Wildlife Service to track the date of the first stocking of trout in Kentucky: one that surprised us and will surprise you.

We quickly realized that the book would be incomplete without illustrations depicting various casting techniques, knot illustrations and maps. Christine Schrodt, Tom's daughter-in-law and professional graphic designer, graciously agreed to prepare all the illustrations for the book. We requested a simple, but painstakingly accurate, approach and she came through for us. A heartfelt thanks to Christine.

Jason Neuswanger, who is completing his PhD in biology at the University of Alaska, sent us a set of colorful, close-up pictures of aquatic insects common to our trout waters. His knowledge of entomology and photography are simply amazing and his pictures are stunning. Jason's generosity and commitment to the environment is commendable.

Finally, we extend our gratitude to Robbie Clark for his copy editing skills and introducing us to that first cold mug of Dunkel. We appreciate his eye for detail and hope to have him fly fishing soon.

Foremost, we thank our spouses, Rita and Ben, who have graciously put up with our absences from our normal home lives while we spent hours on our computers, days fishing and taking pictures, and Thursday mornings in protracted discussions meshing our writings, while sitting in a glassed-in cubicle of the Lexington public library. It has been fun.

A portion of the proceeds from the sale of this book will go to the
Bluegrass Chapter of Trout Unlimited, Trout in the Classroom project.
For more information, please see troutintheclassroom.org

Prologue

Kentucky anglers have been in love with the hard-fighting trout ever since the U.S. Fisheries Department began their stocking efforts in the state. But those efforts began earlier than most of us realize. In 1881, 5,000 eggs of "California Mountain Trout" were provided to William Griffin and five years later Kentucky received its first shipment of lake trout. The first adult (one-year-old) rainbow and brook trout (2,500 and 500 fish, respectively) were stocked in Kentucky in 1888.

The next wave of stocking took place in the early twentieth century. Historians report that 77,000 rainbow and 7,800 brook trout were stocked in Kentucky from 1912-17, but the numbers plummeted to only 1,250 rainbow trout by 1931, two years into The Great Depression.

Biologists mark 1952 as the start of Kentucky's modern trout era. The completion of Wolf Creek Dam on the Cumberland River created a tailwater-habitat necessary for trout to live year round—a rarity in Kentucky. Rainbow trout were later stocked in both the Cumberland and Herrington Lake tailwaters. It was the discovery of healthy trout 60 miles downstream of Wolf Creek Dam, and in the Kentucky River downstream of Herrington in the 1950s that convinced KDFWR Commissioner Minor Clark and Fisheries Director Bernie Carter to stock trout in several other streams. Their three-year experiment not only proved trout could thrive, but it launched an expansion of Kentucky's trout stocking program.

However, getting trout to Kentucky required an arduous 354-mile drive through the mountains to the federal hatchery in Wytheville, VA. Carter and Clark went to Washington in 1962 and convinced Kentucky's congressional delegation to support a federal hatchery in the state. Thirteen years later, Wolf Creek National Fish Hatchery became operational.

Kentucky's modern trout program had a major advocate in Jim Axon, the energetic assistant director of fisheries. "Ax," as he was known around the department, expanded the number of stocked streams and pioneered Kentucky's wintertime catch-and-release seasons for trout before his retirement in 2005. Today, approximately one million rainbow, brown and brook trout are stocked in dozens of streams, lakes and tailwaters throughout the state.

Much effort has gone into Kentucky's trout program over the generations. "Fly Fishing Kentucky" is a fitting capstone to those efforts.

Dave Baker
Editor, Kentucky Afield

Preface

Fly fishing for trout in Kentucky keeps getting better. And it's our goal to get more of you outside enjoying the beautiful angling opportunities that abound across the state. But where are the best places to fly fish? What's the hatch? Do I use an olive Wooly Bugger or a tan Caddisfly? How do I high-stick next to that boulder? We hope to answer these questions and lots more.

This book was written with the novice, intermediate and advanced fly fishermen in mind. Quite frankly, this book has something for everyone. The new angler will walk away with valuable insights on what rods and reels work best in Kentucky waters; what to wear on the creek or river; a primer on basic knot tying for tackle assembly; and knowledge of the rules and regulations that govern this sport.

The intermediate fly angler will see improvements in his or her casting abilities; detailed recommendations on fly selection; and directions to dozens of creek, river and tailwater access points. Advanced anglers will get an enhanced understanding of the life cycles of aquatic insects and matching the hatch; tips on reading water; and the best places to fly fish for those elusive, trophy trout.

Dreaming of fly fishing, some of us only think of legendary western streams such as the Gallatin River in Montana or the North Umpqua in Oregon. Others head east to the Battenkill or Falling Springs or south to a scenic mountain stream in the Smokies. But not all of us are retired, not all of us are independently wealthy, and not all of us have the time to take a week off just to fish.

So let's continue to dream globally and fish locally when we can. Endowed with prolific karst geology, Kentucky has an amazing array of spring-fed creeks all across the state. Browns, rainbows and brookies can and do thrive in the cool waters of the Bluegrass. Throw in an icy cold tailwater or two, and one of those trout could be dangling from your line.

The Kentucky Department of Fish and Wildlife remains committed to running an excellent stocking program, developing and maintaining access points, and improving fish habitats. Importantly, many of the state's stocking efforts rely on federal support and the money generated by trout permits and fishing licenses works hard to further these efforts.

So let's get out and wet a line!

"All the romance of trout fishing exists in the mind of the angler and is in no way shared by the fish." Harold F. Blaisdell

Introduction

What defines the "best" trout streams, lakes and tailwaters in Kentucky? That's a fair question and deserves an honest answer. Basically, we think the best trout streams are where we can catch fish. But we also like to catch fish in picturesque areas where we won't get our vehicle towed and our windows shot out. So our general definition of "best" trout waters would include items such as:

- Top-rated water quality and trout habitat
- Good stocking levels
- Scenic vistas
- Public access with convenient parking

Sometimes we don't like to drive too far, so we threw in a few trout streams that get fished out pretty quickly, but are within close proximity to a large number of local anglers. Conversely, there are a few absolutely gorgeous mountain streams found deep in the Daniel Boone National Forest (DBNF) where the trout are pretty wily, and we frequently go home empty-handed. But that peaceful day in the woods was worth every empty cast we made.

What kind of trout do we find in the Bluegrass state? Rainbows, brown and brook trout. There are some holdover waters, but most of Kentucky's streams must be re-stocked periodically throughout the year. Consequently, most of the larger trout are found in our lakes and tailwaters where water temperatures remain cold year round. Several of our spring-fed creeks provide year-round trout habitat, and in these the trout may be a little hefty and a little wiser than we are.

The book is pretty logically laid out, but if you choose, skip around here and there depending on your interests and skill level. In Part I, we cover all sorts of things that you might need to know before you get out on the water. The first three chapters discuss the equipment and personal gear needed for fly fishing in Kentucky. Chapter 4 covers basic casting and a selection of special fishing techniques written for both the beginners who want to keep their fly line out of their hair and for the more advanced anglers who may need a few tips on mending their fly lines.

Chapter 5 discusses the various trout species found in Kentucky, how to identify them and the stocking procedures used in the state, given its waters have little trout reproduction. Understanding stocking levels and timing is critical to your success out on the water.

Even advanced anglers will want to take a look at Chapter 6, which covers the life cycles of aquatic insects and what trout like to feast upon. Again, we focus on the insects found in Kentucky waters that are meaningful to a trout's diet. While this chapter can be a slightly academic, spending a little time understanding metamorphosis will go a long way in helping you to select the ideal fly to use when, where and how.

Chapter 7 discusses the anatomy of a waterway and the implications for finding fish—which is pretty esoteric for many anglers. But your ability to read water is crucial to your success in landing that big one. If 10 percent of the water holds 90 percent of the trout, you'll want to learn to locate those fish so you can dangle that irresistible fly right before their noses.

But everyone has to follow the rules. Check out Chapter 8 to learn about the rules and laws governing fly fishing in Kentucky. Ignorance will not get you off the hook.

Finally, the heart of the book is in Part II. This section is divided into five regions across the state, with the top five to seven trout streams, lakes and tailwaters identified in each region. For each entry we discuss the ecosystem of the waterway; applicable stockings and regulations; specific recommendations for fishing those waters; and detailed directions to the access points.

Finally, don't forget to glance through the appendices to find other information sources, gear companies and guide services. We also include a glossary and an index for your convenience, because we all forget things.

Importantly, regulations, stocking levels and equipment costs discussed in this book were current at the time of publication in 2014, but are likely to change from year to year. We have provided a multitude of resources to help you keep abreast of these changes.

So pull up a chair and enjoy yourself as you read your way to becoming a better angler. Then grab your waders and your dream box of flies and head to your favorite stream or tailwater for a day of fly fishing fun.

Part I: Tackle and Techniques

We confess—it was hard to write a one-book-fits-all treatise on fly fishing in Kentucky. Some of you are new to the sport, while others can triple-haul us to shame. You might not have any fishing gear. Or you might have been tying flies since you were 9. Consequently, we hope that the first half of this book truly has something for everyone. Beginners might want to read each section in depth, while others might prefer to use the first eight chapters for reference or refining their knowledge base.

Importantly, in each chapter we worked diligently to tailor our recommendations to Kentucky trout waters. Whether we're talking rod and line choices, casting techniques, or fly selection, we constantly focus on what works best in the Bluegrass State. So pull up a comfy seat and beverage of choice as we take you through everything you need to get out on the water for a day of fly fishing in Kentucky.

CDC BWO Emerger

FLY FISHING KENTUCKY

"My biggest worry is that when I am dead and gone, my wife will sell my fishing gear for what I said I paid for it!" Koos Brandt

Chapter 1: Tackle Selection

Tackle selection is just as important to the fly angler as it is to the Green Bay Packers. But selecting fly fishing equipment can be a bewildering experience. From rods to reels to fly line, Kentucky anglers will want to optimize their tackle choices for fishing the waters of the Bluegrass State, while minimizing the amount of money they spend. But, where should you begin?

If you are new to the sport, we recommend seeking advice from an experienced fly fishing friend who sees you as an ally rather than a competitor out on the water. In other words, they *want* to give you good advice. However, while your buddy in Wyoming may know a few tricks and give you several recommendations on fly rods, someone in your local Trout Unlimited chapter may be a more valuable source of local information.

Alternately, you can visit a reputable fly shop, whose clerks will be more than happy to discuss the choice of a balanced set of equipment, and one that matches your skill level and the waters you propose to fish. If you ask, he may even give you a few free casting lessons or let you know about local classes that are being offered. But before you walk in cold and ask an expert for some of their time, it's a good idea to familiarize yourself with some of the terminology and basic pieces of equipment. That's where a good book or Internet search can help immensely.

The purpose of this chapter is to help you wade through the overabundance of choices between various rods, reels and lines. Our focus here is to identify the types of equipment that a fly angler might need for fishing in Kentucky. As noted above, fly fishing for trout in the Bluegrass can be a very different experience from fly fishing for salmon in Alaska or saltwater fishing in the Florida Keys. Therefore, your gear selection might vary significantly.

As is usually the case, cost and quality are directly related and great care should be exercised in the purchase of equipment. Remember, expensive gear should be left for the pros and not for the greenhorn anglers. However, you do want to make wise decisions in selecting the appropriate equipment at that sweet spot where quality and value intersect. Appendix 1 lists some local fly shops, outdoors sporting goods stores and national catalog companies that sell fly fishing equipment and apparel. We have provided estimated gear prices that were accurate at the time of publication, but of course these costs may change over time.

Fly Rods

The most important piece of tackle you might purchase is the fly rod. For some of you, choosing a good fly rod is like choosing a good spouse—you'll want to check out a few different options and carefully consider your final decision. Key parameters to consider include composition; rod length and weight; the number of pieces the rod "breaks down" into; and flex speed or rod action. Let's look at each of these decisions individually.

Rod Composition and Elasticity

Fly rods can be made of bamboo, fiberglass, graphite, or more recently composites containing graphite and fiberglass or graphite and boron. Anglers discuss the merits of each with the same fervor as truck aficionados argue Chevy versus Ford; or geeks bemoan PCs versus Macs. Mostly it's up to personal preference. But there is some general agreement on the advantages and disadvantages of different fly rod materials.

High-quality bamboo rods have that endearing old-school nostalgia, but are hard to find, tend to be heavier and unforgiving, and are more expensive to buy. These are the kinds of rod you might want to inherit one day, but not necessarily purchase outright. Fiberglass rods are a bit lighter than bamboo, heavier and less sensitive than graphite, and are best suited for trolling where sensitivity is not an issue. Graphite rods are rightly in vogue because they have excellent stiffness-to-weight ratios, perform admirably and are moderately priced.

Let's talk a little about that stiffness-to-weight ratio: the "Modulus of Elasticity." A graphite fly rod blank with a high modulus of elasticity has thin walls and the desirable traits of being both lightweight and having excellent sensitivity. The downsides to such rods are they are more sensitive to angler abuse rather than the abuse of a big, fighting fish, and they can be more costly. The newer fly rods made of composites containing boron are touted by manufacturers as being the ultimate piece of equipment, but are extremely expensive and best left for avid anglers and pros. The novice fly angler might want to start with a graphite rod and in a few years ask for a boron-composite for a birthday gift.

Rod Length

Fly rods usually come in lengths from 6-10 feet, but in far-off Scotland a gillie (a Scottish name for fishing guide) might have their client using a 15-foot, two-handed fly rod. But what's best for Kentucky waters? As expected, in tight situations (for instance narrow banks with low over-hanging tree branches), a shorter rod length might be more useful. For most small streams in Kentucky, many of which are only 20-25 feet wide, a rod length of 8 foot would be a reasonable choice. Then again, a 9-foot rod can be thrust through the branches of overhanging bushes to reach that rising trout. And for anglers who like to use high-sticking techniques (discussed in Chapter 4) in these narrow streams, a 9-foot fiberglass rod works very well.

However, in general, longer rod lengths are best suited for large, wide-open expanses of water and experienced anglers. If you think you might spend most of your time fishing tailwaters and lakes, and have developed some good basic casting skills, an 8-1/2 or 9-foot rod would be a good choice for many novice to intermediate anglers for use in all conditions.

Rod Weight, Flex Speed and Pieces

The next rod decision concerns "weight." Fly rods vary from 1- to 15-weight, with 1 being the lightest. This weight has nothing to do with the actual weight of the rod, but rather the fly line that the rod was designed to accommodate (although actual rod weights are sometimes specified.) Typically, the longer the rod, the heavier the rod weight will be, but this is not always the case. In general, you will want to match your rod weight to your line weight. This will be discussed in more detail below, but let's finish with our rod discussion first.

An important characteristic of a rod is what is known as its flex speed or action: slow, medium or fast. A fast rod will flex in the top one-third of the rod and produce a tight loop in the hands of experts; whereas a slow rod will flex across three-fourths of the rod, and will usually result in a more open loop of fly line and will fit the need of the beginner or occasional fisherman. A fast-tipped flex rod should probably be left to the advanced intermediate or expert angler. A medium or moderate flex rod that helps keep the line in control is a good choice for aggressive beginners. Cheap fly rods that are overly stiff and unbalanced will greatly hinder the development of casting skills and should be avoided.

Fly rods come in two, three, four or five pieces. If you expect to hike, back-pack or air travel, a four- or five-piece rod may be a good choice. The segments easily fit together, with male and female ends. Be sure to line the line guides up correctly. Most rods will come with tubes to transport and store them when not in use. Using a tube or carrying case for your rod is a good practice, in order to protect your investment and soon-to-be best friend.

Reel Seats and Grips

At the thickest or butt end of the rod will be the "reel seat" where the reel is mounted onto the rod. While most reel seats are up-locking, some are down-locking, have sliding rings, cork to save weight, and may use stabilized wood to prevent swelling and provide balance to the rod. A small "hook keeper" is usually located just in front of the reel seat.

Nearly all rods have cork grips, but all cork is not the same. Some cork is peppered with holes and several manufacturers try to hide these holes with filler. When the filler eventually falls out, the holey cork makes for poor gripping. So look for quality cork that is smooth and free of filler. Some of the cheapest rods found at the large box stores have a rubber foam material covering the grip. You should avoid the latter.

Rod Weight, Length and Hook Ratios

Above the cork grip, on the butt end of the rod or on its reel seat, you may see inscribed something like: *8-1/2 ft./5 wt/ mid flex/4-1/2 oz*, indicating that this a 8-1/2 foot long rod, designed for a 5-weight fly line, built with a medium flex, and has an actual weight of four and one-half ounces. This rod in two, three or four pieces is ideal for fishing for trout and bass in Kentucky's streams, tailwaters and lakes with flies of most sizes.

The following table shows the recommended rods of various weights and lengths for different fish species and fly sizes. The smallest fly hook would be a #32 and the largest hook would be an 8/0. So in general, the lighter rods are shorter in length and use smaller fly sizes to catch smaller fish. Conversely, longer rods tend to be heavier and are used with larger fly sizes to catch larger fish. Casting a heavy 4/0 fly off a 1-weight rod could break it.

Recommended Rod Weights and Lengths by Fish Species and Fly Size				
Rod Weight / Length	1-2 / 6 to 9 ft	3-7 / 7 to 10 ft	8-11 / 8-1/2 to 10 ft	12-15 / 9 to 10 ft
Species of Fish	Brook Trout, Bream, Bluegill, Crappie	Trout, Small and Large- Mouth Bass	Trout, Carp, Steelhead, Salmon, Gar, Musky, Striped Bass	Tarpon, Tuna, Sturgeon
Fly (Hook) Est. Sizes	#32 - 10	#24 - 1/0	#6 - 2/0	#2/0 - 8/0

A novice should be able to purchase a very nice graphite rod for fishing Kentucky's waters for between $150-200. A $40 rod is just that—a $40 rod; it simply won't work and you'll be wasting your money.

Fly Reels

Once you've decided on your rod, it's time to consider your reel purchase. The primary use of the reel is to hold the fly line and to assist in playing a fish. The best and most expensive fresh water reels are carefully crafted from aluminum bar stock, fitted with disc drags, and supplied with instructions for an easy switch for left-handed fishermen. Nearly equally good reels are machined from aluminum and usually have all the characteristics of the very expensive reels. When buying a reel, check to see that the spool works freely and it fits the rod seat securely. You can buy a good freshwater reel for about $100 or a little less.

But, given the choice of spending money on either the rod or on the reel, put your hard-earned dollars into the rod. Novice fly fishing enthusiasts may also choose to purchase a good rod and reel combo from a reputable company. This should set you back about $250 or less.

Importantly, fly reels should be weighted to match the rod. Reels are usually marked with weights stamped into the metal such as "5/6" meaning that it is suitable for either a 5- or 6-weight rod or fly line. Alternately, if you have either a 4- or 5-weight rod, you will want to purchase a 4/5-weight reel. If purchasing a rod and reel combo, the manufacturer will have taken care of that decision for you, as they will come pre-matched.

Most fly reels come with either a disc or pawl drag that can be adjusted by turning a small button on the side of the reel. The pawl drag must be set to accommodate right- or left-handedness, as explained in the directions that come with the reel. Usually, a clockwise turn of the button will increase the drag (tension on the escaping line), and conversely a counterclockwise turn will loosen the drag. By pulling on the line you can test the tension of the drag you set. Set it too tight and a fish might break your tippet (the end of your line). Set it too loose and a big fish may run out lots of loose line and then spit out the fly. It is a judgment call, because we are forced to guess the strength of the fish we might hook.

Most reels do not come preloaded with line. Extra spools of line may be purchased for some reels, so that different kinds of fly lines can be used on the same reel. This is a very cost-effective way for the angler to multi-purpose the same reel case with multiple spools loaded with different lines to be used under various fishing conditions.

Now that you have selected your rod and reel, what type of fly line should you be using? No one really knows, but it would be a fair to say that there are hundreds, if not thousands, of different kinds of fly line. Confusing? You bet! But, let's take a closer look at line choices in the following section.

Fly and other Lines

Unlike traditional spinning reels that use a single clear (e.g. monofilament) fishing line, fly reels are typically loaded with four different kinds of line–backing, fly, leader and tippet. These four lines are loaded and tied consecutively onto the fly reel in the order given. Take a look at the illustration below to get a better sense of the order of each line loaded onto the reel. Chapter 3 discusses in detail how to tie all these lines together using the appropriate knots. But for now let's examine the function of each of these lines individually, starting with the line first loaded onto the reel—backing.

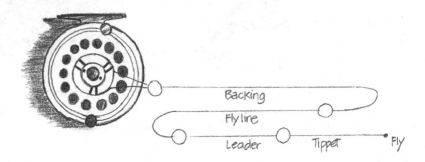

Backing

Backing must first be spooled onto the reel and then attached to the fly line. Most fly lines from 30-40 yards in length and the backing allows you to fill a reel with less expensive line, and provide for long runs of fighting fish. Many anglers will never even see the backing unless they are playing a very strong fish and have a lot of line out. Backing is frequently made of braided Dacron with a breaking strength of 20 pounds or more. The yards added to the reel should be sufficient to bring the end of the fly line to nearly the top of the reel, which usually requires about 30-40 yards of backing for a medium-sized reel. The backing is relatively inexpensive: no more than several dollars for 100 yards.

Fly Line

The fly line is that line you can typically see when you cast. Unlike the leader and tippet lines (discussed below), the fly line actually has some heft or weight to it, allowing the angler to put his or her lightweight fly into the desired part of the stream or lake.

Again, let's consider traditional spinning rods loaded with monofilament line. Spin casting uses the weight of the artificial lure or some type of lead weight attached above the bait to add heft to the fishing line to enable the angler to cast effectively.

But with fly fishing, you might be trying to cast an artificial fly weighing less than a gram, 30 yards across a stream in breezy conditions. The intent is to quietly drop that fly on the surface, without scaring that elusive trout looking up from the deep. Without any weight on the end of your line, it is the fly line itself that allows you to place the fly where you want it. In essence the fly is just along for the ride as the kinetic energy released from the rod propels the fly line and its rider to the intended target.

One would think that the selection of fly line for a fly rod of a specified weight would be simple. Unfortunately, it can be confusing. Fly lines come in an assortment of designs, lengths, colors, materials, tapers and, of course, costs. Each of these choices can alter the performance of the fly line, as some seem to cast better, some are stiffer, some turn over better, and so on. Manufacturers are always touting that their lines are slicker than their competitors and result in greater casting distances. Of course this creates strong disagreements between fly fishermen, which can be great fun for the experts and frustrating for the novice.

If you purchase a line from a reputable fly shop, the clerk will help you in selecting the correct line for your rod and fishing intentions. The following discussion should help you in selecting fly line as your skills improve and you start to fish other types of waters.

In general, fly lines have a solid core and are thickly coated with a polymer, usually polyvinylchloride. This polymer may have air bubbles in it to make the line float or be weighted to make it sink at a specified rate of descent.

When you pick up a box containing a spool of fly line you may see something similar to the following: *Orange, 90' WF-5-F.* This tells you that the line is colored orange, is 90 feet long, has a weight forward taper for a 5-weight rod, and will float. All of these parameters add up to a good choice for the beginning fly fisherman using a 5-weight rod who is likely to be fishing Kentucky's streams, shallow lakes and tailwaters and using dry flies and nymphs. Let's look at these parameters in more detail.

There are ongoing discussions as to whether the color of the line is important. Do bright colors such as yellow or orange scare the fish? Notably all lines, regardless of color, cast a shadow that fish can see. But with a 9-foot length of leader it is unlikely they can detect the fly line if the leader is straight out. If seeing the line on the water is no problem for you, pick a green or gray line color to be on the safe side. Like other fish, trout can be quite skittish and camouflaging your gear and your intentions can be advantageous.

After the yardage, the spool will tell you if the line is Weight Forward (WF), Double Taper (DT), Level Taper (LT), Sink Tip (ST), or one of several other specialty lines. Basically, these descriptors tell you how the weight of the line is distributed across the line itself from one end to the other. The sophistication of fly line construction helps explain its relative high-cost, as compared to simple monofilament fishing line.

Weight Forward (WF)—This line has additional weight and thickness in the first 30 feet (closest to the fly end of the line). The remainder of the line is lighter and thinner and easily runs through the guides for longer casts. A WF line is the most common fly line and great for a beginner.

Double Taper (DT)—The front and back of this line are identical with a uniform 12-foot taper of diameter and weight to each tip. The center portion remains a constant weight and width. This line is suited for medium to short casts, but has the benefit that it can be turned around when one end wears out.

Level Taper (LT)—This is a level floating line that has no taper because it has a uniform thickness and weight along its entire length. While these lines are the least expensive, they are difficult to cast and cause great problems for the beginner.

Sink Tip (ST)—The first section of this line (which can range from three to 30 feet) is weighted so that it sinks. Generally speaking, sink tip length is a function of river depth, speed and personal preference. The rest of the line floats. These lines are used to get wet flies near the bottom quickly or to get streamers below the surface for line stripping.

Specialty Lines—These include shooting tapers and lines with specialized sink rates measured in inches per second. Really heavy sink (and sink tip) lines are rated in grains, e.g. 500 or 600 grains.

Because of the wide variation of fly lines, as suggested above, many anglers carry multiple spools loaded with various fly lines. These extra spools can be purchased and used for the better reel cases. This allows relatively quick changes of line for use in different fishing circumstances. This is particularly true for a waterway such as the Cumberland River tailwater where a wide-variety of fishing techniques might come into play as the angler changes from nymph fishing to streamer fishing.

Leader and Tippet

To the end of the fly line, one attaches two other kinds of line known as a tapered leader and some tippet. Each fly line will have about six inches of uniform line in front of the taper. This provides ample line for installing several changes of leader before cutting into the taper. Some line manufacturers will specify on the box the species of fish for which they think the line is most suited, e.g. bass, trout, pike, steelhead, etc. It's always a good idea to carry extra leaders of different ratings and tippet materials with you while out fishing for the day.

      The purpose of the leader is two-fold. First, your fly line is highly visible to fish underwater, whereas the leader is nearly invisible. Second, the leader is a bit more durable than the tippet, which is the last line attached to your reel and what is actually tied to the fly. Usually about 7-9 feet of leader is required and 12-36 inches of tippet.

Leaders come in lengths of 7-15 feet and in tip diameters from .003 inches (8X, with test strength of about 1.2 pounds) and up to .010 inches (1X, with test strength of about 12 pounds). The leaders are uniformly tapered, the butt being much thicker than the tip. Tippet material typically comes in spools of 30 yards and in the same diameter and approximate test strengths as the leaders. A chart describing leader ratings by diameter, strength and estimated fly sizes follows:

Leader Ratings, Parameters and Estimated Fly Sizes							
X-rating	8X	7X	6X	5X	4X	3X	2X
Diameter (inches)	.003	.004	.005	.006	.007	.008	.009
Est. Strength (pounds)	1.2	2.2	3.8	5.2	6.2	7.8	9.0
Est. Fly Size #	14-32	10-28	6-22	6-20	1/0-18	2/0-14	4/0-10

Several factors will influence the selection of leader and tippet length and size, but the most important of these are the kind, size and wariness of the fish sought and the clarity of the water. For small brook trout in very clear water one might select a 7-1/2 foot 8X leader and 18 inches of tippet in size 8X. On the other hand if one were fishing for 16-inch brown trout using nymphs under an indicator in murky water, one might want to use a 6X leader of 9 feet and 12-18 inches of 6X tippet.

For years most leaders sold in the U.S. were made of clear monofilament nylon, but with the advent of fluorocarbon, a material that is nearly invisible to the fish, the best leaders and tippet material are made with fluorocarbon. It is important to note that fluorocarbon is slightly heavier than nylon and should be avoided when fishing with dry flies. However it is advantageous to use fluorocarbon with wet flies.

Fluorocarbon is also more expensive than the nylon and therefore its use is sometimes confined only to the tippet. Tapered 7-1/2 to 9-foot nylon leaders in sizes 1X to 8X costs about $4 each, while those made of fluorocarbon will run you about $14. A 30-yard spool of nylon tippet material can be purchased for as little as $5, but be prepared to spend $14 for the same length in fluorocarbon.

In summary, the fly rod assembly is composed of the rod, reel, backing, fly line, leader and tippet. To this we add the fly and off we go fishing. But first we need some tools of the trade to assemble it all and catch those trophy fish.

"Even a fish wouldn't get into trouble if he kept his mouth shut. "
Author Unknown

Chapter 2: Tools and Gear Selection

As discussed in the last chapter, the choice of an appropriate rod and reel outfit is a crucial decision for the fly angler. This chapter continues our discussion of what to buy before heading out for a day of fishing and focuses on the selection of some of the tools and other personal gear required for a successful and comfortable day of fly angling. First, we'll make some suggestions regarding what pocket tools an angler might take on the water–a personal "tool box" so to speak or tools of the trade. Second, we'll take a look at other personal gear you might want to purchase (or you may already own), such as waders, boots, outdoors clothing, wading staff, sunglasses and the like. Our aim is not to make you look particularly fashionable, but to keep you warm (or cool) and dry while fishing your favorite stream or tailwater without spending a fortune.

On-the-Water Toolbox

Whether bank fishing or stream wading, many anglers like to keep a small set of tools within easy reach. The following items should be kept handy and make great stocking stuffers:

Forceps are used for removing hooks from the mouth of fish, holding flies while threading, and flattening barbs on hooks for barbless catch-and-release fishing. This handy tool runs less than $15, and comes in a variety of sizes, with locking handles, smooth or striated jaws, and curved or straight tips. If you have large hands, it may be worth scouting out a pair of forceps with extra large thumbholes.

Nippers (or snippets), similar to a pair of nail clippers, will snip fishing line with ease. Some models also have a small needle attached that can be used for clearing hook-eyes. These will run you less than $10.

Floatants are an essential part of dry fly casting when you want the fly to stay on the surface of the water. Typically a silicone product, floatant comes in a paste (rub on with your fingers); liquid gel or spray form (simply squirt a small amount on a knuckle and apply to the fly); or as a dry powder (add the fly to the small canister, shake several times, and remove the fly). Be careful not to add too much floatant, causing the hairs or hackles of the fly to stick together. A little goes a long way and prices generally run between $5-15.

Dessicants are used for cleaning flies after you have caught a fish (and let's hope you need to buy a lot of this stuff!) or after a dry fly has become waterlogged and floatant can no longer be effectively applied. Some products on the market serve as both floatants and dessicants in one. Dessicants typically run about $10.

Strike indicators are tied to the leader and help the angler know if a strike has taken place—if you can't feel the strike you may lose the fish. Indicators come in various types and each has their advantages and disadvantages. Most common for Kentucky fly fishing are yarn indicators, foams and plastic bobbers. *Yarn indicators* are easily tied onto the leader and can be either wool (which is naturally waterproof) or synthetic (treated with waterproofing). These indicators are good for water with relatively little current, and their neutral colors may be advantageous with skittish fish. *Foam indicators*, particularly the smaller pinch-on foam products, are extremely easy to attach to the leader and very buoyant. However, the larger foam indicators are much more difficult to cast, and the bright colors and large shadows tend to scare shy trout. *Plastic bobbers* float high in the water and are easily seen in fast-moving or choppy water. However, again their bright colors can spook the fish, particularly in clear, shallow water. For fly fishing a one or two centimeter bobber should be used to keep it hidden from the fish. Prices vary from cheap to inexpensive.

Adjustable indicators make it easy to change the position on the leader without having to re-tie your fly. For example, if fishing tailwaters using nymphs, using an adjustable indicator is preferred because as you go from shallow water to deeper water you will want to change the position of the indictor on the leader. One popular and effective style is a small (one inch or less) Styrofoam® indicator with a slit cut vertically through the slide (sometimes called a slot indicator). Simply remove the wood "pin," insert your leader into the slit, and then replace the pin. White and yellow are good colors to use since they are less visible to the fish below.

Fly line cleaners (or dressing) will help keep your fly line clean, supple and buoyant. However, before applying any product, wash your fly line in a bucket or sink of clean, warm water in which a few drops of mild soap (such as Ivory®) has been added. After soaking for one-half hour or so, start with one end and remove the line from the water by holding a clean cloth in one hand and running the line through with your other hand. This should remove most of the dirt that has accumulated on the line (either from the ground itself, or from fishing lakes and streams with a lot of algae or other microorganisms present). If your fly line still looks and feels dirty or gritty, you can use a specially designed product called fly line cleaner or dressing, or a simple silicon spray. These cleaners can add a layer of protection to your fly line by coating it with a surfactant, rendering the line more durable and slick in the water.

Landing nets are useful when you need one and only get in the way when you don't. Prices range from $10 (easily broken the first time) to $150 (for a hand-crafted net and knotless nylon construction). The telescoping handles are nice for storage or when reaching out over a muddy bank or the gunnel (gunwale, in old English) of a boat. Most anglers prefer a net constructed of rubber, polyester or another soft fiber; stiff nylon nets tend to be too rough and can damage the external coating of the trout which can kill the fish before it can be released. For most Kentucky stream fishing, a 14-16 inch net is sufficient.

Zingers, retractors, tie-ons...or whatever you want to call these gadgets, they are heaven's gift to the clumsy at heart. For about $5-10 apiece, this small contraption easily hooks onto your vest or pack, and connects to the tool of your choice by a heavyweight, retractable line. You can have one for each tool or some models have a large ring that serves more like a key chain (enabling you to attach several tools to the same gadget.)

Fly boxes (cases) are essential for keeping your growing collection of flies clean, well-organized and out of your hair. Beginning anglers may have one carefully selected box, while advanced fly fishers may have tens of those little boxes tucked here and there amongst their gear. The typical fly box will be relatively small; square or rectangular in shape; and shallow with rows of small slits or compartments to individually hold each fly. You can buy a decent box for $12-15, or a really nice waterproof one for $35. But be sure to get one that floats. As you amass more flies, you may find yourself categorizing your collection by type of fly, by a particular waterway, or by geographic region.

Emergency first-aid kits are only for those people whom "never get hurt" on the water. The kit may never be used, but a small collection of items could be worth their weight in gold. Of course, if you're out on a boat, the vessel should (legally) be fully equipped. And if you're bank fishing only a few yards from your vehicle, a first-aid kit might not be necessary. But if you're intending to spend four to eight hours wading a creek, be sure to pack some high-energy snacks, bottled water, lighter or waterproof matches, anti-bacterial ointment, a few band-aids, and some duct tape (useful for many things, including splinting body parts.) A little food, water and basic supplies can go a long way in warding off hypo- or hyperthermia.

Personal Gear

Having the right personal gear can make all the difference between a successful day out on the water and a fly fishing fiasco. This section takes a look at the advantages of using a vest versus a pack; the need for waders and wading boots; and the choice of clothing while fly fishing. Again, our intent is not to get you on the cover of an Orvis® catalog or break the bank, but to make your angling day as productive and comfortable as possible.

Vests Versus Chest and Lumbar Packs

Now that you've invested a lot of thought into assembling your "on-the-water tool-box", you'll want a place to keep all those tools handy and hopefully not at the bottom of the river. Traditional fly anglers have opted for fly fishing vests. Many of the newer vests on the market have all sorts of built-in retractors, pockets for various tools, and fly patches to keep those Wooly Buggers and Caddisflies nearby. A good vest can run you anywhere from $60-220.

Conventional canvas vests tend to be a bit too warm for many anglers in the heat of summer, but the newer mesh and other breathable fabric vests have eliminated that problem. Conversely, if you do most of your fishing on cool spring or fall days, a waxed cotton, polyester/cotton, or waterproof/breathable fabric might be a better choice. It is important to keep in mind when buying a vest that you buy a large enough size to accommodate whatever layers you will want to wear underneath it. The vest must be able to fit comfortably over all base layers, waders and jackets or raincoats you might be wearing. Some of these vests can also double as backpacks or creel bags, but you want to be sure that you have easy access to all of your tools, lines and flies while fishing. An added bonus of some vests is that many of them have built-in fleece-lined pocket warmers.

Another option for holding personal gear is a chest pack. The downside is that most chest packs don't hold as much gear as a vest does. The upside is that most chest packs keep you traveling light and some models have a small "table" built in (a supported flap, really) that you can use to help tie flies onto a tippet. They are definitely cooler than most vests, but again, it all depends on the time of year and conditions that you like to fish. Chest packs are in a similar price range as vests, but tend to be a tad cheaper.

A final choice is the lumbar pack, which attaches like a fanny pack, but can also be turned around and positioned on your belly. While lumbar packs give you more freedom of movement when casting, they also sit closer to the water line when wading. Lumbar packs are easily adjusted to a variety of clothing layers.
In making your purchase decision, several key questions you might want to ask yourself are: Are you expecting the vest to keep you warm or the pack to keep you cool? How many layers do you want to wear underneath? How much gear do you really want to take while on the water? Are you wade, bank, or boat fishing? Do you also like room for a water bottle and sandwich? The answers might help you determine which option is best for you.

Waders

Fly anglers who like to wade fish out into the current as it rushes over shoals or through deeper pools without getting wet typically use waders. While some models only reach thigh high, many anglers opt for waders that reach mid-chest. However, waders that reach chest-high can give the wading angler a false sense of security and encourage fishermen to literally get in over their heads. Another alternative is to wear waist-high wader "pants." Once again, this is personal preference. The whole idea here is to keep from getting wet, both from a comfort perspective and to avoid hypothermia which can quickly set in even if you're standing in cold water for only a few minutes. Alternately, if fishing from shore or a boat, waders typically aren't required.

If you are considering purchasing waders, you have several choices and price levels. Nylon waders are fairly inexpensive and some fabrics are 2- and 3-ply with stretch added. Even so, few nylon waders can really be considered waterproof because they tend to leak along their seams. Unfortunately, you may also end up sweating up a storm in these and still getting wet.

Waders made of neoprene (a family of synthetic rubbers), are waterproof and typically the warmest of all waders. Several models have fleece-lined pockets, which can be greatly appreciated in very cold water. However, neoprene has its drawbacks, and on warm, sunny days you may quickly overheat. Neoprene is also very vulnerable to the sun's ultraviolet (UV) radiation, which will cause the rubber to deteriorate and lose its waterproofness. You can get a good pair of neoprene waders for about $125.

The waterproof/breathable waders out on the market tend to be a trifle more expensive but frequently are the best choice for the fly angler. Gore-Tex® waders and other imitators have a multitude of different models out there and they really do work well. Even the seams of these waders have been taped to keep water from coming in. Although you'll still sweat some on a warm day, the breathability factor helps tremendously by allowing water molecules to escape (but act as one-way valves, by not letting water come in). While authentic Gore-Tex® waders can set you back $400-500, other manufacturers offer very similar fabrics and models for as low as $125 or less.

All waders are prone to develop seam leaks over time or holes from use. Frequently this damage can be repaired with patches and/or the use of Aquaseal®, a flexible waterproof glue.

Many waders have built in neoprene "booties" that are worn over socks. You can also buy waders with built-in wading boots. All of these are personal preference and may depend on the type of fishing you like to do. When trying on waders be sure to get a large enough size in which you can bend your legs and sit down comfortably. You will also want to have enough room both top and bottom in which to wear your base layers and perhaps even a jacket or raincoat.

One alternative to waders is to simply wear rubber boots. If you don't mind water occasionally coming in over the top, limiting how deep you wade out, and sweating profusely, this could be your least expensive option.

Wading Boots

Most wading boots are very similar to hiking boots in appearance, and serve a similar function–protecting your feet and providing stability over rough, uneven terrain. Wading boots frequently have "holes" to release water, since some water does enter the boot. However, the neoprene bootie mentioned above works to keep your feet dry and warm while wading. Finally, wading boots are much lighter in weight than hiking boots and are never made of leather.

Always try your wading boots on over the waders you will be using to ensure proper fit. A thin pair of smart wool or polypropylene socks under your neoprene booties will provide you with an extra layer of warmth and slightly more cushion from the taped toe seams of your booties. Last, it may be easier to put your wading boots on if you wet them first.

Wading boots tend to offer a choice of sole, namely rubber or felt. Rubber soles tend to have a track pattern similar to hiking boots and they will give you excellent durability over time and stability on uneven, rocky surfaces. Some anglers prefer felt soles for flat rock surfaces that can be coated with slippery moss or silt, commonly found in many Kentucky streams. One compromise that some manufacturers have come up with is a felt sole with rubber or metal studs, but these are not overly popular. However, some companies (Korker® footwear manufacturer, in particular) are now making wading boots with an interchangeable rubber to felt sole. The soles are relatively easy to switch out and it makes cleaning the felt soles much easier, as discussed below.

Importantly, anglers wearing felt soles should take good care to wash and bleach their boots after every fishing trip. Invasive species tend to cling to the surface of the felt and can be transported from one waterway to another. Four states have outlawed felt soled boots for this reason —Alaska, Maryland, Rhode Island and Vermont.

In warm weather and waters, many anglers opt for wet wading sandals. These sandals typically offer excellent rubber treads, secure straps, and an enclosed rubber rand across the front of the toe box. Water can easily flow out of the sandals, but on the flip side, gravel can sometimes lodge inside the shoe and under the foot bed. Of course you can also wear old tennis shoes.

Wading Staff

Some fly anglers have come to rely on a wading staff, similar to a hiking staff, to help them navigate swift currents. A good wading staff will run between $50-150; frequently is collapsible, but will sometimes be telescoping; and should always have a wristband. Some of the upper-end staffs tout magnetic tips for added stability, fly retrievers and high-quality cork handgrips.

Clothing

Since trout season in Kentucky typically begins in the cooler spring months and ends in late fall, staying warm and dry can be a challenge. The number one danger is hypothermia in which the core body temperature drops below 95°F, the rate typically required for basic human function. Characteristic symptoms include shivering; slurred speech; loss of coordination; mental confusion; and reduced heart rate, respiratory rate and blood pressure. Hypothermia can occur after even very brief periods of exposure to cold water and is very difficult to self-diagnose.

Obviously, the main way to avoid hypothermia is to stay warm and dry, and to consume plenty of fluids and high-energy snacks. In the section above we discussed the advantages of wearing waders and wading boots. What you wear under those layers is also important in avoiding hypothermia.

Anglers should begin with one or more base layers next to their skin. In cold or cool weather conditions, anglers should avoid wearing cotton and instead opt for materials such as polypropylene, fleece or lightweight wools. Some of the brand names you might see are Patagonia® Capilene, Smartwool® , Mountain Hardwear® and Icebreaker® , but there are lots of other good companies out there. Basically you want to avoid fabrics that absorb water (including body moisture), and wear clothes that dry quickly and have high warmth-to-weight ratios.

Over the base layer, choose one or more outer layers that provide warmth, and wind plus rain protection. The outer layer may be a heavier layer of fleece, topped with a lightweight Gore-Tex® or similar jacket. If wearing chest waders, be sure to cinch the belt tightly around your waist to prevent cold water from entering your waders should you take a dunking. Standing in cold water with constant wind exposure, as well as frequently getting your hands wet, can wear out even the toughest outdoorsmen. If you have the misfortune to fall into cold water, get to the shore quickly, replace your wet clothes with dry ones, drink plenty of fluids, eat a high-energy snack, and exercise to increase body heat.

On the other end of the spectrum, hyperthermia is an elevated body temperature that occurs when the body produces or absorbs more heat than it expends. By dressing in layers, you can more easily regulate your body temperature by removing layers as necessary.

Regardless of the time of the year, a good hat with a brim can be invaluable in keeping the sun and the rain off your face and out of your eyes. Some anglers are even using sun masks to minimize exposure.

And be sure to lather on that sunscreen 30 minutes before getting on the water, paying special attention to the tops of your hands, the back of your neck, ears and your face. Finally, some anglers try to wear fingerless gloves during extremely cold days, but that can also be a challenge.

Polarized sunglasses are a must. Again, we're not trying to make a fashion statement here, but are trying to provide good eye protection from UV rays, while enhancing your visibility out on the water. Unlike tinted sunglasses that simply reduce brightness, polarized glasses actually reduce glare and eye strain, allowing you to look at the surface of an object that is reflecting large amounts of light. Polarized sunglasses also improve the viewer's ability to look through the water, showing more detail, deeper colors and better contrast as compared with simple tinted glasses. Polarized glasses also come in a variety of colors: brown, gray or green lenses are better for bright conditions, while yellow is favored for low-light conditions.

Don't forget to carry an extra set of clothing, including footwear, for when you get off the water. You'll appreciate some dry duds for the drive home. Also be sure to hang up and properly dry all your fishing gear upon returning home, including providing lots of good air circulation. Stinky neoprene and moldy boots may result in you driving alone next time and may even cause you to lose a few fishing buddies.

Well, here you are all dressed up with nowhere to go. Let's give those empty hands something to do by getting your rod, reel and lines assembled. Chapter 3 will help you tie it all together so you can get out on the water, which is where we'd all rather be.

"There's a fine line between fishing and just standing on the shore like an idiot."
Steven Wright

Chapter 3: Rod, Reel and Line Assembly

Having collected all your gear, including tackle and tools, we need to literally tie everything together. As we discussed in Chapter 1, while some rod and reel combos come pre-packaged off the shelf, most anglers prefer to hand-select various components to their own liking. It's very much like buying a car off the lot versus ordering one with only the options *you* want. Plus, even with combo packages in which reels come pre-loaded with line, you'll need to know how to properly assemble your rod and reel, and how to replace line as needed.

Assembling your rod, reel and various lines also allows you to "custom build" your tackle set-up for various fishing conditions, including the type of water, the fish you are going after, and the flies you'll be using. For example, one day you might be after smallmouth bass below riffles in a stream and another day you might be fishing for large browns under logs in a tailwater below a dam. Consequently, as your knowledge of fly fishing increases, you'll find yourself periodically altering your set-up by swapping out different fly lines, perhaps switching spools in a reel, or replacing leader and tippet material.

The first part of this chapter takes a brief look at the structure of a fly rod and reel, how to carefully assemble the two, and then disassemble the rod once again. One would think that the latter is a no brainer, but a wrong step here could lead to some costly rod repairs.

In the second part of the chapter we will show you how to tie four basic knots and use them to assemble your tackle. Some people just love to tie knots. Maybe this goes back to their scouting days or they simply have great finger dexterity. Other people seem to be all thumbs and the only things they can tie up are traffic or their tongues. Maybe these folks are like us and simply need to get a better pair of reading glasses so they can see the darn line. Regardless, tying knots is a fact of life for the intrepid angler. But before we start tying things up, let's make sure you can properly assemble your rod and reel.

Rod and Reel Assembly

The most important thing in putting the rod together is securing the individual sections so that the stripping and snake guides are lined up and the ferrules are snug. If we're speaking in a foreign language, let's first dissect the parts of your rod. It may be easier if you pull out your own fly rod and examine it while we discuss each component. This isn't rocket science–just new terminology for some of you. If your eyes are already rolling, simply jump ahead a few paragraphs and we'll move on.

Nearly all fly rods come in two or more sections. The rod section with the thickest diameter is the butt-end where the reel will be mounted. Just past the reel mount will be a cork handgrip and approximately one-half to three-fourths of an inch past the handgrip is a very small stainless steel loop called the hook keeper. Beyond the hook keeper is the stripping guide, which is the largest "eye" on the rod, typically located two feet or so from the cork handle. Past the stripping guide and extending up the rod are the snake guides (also referred to as the running guides), spaced every 5-14 inches along the rod, with the furthest spacing closest to the handle end and getting closer together towards the tip end of the rod. If you look carefully, you can see that the guides are tied to the rod using very fine, strong nylon thread, coated with a color preservative, and sealed with a flexible, plastic resin varnish. The very last eye is referred to as the tiptop. On the best rods this and the stripping guide may have hard ceramic inserts. Eventually you'll run your fishing line from the reel, through the guides, and out the tiptop. Now let's move on to assembly.

If your rod sections came in a cloth bag and tube, remove them, stuff the bag back in the tube so you don't lose it, and replace the top. The ferrules are the ends of the sections where the rod joins via male and female parts. If available, rub a little paraffin on the male ferrules so they will fit snuggly into the female ferrules and can be easily removed later. It's a good idea to lightly assemble the rod, making sure all the guides are properly aligned, before snuggly seating the ferrules. Mis-aligned guides will also cause the fly line to drag as it passes through them, thereby reducing line speed. Once the ferrules are firmly seated, do not twist them, as that will cause the ferrules to wear out prematurely or even split, a common mistake of the novice angler. Do not over tighten the ferrules either, making them excessively difficult to pull apart at the end of the day.

Let's take a look at the reel. As you know, fly reels come in an assortment of designs, materials, diameters, weights and colors. Most importantly, the diameter and weight should match the weight of the rod, as discussed in Chapter 1. The piec-es holding the sides of a reel case together are called the frame posts and the part that holds the line is called the spool. You will also notice the fly reel drag that can be adjusted to provide some line tension to prevent a fighting fish from stripping all the line from the reel.

After assembling the rod, you will want to seat and secure the reel foot tightly with the rod hardware. First double-check that the reel will fit the rod. On most rods, the size of the opening to accommodate the foot of the reel can be ad-justed by simply twisting open the metal nut near the butt end of the rod. Carefully unscrew the nut (turning the nut counterclockwise or left to loosen) to widen the opening between the butt and the handle. The "foot" of the reel should not be too wide to fit into the opening, nor should it be too high to fit under the handle. Basically, the concave reel foot should fit snuggly against the concavity of the rod itself. Once the foot of the reel is seated, *firmly* screw the nut clockwise (right to tighten) to close the opening around the foot. There is no need to over tighten given that you may want to remove the reel again.

Now rotate the rod so the reel hangs below the rod. For a right-handed person, the reel should be mounted on the reel seat so that the handle is on the left side when the reel is hanging under the rod. Conversely, for a left-handed person the reel should be mounted on the seat so that the handle is on the right side when it is hanging under the rod. Right-handers will want to reel with their left hand and southpaws with their right hand.

Line Assembly

Once your rod and reel are assembled, let's take a look at loading line onto the reel. As noted above, some reels come pre-loaded with backing and fly line. However, if your reel did not come pre-loaded with line or if you want to change the line on your reel, follow the easy instructions below.

Since fly fishing requires the use of four different kinds of line loaded onto the reel, we'll need to tie all these lines together using the following basic knots. There are countless other knots, but these four are all we need to assemble a complete fly fishing outfit and secure flies to tippets. These knots are strong and will not break or fail if properly tied. They include:

- Arbor knot – Used for tying the backing line to your reel
- Nail or Tube knot – For tying the backing line and leader to the two ends of your fly line
- Double Surgeon's knot – For tying leaders to tippets
- Improved Clinch knot – For tying tippets to flies

The arbor and nail (or tube) knots are used infrequently. However, the double surgeon's and improved clinch knots are used repeatedly in the course of fishing, and you should practice both knots until you can tie them blindfolded. Quite simply, you don't want to be out in the middle of a stream and suddenly forget how to tie a clinch knot; otherwise, you may find yourself uttering a volley of invectives. In addition to our directions and illustrations below, you can also explore various Internet sites such as YouTube to find video tutorials on knot tying by simply searching for a particular knot type.

The illustration on the following page illustrates the order in which the lines are loaded onto the reel and the knots that are needed to connect the lines together. Let's take each of these in sequential steps, beginning with the backing line.

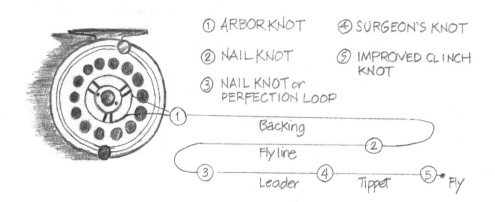

① ARBOR KNOT   ④ SURGEON'S KNOT

② NAIL KNOT   ⑤ IMPROVED CLINCH KNOT

③ NAIL KNOT or PERFECTION LOOP

Loading Backing Onto Your Reel

Loading backing onto your reel requires a few preparatory steps. Locate an arm-free chair, table and a well-lighted area to work in. On the table lay out your snippet, a six to eight inch long pencil with a dull point, and a one inch section of a plastic hollow tube cut from a Q-tip® cotton swab. Add to this your rod, reel, spools of backing and fly line, a package of leader, and some tippet material. Several of you might also want to locate your reading glasses and a steady hand.

At this point, you must revisit your decision as to whether you want to reel in with your left hand or your right. It is important to note that once the line is loaded onto the reel, you cannot simply mount the reel to accommodate a switch from one-handedness to another.

As noted above, most right-handers cast with their right hand and reel in with their left. Conversely, left-handers do just the opposite. Now, stop and look straight at the side of the reel with the handle. If you are retrieving (or reeling in) with your left hand, you will reel in the line with a counter-clockwise motion. For left-handers who reel in with their right, you will reel in the line with a clockwise motion. This is important in determining which way you want the line to wrap around the reel. Now that you know which way you want your line to wrap, let's start to load the backing.

Using only the butt section of your rod, attach your reel and rotate the two so the reel is on top. Importantly, you should not have all of the parts of your rod fully assembled when loading line onto your reel. While sitting in the chair, pass the pencil through the center opening of your spool of backing line, place the pencil and spool between your knees, and strip off (but do not cut) about six feet of backing. Feed the backing through the rod's stripping guide so that the tag end is pointing towards the reel.

Carefully thread the end of the backing line around the spindle of your reel, being careful to go under the top frame post of the reel. Pull about six inches of line beyond where the lines overlap. Using the tag end, tie one overhand knot over the backing line. Tightly tie a second overhand knot on the tag end itself. Slowly pull the backing line snug against the reel, allowing the overhand knot to slide along the backing line. Trim the tag end.

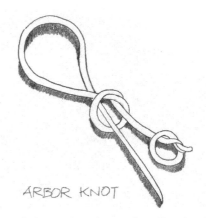

ARBOR KNOT

Now, lightly pinch the line in front of the reel with one hand and, while allowing the spool of backing to rotate on the pencil, with the other hand carefully turn the reel's handle counterclockwise (clockwise for lefties) so that the backing is firmly and uniformly loaded on the reel until there is about one inch of uncovered spool left for the fly line. The line should collect on the top, not the bottom, of the spool (or the opposite side of the foot). Without removing the backing line from the stripping guide, snip the backing line leaving about four feet dangling from the guide. Set the extra backing and pencil aside. You are now ready to attach the fly line to the backing.

Tying Fly Line to Your Backing

The next step is to attach the fly line to the backing with a tube or a nail knot. The main difference between these knots is that the tube knot actually uses a small tube to aid in tying the knot, while the nail knot uses a small nail to achieve the same basic purpose. While these knots are a bit complicated and you could buy a little $5 device to help out, the knots are easily mastered and fun to show off to your friends. Personally we prefer the tube knot because we think it's a little easier to tie.

The core of this knot should be the fly line and the backing will be the wrap. The thinner, more flexible backing will tend to bite into the thicker, softer fly line and make for a tight knot. The beauty of this knot is its slim profile, which allows your lines to glide effortlessly through the guides of your rod.

To begin, pierce the spool of fly line with the pencil, brace it between your knees and pull off several feet of fly line. With a weight forward fly line (WF), make sure that that you attach only the back end of the fly line to the backing line. There should be a small tab on the line that reads "*end to reel*" to indicate the back end.

With the little hollow tube in hand, peruse the illustrations and follow the directions on the next page, and you will end up with a compact and secure knot. In the illustration, the fly line should be the core (the black line in the figure); the backing should be the wrap (the white line in the figure.)

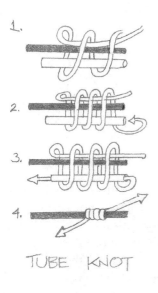

TUBE KNOT

1. Take both tag ends of the lines you are tying together and overlap each one adjacent to the tube. The fly tag end should extend just beyond the tube and the backing tag end should be about 4" long.

2. Wrap the backing around the tube and the fly line 4 or 5 times, keeping each wrap neatly adjacent to the previous wrap (figures 1 and 2.)

3. Insert the longer tag end of the backing through the tube (figures 2 and 3.)

4. Remove the tube and gently but firmly pull the tag end and continuous section of the backing in opposite direction, until all lines and wraps are snug. Trim both tag ends close to the knot.

After you have trimmed off the tag ends, evenly spool the line onto the reel leaving about a yard of it outside of the stripping guide. Ultimately, you want to have the backing and the fly line to fill the reel, until both lines combined are one-eighth of an inch (or one-fourth of an inch at the most) short of the outside edge of the reel. The leader can now be attached to the fly line.

Tying Leader to Your Fly Line

Carefully unwind the leader from its package so that it does not tangle. Untangling an unused leader is not much fun and tends to elevate the blood pressure. If there is a loop on the butt (thicker) end of the leader, cut it off as close to the loop as possible. Now attach the butt end to the fly line using the tube knot shown above. The fly line should be the core of the knot and the leader will be the wrap. Again, follow the tube knot illustrations and tying directions above. Snug the knot and trim the tags as close as possible without threatening the integrity of the knot. It is essential that this knot be compact to avoid the leader, tippet and fly from catching on the fly rod guides as you take up fly-casting.

Tying Tippet to Your Leader

The double surgeon's knot is used when tying together two lines that are of slightly different diameter, such as a leader and tippet. Tippets, rated no more that +/- 2 sizes from the leader size, can be attached to the leader before or during fishing. Typically tippets should be at least 12 inches long, but are seldom more than two feet in length. Follow the illustrations and directions found below for the double surgeon's knot. Your reel is now loaded with backing, fly line, leader and tippet. Reel in most of the leader and tippet, but leave about three to four inches off the spool so that you can locate the end when you go fishing.

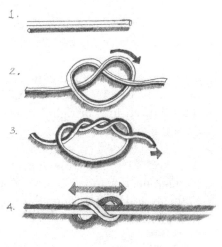

DOUBLE SURGEON'S KNOT

1. Overlap the ends of each line 3 to 4", with each line pointing in the opposite direction.

2. Holding both lines, make a simple overhand knot, but do not tighten.

3. Pull both lines through a second time. As you pull the tag ends, wet the knot so that it tightens snugly.

4. Pull both ends securely. Trim both tag ends.

Tying a Fly to Your Tippet

There is no need to tie a fly on to the tippet until you go fishing. But let's jump ahead and see how to do that so you are set to go when fishing time comes. Knot selection can be mildly controversial at times, but we prefer the use of the improved clinch knot when tying flies to tippet material.

After you have fully assembled your rod and reel, pull about six to nine feet of fly line from your reel and near the end of the fly line make a little fold in the last few inches of line (doubling over the last bit of line.) Pass this and the trailing fly line and leader through all the guides and out through the tiptop. Believe us—this beats trying to feed the end of the limp tippet through all those guides. The leader is likely to have set a curl on the reel, so to straighten it grasp the leader/fly line tube knot. With the index finger and thumb of the other hand, tightly stroke the leader several times until you feel it warm up in a section. *Lightly* stretch this section to remove the curl. Repeat this action moving down the leader to its end. You may need to do this each time you fish.

The improved clinch knot is a knot you will be tying over and over and over again. There is nothing worse than hooking a nice trout, only to have the knot fail and you lose the fly as the fish simply swims off. It's a relatively simple knot that soon will become second nature. Make note that 6X and larger tippets will not pass through the eye of flies smaller than #28. We don't worry about this much since neither of us can see a #28, much less its eye. If needed, clean the eye of the fly with the needle on your nippers. Follow the directions and as you snug the knot, wet it a little and pull on both the tag end and the tippet.

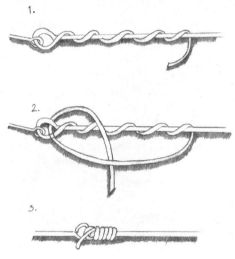

1. Pull the tippet line through the eye of your fly, extending out 4" or so.

2. Wrap the tag end of the tippet around the line 3-4 times (or hold the lines securely in your right hand and twist the fly in your left hand 3-4 times).

3. Take the tag end of the tippet back through the first loop next to the eye of the fly and back through the loop formed next to the wraps.

4. Hold the tag end with one hand and pull out on the tippet with the other causing the wraps to securely tighten as they slide down towards the eye. Trim the tag end.

IMPROVED CLINCH KNOT

It always appears that artificial flies seem to fly around on their own and end up where you thought they never would, such as hung in a tree or embedded in the rear of our waders. When you are in a stream or walking along the shore, but are not fishing, carefully place the hook of the fly in the hook keeper above the cork grip and spool up any dangling line. If your leader is longer than your rod, slip the leader behind the reel's lower frame post, hang the fly on the keeper, and then take up the slack. This keeps the fly line and not the leader outside the tiptop. Watch where you place your rod. Keep it away from car doors and places where it might easily fall on a rock and crack. Never, and we repeat never, pick up your rod above the stripping guide; it can break, especially with the reel attached.

At the End of the Day

After a day of fishing, remove your reel and disassemble your rod by carefully pulling apart the individual sections of the rod. *Do not* hold the rod horizontal in front of you, with elbows fully extended left and right, and begin pulling the rod sections in opposite directions. Instead, hold the rod perpendicular off to one side, lining your arms up and gently pull in opposite directions. Keep the rod (and adjacent sections) as straight as possible so there is no twisting or bending of the ferrules. Again, you do not want to end up with cracked or worn out ferrules. Dry the individual rod sections and return them to their bag and tube.

Before storing your reel, it's a good idea to clean your fly line with a mild solution of soap and water and let it dry, or use a fly line cleaner. Open your box of flies and air dry before storing. More information regarding cleaning your lines and flies can be found in Chapter 2.

Now that you have all your gear and tackle assembled, what next? Well, let's check out your casting skills. Chapter 4 contains lots of great information for beginners, plus many specialized techniques for the more advanced fly anglers.

"Many men go fishing all of their lives without knowing that it is not fish they are after."   Henry David Thoreau

Chapter 4: Basics of Casting
and Special Techniques

Most of us have a romantic image of the lone angler diligently casting a fly line across the swift waters of a crystal-clear stream or into the deep blue of a high-elevation lake. The angler becomes one with the fly, an artist with a paintbrush, a Zen master at work. But as we put ourselves into that picture, all too frequently the line becomes entangled, the hook catches our jacket, and the fish dart swiftly away, seeking safe harbor from the nut with the rod. Kapow. Imagery is savagely attacked by reality. So how do we make amends between the angler we are and the one we want to be?

Obviously there are many, many books that detail both the basics and the subtle nuances of fly casting. It is not our intent to reinvent the wheel or to provide a written substitute for good personalized instruction. But for the novice, the following directions will provide a good overview of the casting process and the intermediate angler may be able to troubleshoot some shortcomings he or she might have to improve their technique. Practice, practice, practice these skills until they become second nature. And if possible, have an experienced fly angler or two critique your technique. It is amazing what other people can see in you.

The chapter begins with the basics of fly casting, focusing on the overhead, distance and roll cast. We also talk a little about the differences between practice casting in the grass versus real-life casting out on the water, as well as techniques to manage casting in windy conditions. Our attention then turns to special fishing techniques useful in Kentucky waters, including both surface and subsurface skills. Lastly we cover the basics of hooking, playing, landing and releasing fish. Skillful casting is rewarding. But pulling in that fighting rainbow is a hoot!

Basics of Casting

The steps one takes to become first-rate in both fly casting and golfing are astonishingly similar. In golf one imparts momentum to the club head in order to drive the ball to a desired spot; whereas in fly casting one imparts momentum to the fly rod to drive the fly line and fly to the desired spot. Whether stroking the golf club or fly rod, there are certain techniques one must learn and certain motions (and perhaps emotions) to avoid. For beginners these techniques are best learned from someone who is very good at their sport. Without good instruction, learning can be difficult, but not impossible. However, there are excellent fly casters who have never had a formal lesson. Regardless, reading books and watching videos is a good alternative, but no substitute for practice.

In casting with a spinning or casting rod, the lure strips line from the reel and the rod propels the lure to the intended spot; whereas in fly casting, the rod imparts momentum to the fly line and the fly merely goes along for the ride. A short piece of fly line has little weight, but the weight of 30 feet of fly line moving with ample velocity, i.e. speed and direction, will give considerable momentum to the line and direct the fly to that point where the tip of the rod is pointed. Great energy on the part of the caster is not required to do this.

As you watch a skilled fly caster you will see that the fly line moves from front to back to front, and as it does so it forms narrow or tight loops that uncoil at the end of each of the back and front strokes. As the rod motion is stopped at about the 1 o'clock position behind the head of the caster, energy is unloaded into the fly line and it will be driven in an uncoiling narrow loop behind the caster and then straighten out. The weight and momentum of the line will begin to flex the rod backwards, and additional flex and energy will be imparted to the rod as the caster moves the rod forward.

With the arm moving in a rapid, accelerating, continuous forward motion, the fly line continues to gain momentum, the rod flexes backwards and energy is loaded into the rod. The tip of the rod will be seen to move first to about 11 o'clock; stop abruptly forcing the fly line to begin to uncoil and form a straight line; and as the caster dips the rod to a 9:30 position the line becomes completely straight over the grass or water. The energy stored in the flexed rod has been released into the fly line.

Sounds simple, doesn't it? Maybe deceptively simple! In the paragraphs below, we'll try and dissect the mechanics behind the skill and grace of an expert fly angler. Fortunately, one seldom needs to cast more than 30 feet in Kentucky's streams and not more than 50 feet in its tail waters. Learn to cast well at 30 feet and then slowly increase your distance as you improve. We'll start you off with the basic cast, before moving to distance and roll casting. With these three casts you will be able to fish all the streams, tailwaters and lakes in Kentucky.

Practice Casting on the Grass

First practice casts should take place on grass. You will need about 60 or 70 feet in both the front and back directions, and plenty of overhead clearance from trees and power lines. If your backyard will not suffice, you may find ample room at a nearby park, golf course, church or schoolyard. It is a good idea to mark the spot you would like to aim your cast using something like a Frisbee® or other similarly sized object.

After you have properly assembled your rod, reel and fly line, strip all the leader and about nine feet of fly line from the reel under the front of the top reel tube that holds the sides of the reel together. The line should be wound clockwise on the spool and trailing out from the top of the reel case. Make a small loop in the fly line and pass this through the stripping guide and each of the snake guides, and finally out through the tiptop of the rod. Pull about 40 feet of line out, and to the end of the leader attach a small one inch strip of brightly colored yarn. No tippet on the end of your leader is required for this exercise.

Proper grip of the fly rod is very important. If you are right handed, position the rod in your right hand with the reel hanging downward under the rod. Grasp the cork handle as you would a bicycle handlebar with your thumb on top and extended towards the rod tip.

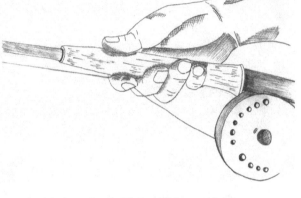

Before attempting the overhead cast, try casting while keeping your arm and rod chest high. This will be a side-arm cast, allowing you to continuously maintain eye contact with the path of the fly line during the entire cast. Keep your forearm parallel to (or in line with) the rod, as if your arm were an extension of the rod itself. When practicing, position yourself so that the outside of your left shoulder is pointing in the direction you wish to cast; the Frisbee target is at about the 9:30 position (assuming you are facing the noon position); and your right shoulder in the direction of your back cast. Your feet should be about 18 inches apart. This position will allow you to see the forward cast and the backward cast as well.

If you are left handed, position the rod in your left hand with the reel hanging downward under the rod. Grasp the cork handle as you would a bicycle handlebar with your thumb on top and extended towards the rod tip. Keep your forearm parallel to (or in line with) the rod as if your arm were an extension of the rod itself. Your arm and rod should remain about chest high. When practicing, position yourself so that the outside of your right shoulder is pointing in the direction you wish to cast; the target is at about the 2:30 position (assuming you are facing the noon position); and your left shoulder in the direction of your back cast. Your feet should be about 18 inches apart. This position will allow you to see the forward cast and the backward cast as well.

35

Now place the piece of yarn on the target with the line lying straight out and the rod tip pointing to it. Securely tuck the fly line coming out of the reel under your index finger resting under the cork handle. Using a continuous motion raise the tip of the rod up 45 degrees keeping your wrist straight, your forearm parallel to (or in line with) the rod, and your elbow fairly close to your waist. If you are right handed, quickly and forcefully move the rod through an arc from left to right stopping it abruptly at 1 o'clock as depicted in Step 1 of the side-arm cast below.

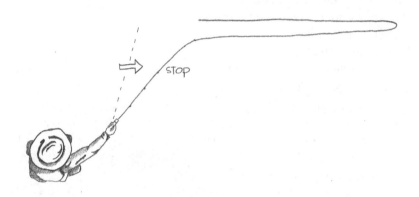

Side-arm Cast: Step 1 – *Stopping abruptly at 1 o'clock*

Carefully watch the line uncoil and when straightened out quickly move the rod tip through the same arc in the opposite direction stopping it abruptly at 11 o'clock and watch the line uncoil. The yarn should come to rest on the target. See the illustration of Step 2 of the side-arm cast below.

Side-arm Cast: Step 2 – *Stopping abruptly at 11 o'clock*

To become a good caster you must stop the backward and forward casts abruptly. This will make for tight loops. Practice until you are satisfied with your casts and their loops.

Now let's try an overhead cast. Turn your shoulders until your chest is facing the direction you wish to cast. Try casting again, lifting the fly line off the grass with an up and backward motion of the fly rod as shown in the figures in Step 1, 2 and 3 below.

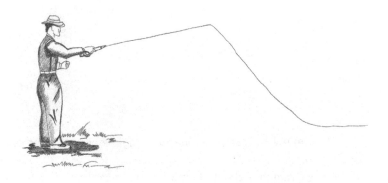

Overhead Cast: Step 1 – *Chest perpendicular to direction of cast*

Keep the rod 10 degrees out from your shoulder. Rapidly and continuously power the rod in the backward direction stopping abruptly at 1 o' clock allowing the line to uncoil and straighten out behind you as shown in Steps 2 and 3.

Overhead Cast: Step 2 – *Powering the rod in the backward direction*

Overhead Cast: Step 3 – *Line has straightened out behind you*

Once the fly line has straightened out behind you, reverse the power stroke moving the rod straight forward and halt this motion abruptly at 10 o'clock allowing the fly line to begin to uncoil, and, as it does so, drop the rod tip to 9:30. These motions are shown in Steps 4, 5 and 6. Your piece of yarn should come to rest on or near the target.

Overhead Cast: Step 4 – *Begin to accelerate the rod forward;*
then put power into your stoke

Overhead Cast: Step 5 – *Line uncoils and rod moves to 9:30 position*

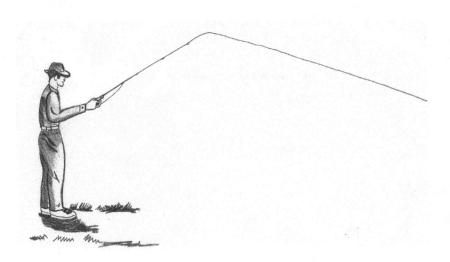

Overhead Cast: Step 6 – *Line straightens with rod at the 9:30 position*

We have shown these strokes for the right-handed angler, but southpaws should have no problem converting them to opposite motions. In time you will become sufficiently comfortable with your casting ability that you will sense when to begin the forward power stroke and not have to follow your back cast with your eyes at all.

Errant motions such as slow, looping arcs and reversing the stroke before the line straightens out will cause wind knots to develop in the leader and flies to snap off. If your cast results in line falling before it has straightened out, you need to put more power into your cast. For longer casts, finish holding the rod tip higher. Practice 20 minutes each day and in four weeks you will feel confident enough to add distance to your casts with an added technique known as the single-haul cast.

The Single Haul Cast: Adding Distance

With the fly line extended in front, strip six more feet of line from the reel using your free hand and clinch in your palm that portion of the line about 12 inches closest to your index finger on the rod. Make a normal back cast and as you power the rod forward release the line under your index finger and pull downward with your hand holding the extra fly line as shown in Step 1 shown below. This will impart extra energy into the forward stroke, and at about 10 o'clock let the fly line slip through that hand and out through the stripping guide, as shown in Step 2 on the following page. You will need to impart some additional energy into the forward cast to allow the loop to uncoil and the line to straighten. The downward *single haul* and forward power stoke must occur simultaneously.

As you let more line out, you may want to keep your rod tip slightly raised to help the extra fly line clear the guides. You will also want to take a little more time with your forward and back motions to allow the extra line to fully coil and uncoil. Some anglers with their back casts go closer to the 2 o'clock position behind the head to get that extra bit of energy transferred from the rod to the line.

Single-haul Cast: Step 1 – *Simultaneously the fly line is hauled downward while powering the rod forward*

Single-haul Cast: Step 2 – *Just as the fly line uncoils, the line slips from the left hand*

Practice Casting on the Water

Later, if you should practice on water, wet the yarn with a little oil to keep it afloat. Beginners should look for flat, unmoving water or a gentle current, with no obstructions. Follow the general instructions above for practicing on grass, replacing the target with something in your mind's eye or a water feature such as the head of an eddy. With the fly line lying atop the water, the caster slowly lifts the tip of the rod, removing a portion of the line off the surface, with the remaining portion still attached to the top of the water by its surface tension.

The caster may flip his wrist at the very end of the forward stroke to impart a little more momentum into the line to let the leader and tippet straighten out and turn over the fly so it lands in the water before the line does. The line will go where the rod tip was pointed. In the backwards motion, if the tip was allowed to drop to the 3 o'clock position, the fly line will fall into the water and completely disrupt the forward cast. If the rod tip has dipped too low in the forward cast, the fly will dive into the water, spooking the fish. Stopping the rod at the 1 o'clock back position, and again in the forward 9:30 position, will allow the rod to unload and form good narrow loops. Again practice will do wonders to avoid the embarrassment of a wayward cast or hooking an innocent bystander.

The Roll Cast

One other cast found useful on Kentucky's streams is the roll cast. It is very simple and useful when brush or other obstructions limit your back cast or when you have a large pile of line at your feet. With the fly line fully extended in front and the rod tip pointing to the end of the fly line, slowly raise the tip of the rod until it is at the 1 o'clock position behind your shoulder as shown below in Step 1. If you begin the cast with the rod in front of you, it will not load.

Now quickly snap the rod forward and downward (Step 2). The line will form a large loop and the end of the line will roll over and shoot outwards (Step 3), with your line coming to rest on the water. Remember the end of the line will end up where you point the tip of the rod.

Roll Cast: Step 1 – *Raise the rod tip to the 1 o'clock position*

Roll Cast: Step 2 – *Quickly snap the rod forward and downward*

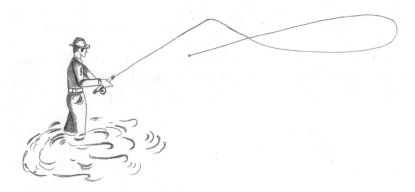

Roll Cast: Step 3 - *Line forms large loop; end of line rolls over and shoot outs*

Casting Around the Wind

Windy conditions can play havoc when fly fishing. Even light winds can foil the beginning fly angler and anything heavier can cause the most intrepid angler to make adjustments in their casting techniques. A wind-buffeted fly is all the more reason to wear a hat and sunglasses to provide some protection from errant flies that could end up hooking us and not the fish. If a rocketing fly is about to hit you or a buddy do not set the hook; it is better to just let it strike you.

Generally speaking, on windy days it is best to simply get closer to the fish. Fortunately, breezy conditions will also set a ripple on the surface of the water, making it more difficult for the fish to see you. So instead of fighting the wind, try and position yourself so that shorter casts are more effective and use the power of the wind to complement your efforts.

Winds affect the motion of a fly line and you must alter your casting strokes from their norms to better control line direction. Your cast will require more force and timing, and different wind directions will determine the tactics you should use.

If casting with a light tailwind, aim a little higher, and put more energy into the backcast and less into your forecast. Basically you want to use the wind's energy to supplement your own. However, with moderate to heavy tailwinds you will never be able to get your line to straighten out behind you. Alternately, use an extended arm, upward back cast and when the fly reaches over your head, move your forearm forward and let the wind propel the line and fly to where you point the tip. This works best for short casts between 25 and 35 feet.

Casting into a headwind is a challenge for just about anyone and should be avoided if possible. Powering a cast into a headwind is nearly impossible unless you are an expert in multiple hauls, which few of us are. If trying to cast directly into a light wind, put less energy into your back cast while pumping up that forward cast.

In heavier winds, an effective technique to use is a side arm cast, keeping your rod and line closer to the water. Wind speed is lowest near the ground and water surfaces, so using a side arm cast with a low angle will help you to work under the headwinds. Keep your rod about 90 degrees, rather than directly overhead, to minimize the impact of the wind. Longer fly rods (such as a 9 foot) and heavier fly lines (a #7 or #8) also work better in windy conditions. Other suggestions include keeping your casts shorter; shortening your leader and tippet; and using heavier or lower profile flies.

If the wind is coming from the same side as your casting arm, it will tend to blow the line and fly into you. Here are two techniques to overcome this effect: (1) Place your casting forearm across your chest and make a normal overhead cast; now the line and fly will move away from you. (2) Simply turn around in the opposite direction and make a normal cast, looking over your shoulder to where you want the cast to go. If the wind is coming from the opposite side of your casting arm, the line and fly will naturally fall away from you.

Practice casting in various wind conditions with each of these techniques so you'll be ready out on the water when a wind comes up. However, we all know there are basically two kinds of anglers: those who have been stuck with a hook and those that have stuck others with a hook. And most of us fall into both categories.

Managing Hang-ups

If you have a hang-up, it may be best to see your psychologist. But, if your hook is hung up, there are several ways to manage that dilemma. More often than we would care to admit, we manage to get our flies hooked on something other than fish nearly every time we go fly fishing. But losing flies can be just as costly as losing friends. Let's look at some various ways to get our hooks out of sticky situations. None of these suggestions are foolproof, but they may help as even hookless flies can get hung up.

If your fly is embedded in a low-hanging tree branch, wedged under a rock, or stuck on a log, you may be able to easily walk over or wade close enough to release it. This is much preferred over repeatedly jerking your rod in hopes that will somehow magically release the hook. Banging your rod against a tightly held fly will result in either (1) breaking your tippet and maybe losing your fly, or (2) breaking your rod, probably near the tip or at a female ferrule. Both are costly lessons in what not to do when attempting to dislodge a fly.

If your hung-up fly is out of reach in the water, pull about six feet of fly line from your reel, raise your rod tip, and make a hefty roll cast directly at the hung up fly. Pray a little bit and there is a 50/50 chance the hook will come free as the heavy fly line pulls the fly in the opposite direction of your stance.

If your fly is way up in a tree or hung up in deep water, you will not be able to retrieve it unless you have either brought a ladder along or you want to go swimming. Barring these options you are most likely going to kiss the fly goodbye. However, there is a slim chance you may save it, your rod and the tippet. Hold your rod in your casting hand below waist level and point the rod directly at the hung-up fly (avoid at all cost flexing the rod.) With your other hand grasp your fly line and pull on it until either the fly comes loose or the tippet breaks. The fly line will come zinging back towards your waist, so be prepared for that. The worse that can happen is you will lose your fly and tippet.

If your fly should become embedded in your clothes or worse your skin (but not your eye), most times that can be easily handled. With a barbless hook simply rotate the hook following the hook's curvature, and it will come out. If the hook has a barb that is not embedded, do the same thing. However, if the fly has a barb and it is embedded, and you have a buddy to help, you have at least three options: (1) Either you or your buddy can take a one foot piece of monofilament line and thread it around the hook at the bend. Simultaneously, pull down perpendicular to the hook's shaft and push forward and away on the hook's eye. This will dislodge the barb and the rotation will free the hook without tearing flesh or fabric. (2) If you are not too squeamish and the barb is embedded in your skin, rotate the hook so that the point and barb of the hook pass out of the surface of the skin. Either cut the point and barb off with a needle-nose set of pliers, or mash the barb with your forceps and rotate the fly out. (3) Clip the tippet off the fly, cover the fly with a Band-Aid, and see a physician later. If the hook was removed from flesh, rinse the spot with clean water, apply some antiseptic, and cover it.

If the fly is lodged in your eye, do not touch the fly or your eye and without any hesitation, immediately go to the nearest physician. This situation calls for professional help.

Special Fishing Techniques

Now that you have mastered some basic casting skills, let's discuss some special fishing techniques that are more site-specific to where you are fishing. To become a good trout fisherman, it is imperative that the fly be presented to the fish in a natural way and that the trout not detect the presence of either the fly line or the angler, otherwise it will reject the fly.

How we present a dry fly to rising trout in a flowing stream is quite different than how we present a nymph below the surface to trout feeding off the bottom of a tailwater, or how we entice a trout feeding on shad in a lake to strike our streamer. In each case we select different techniques and couple these to basic casting. The trout will strike the fly differently and we must be prepared to set the hook. How we play the fish, land it and then, if we choose, release it so that it survives is all-important to the sport. Each species of fish we pursue and each piece of water we fish will present new challenges to our repertoire of skills.

In the pages below, we divide these "special fishing techniques" into surface and sub-surface fishing. We then wrap up with a section on hooking, playing, landing and releasing trout.

Surface Fishing

It is exciting to see a trout hurdle itself out of the water and take a dry fly. That may be the reason so many anglers fish dries even though they see no fish rising (also known as "rises"). Surface fishing is simply presenting a fly on the surface of the water, be it a lake or a stream, and enticing the trout to rise from below and take the fly. Consequently, surface fishing requires the angler to carefully select the choice of flies, rethink the type of lines and floatant used, and to alter his or her casting and other fishing techniques.

On any kind of water, if you see fish either sipping at the surface or breaking the water, that is a good indication they are either feeding on duns, spinners or emergers. You may need to refer to Chapter 6 for more detailed discussion about various kinds of aquatics and flies. Ideally, you will want to examine the surface of the water to "match the hatch" or use an imitator that will best attract the trout feeding off the surface of the water. By their nature, dry flies are fished on the surface; however, it is not unusual for a trout to take a dry that has sunk below the surface.

Typically, if the water is ultra clear and slick, a 12 ft 6X leader and 24 inches of 6X tippet will be called for; otherwise a 7-1/2 or 9 ft 5X leader and 18 inches of 6X tippet will suffice. Of course, various conditions can dictate much broader leader and tippet choices. Attach the fly to the tippet using an improved clinch knot and place a dab of floatant on a knuckle, and from there rub a little on the hackle and upper body of the fly. With no floatant on the thorax, the fly will rest *in* the water like a natural.

There are at least four ways of presenting a dry fly to surface feeding trout in a flowing stream or tailwater: (1) across and upstream, (2) across and downstream, (3) directly upstream and (4) directly downstream. In each of these four casts the fly is presented so that the fish detects neither fly line nor angler. This greatly improves your chance of getting a fish to strike.

Across and upstream: If the fish are rising in the current of a stream or tailwater, if possible, position yourself so you can pick a target up and across from the fish; they will be facing into the current. Direct your cast a little beyond and above your target. If the current is rather stiff you may need a *reach cast.* Just after the fly line has straightened out and the fly is on its way to the target, move your casting arm out and upstream, i.e. *reach.* The fly will continue to your target on the water, but the fly line will bow upstream above the fly eliminating any drag of line or fly that may otherwise spook the fish. If either the fly or line begin to drag before the fly reaches the fish, simply reach again, or as some say "mend" the line upstream. The idea is to have your fly come to the fish like the naturals they are feeding on. Keep the tip of your rod pointed at the fly at all times, the fly line under your index finger, and take in any slack that occurs.

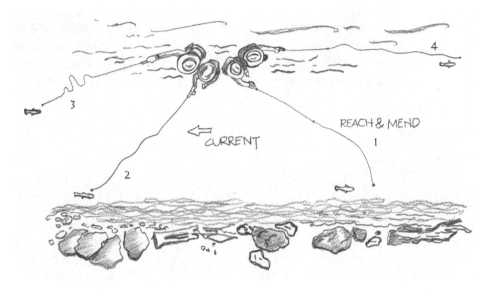

Four Casting Strokes: *(1) Reach across and mend; (2) Across downstream; (3) Pull cast downstream; (4) No spook upstream cast.*

Across and downstream: Casting across and downstream is not as complicated. Pick your target above any feeding fish and make a basic cast to it. After the fly and line are on the water, strip some extra line from the reel, and gently shaking the tip of the rod back and forth let some slack line out. As the fly floats downstream naturally over the fish, the slack will stretch out. This is a good method to fish terrestrials along banks or over sunken depressions.

Directly downstream: If you are located above feeding fish and are unable to position yourself to either side of them for various reasons, a *pull cast* may be used to reach them. Select a target above the fish and make a basic cast, and while the line is in the air quickly raise the rod tip and then drop it. The consequence of this move will be that the fly will drop in front of the fish with some slack in the line and the fly will drift naturally downstream to the waiting fish. If needed, additional line may be stripped from the reel, and again moving the tip back and forth feed this out on the water.

Directly upstream: If you are located below feeding fish (and the fish are feeding above you) an upstream cast is called for. Select a target above the feeding fish, but only so far that the leader falls over them and not the fly line, otherwise they will be spooked. The fish will be facing upstream and will not detect your presence. With this upstream presentation the fly will drift naturally.

Sometimes we see fish rising in total quiescent water. Then we must position ourselves so the trout do not see us. That may mean crouching down on our knees or sitting in a boat and using a long leader. Make a simple basic cast to the fish in the pod. If you need to make a false cast do not do this over the fish, but off to one side. Keep the fly line out of the pod and let only the leader enter it. Punch the rod tip at the end of the cast and that will turn the fly over so it lands on the water first. Keep the rod tip low and pointed at the pod. This will increase a chance for a quick strike.

Another technique that sometimes entices a fish to strike is to skitter the fly over the water. Simply use quick 6-inch strips and fold them in the palm of your left hand. If your dry fly should sink, retrieve it while under the water; it is not uncommon for a trout to take a dry that has sunk below the surface.

Subsurface Fishing

Nearly 80 percent of the food that trout feed on is taken below the surface, such as nymphs, crustaceans and live fish. Anglers merely fish replicas of these aquatics below the surface of the water. Let's take a look at some of these techniques.

Subsurface fishing from a boat provides the advantage that a lot of water can be covered. One highly effective way of fishing a tailwater, like the Cumberland River, is to drift with the current and fish with one or two nymphs below an adjustable indicator. Use a 9 ft 5X or 6X leader and 24 inches of matching tippet. To fish two nymphs, tie the larger one, say a #12 or #14, to the tippet and then attach about 14 inches of tippet to the bend of this nymph with a clinch knot. To the end of that tie a much smaller nymph, say an #18 or #20. Adjust the indicator so that the bottom nymph drifts just above the bottom of the river. This may require using either bead-headed nymphs or attaching weight to the leader just above the tippet knot. Cast this in front and to either side of the boat and keep the fly line mended upstream so that the fish first sights the nymphs and not the line or boat. When wading in big water use this rig and the *single or mend* method discussed above, but let the nymphs drift all the way downstream until it is directly below you. Do not re-cast until you see the nymphs rise to the surface. At times a fish will take the nymphs as they rise thinking they are emergers.

When wading in a stream with deep pools or pocket water, either one or two nymphs can be used, with or without an indicator. Stay clear of the deep water and use a *high stick or short line* method of presentation. Shorten your extended fly line so that it is slightly longer than the length of your rod. Standing beside the pocket water or pool, flip the rig upstream, dropping the tip down as you do so. This is shown in Step 1 on the following page.

High-Sticking: Step 1 – *Flip or roll cast a short line upstream*

As the nymph(s) drift downstream into the pool or pocket water, raise the rod tip *high* and over the nymphs, keeping the line taut and out of the water. Carefully watch your indicator or, if not using one, watch the end of your fly line for a strike. This method can also be used along dead trees, boulders, root wads, riffles or deep banks as shown in Step 2.

High-Sticking: Step 2 – *Follow a natural drift, raising the tip of the rod over it*

49

Another type of subsurface fishing involves fishing streamers in the center of a lake by slow trolling at about six feet per second (four miles/per hour) from a boat and using a sink-tip line and heavy leaders. The depth to fish will depend greatly on the temperature of the water. Your streamer needs to be in water below 70°F and that may mean at a depth of 15-20 feet in the hot summer months. Keep all the fly line in the water and the rod tip elevated and to one side of the boat. The rod tip will dip from a striking fish.

Streamers can also be fished along the banks of lakes and around fallen trees, root wads and over sunken depressions in big tailwaters. Following a basic cast, wait for the streamer to sink, about two or three seconds, and then retrieve it with short strips that you can fold in your left hand. Alter the timing and length of these strips.

Hooking, Playing, Landing and Releasing Fish

When a fish takes your fly, quickly raise the tip of your rod upwards about three feet, and then raise it up to about 10 o'clock. This is adequate to set the hook without breaking the tippet. Do not jerk the rod so hard that it might break the tippet. If the fish moves to your right, move the rod to your left and vice versa. Avoid any slack in the line, and keep a small amount of pressure on the fish. If the fish should jump, tip your rod downward; this avoids tippet breaks.

If you judge you have a big fish hooked, with the line lightly closed under your index finger, reel in all the slack line and then play the fish off of the reel. Adjust the drag so that if the fish makes a run it will strip line from the reel without unduly pressuring the rod or breaking the tippet. If it is a small fish, you can strip line in under your index finger.

If you have a landing net, lead the fish headfirst with your fly rod hand and net it with your other hand. Wetting your hands first will minimize or eliminate the natural protective coating of the fish and improve their survivability. While the fish is still in the net use your forceps to remove the hook. Turn the fish upside down as you remove it from the net, as this will calm the fish. If you wish to release it, turn it back up and place it in the water and hold it gently by its tail facing upstream until it is fully revived and it swims off. Keep it out of the water for as short of time as possible. Lastly, rinse the fly of fish saliva, and then squeeze the water out and use desiccant to dry it before applying new floatant if it is a dry fly.

By now you should have a decent rod and reel assembly, be fairly confident of your casting ability, and know a few special fly fishing techniques to impress your friends. In the next chapter we'll talk more about what species of trout live in Kentucky waters and the state's stocking program.

"There's more B.S. in fly fishing than there is in a Kansas feedlot."
Lefty Kreh

Chapter 5: Trout Species and Stocking

There are no indigenous trout in Kentucky: That is, there are no native trout that naturally reproduce and live out their life cycle in the state. None! So where did our trout come from? To answer that question, we have to go back in time and trace the stocking history for the state.

The earliest records from the U.S. Department of Fisheries for Kentucky indicate that 5,000 eggs of "California Mountain Trout" were provided to William Griffin in 1881. A few years later, Kentucky received its first lake trout stocking in 1886, which was followed by a stocking of 2,500 rainbow and 500 brook trout in 1888.

On May 24, 1912 the Mountain Advocate, published in Barbourville, KY, reported that the U.S. Department of Fisheries had released 14,670 rainbow trout into the headwaters of the Cumberland River. In addition, the early annals of the Kentucky Game and Fish Commission indicate that in 1914 the U.S. Bureau of Fisheries released 1,800 rainbow trout into two ponds, a lake and a stream in Kentucky. There may have been sporadic releases of rainbows between then and the middle of the last century, but it is unlikely they survived the state's hot summers and reproduced to establish ongoing wild trout fisheries.

Kentucky's neighboring states to the east and south had struggling native populations of Appalachian brook trout. But the brookies were under pressure from ill-considered logging and the stocking of non-native West Coast rainbow and European brown trout that had been stocked. The rainbows and browns were more predatory in nature and had moved into the higher elevations that were the preferred habitat of the brook trout. Over time, the rainbows and browns reproduced vigorously, establishing broods of wild trout. It took several decades of hard work by cold-water conservationists to clean out the rainbows and browns from these higher elevations, particularly above waterfalls that served as natural barriers to their passage, in order to allow the brook trout to recover.

Back in Kentucky, bass, walleye, bluegill and many other warm water species of fish flourished and reproduced, providing anglers with a seemingly endless variety of fishing options. But some of the streams, lakes and tailwaters in the state harbor enough cold, clear water through most of the year to support trout, and in the early 1950s Kentucky began developing a trout-stocking program in earnest.

Consequently, because Kentucky has no indigenous trout populations, there are only stocked trout in her waterways. Rainbow and brown trout are stocked each year in select rivers, streams and lakes. In 1980 and 1981, Owhi brook trout were released into a half dozen streams in the DBNF and in higher elevation creeks of the Cumberland Mountains. When this book was published, there were no cut-throat trout in Kentucky and probably only remnants of the lake trout that had been stocked in Dale Hollow Lake and Lake Cumberland over 30 years ago. Each trout species has a different origin, prefers a slightly different habitat, and displays distinct markings. Perhaps surprising to some, rainbow, brown, brook and lake trout are all members of the salmon family.

Trout Species

Rainbows

Over 100 varieties of rainbow trout are native to the western coastal states, many of which are now distributed across the United States. Rainbows were first stocked in the Cumberland and Herrington Lake tailwaters in 1952.

Rainbow trout are identified by the red or pink lateral stripe along their sides; a dark green back; and small black spots on their top, sides and tails. However, their coloration can change throughout the year, especially during the spawning season. Rainbows begin to breed between the ages of one and five years. In the spring the female fans out a nest, called a redd, and lays up to 100 eggs. Unfortunately, Kentucky's rainbows do not spawn because of the state's deleterious water conditions.

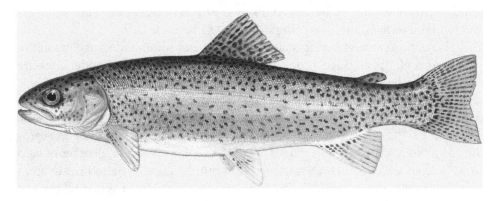

With regard to size, rainbows typically grow 12-18 inches in length, but can reach lengths up to 30 inches and weights up to 17 pounds. The largest rainbow caught in Kentucky weighed 14 and three-eighths pounds and was caught in the Cumberland River tailwater in 1972.

Rainbow trout are a hardy fish that thrive in cold (52° to 68°F), clean water and prefer a complex stream habitat that includes riffles or swift running water over one- to three-inch diameter gravel; deep pools; submerged wood (such as logs, branches and root masses); boulders or rock piles; and undercut banks with over-hanging vegetation. Since rainbows are more solitary than social in nature, they like the partitions that a complex habitat can provide. Notably, rainbows are skittish and will avoid all predators, including anglers.

Rainbow trout are opportunistic feeders that sustain themselves on a wide-variety of foods and generally feed close to the bottom of their habitat. In streams passing through riparian vegetation, rainbows will feed on terrestrial insects such as grasshoppers, ants and beetles that fall into the water. Rocky streams with riffles provide rainbows with bottom-dwelling invertebrates including a variety of insects and crustaceans. Finally, both streams and lakes provide rainbows a rich diet of crayfish; small fish and fish eggs; worms; and both the larval and aquatic stages of dragonflies, mayflies, and caddis flies for the trout to feast upon.

Browns

In 1883 this species was first introduced into U.S. waters from Germany. The Plymouth Rock strain of three- to four-inch browns was first stocked in Kentucky's Laurel Creek in 1981 as a put-grow-take endeavor. Eleven additional streams have since been added with good success.

You can identify brown trout by the large black spots on their backs; red spots and at times halos around dark spots on their sides; and few if any spots on their tails. They have white to cream colored underbellies. A brown trout will spawn in the fall typically laying several hundred eggs. Some browns are known to spawn in the Cumberland tailwaters.

The average brown trout grows to 16 inches in length. The largest brown caught in Kentucky also came from the Cumberland tailwater and weighed 21 pounds. It was caught in 2000.

Compared to rainbows, browns can stand slightly warmer water (54° to 69°F) and a wider range of habitat conditions, including more deeply stained water

53

that carries less current. They shun sunlight, and can frequently be found under dead falls and root wads. More than other species of trout, browns prefer significant amounts of cover as provided by large piles of woody debris, boulders and undercut banks. Browns can also be found in deep trench pools (at least three to six feet in depth) and along meandering channels.

Brown trout have developed a keen sense of sight and underwater hearing, and are viewed as both opportunistic and specialized feeders, depending on habitat and food availability. Browns sport rows of sharp, pointed teeth and feed off aquatics and terrestrial insects, crayfish, salamanders, small rodents and other fish. Adult browns also have the tendency to become nocturnal, preferring to feed at night, creating even more challenging conditions for the angler. Consequently, you may have better luck fishing for browns on gray or even drizzly days.

Brooks

Brook trout are native to eastern North America, from Canada's Hudson Bay to northern Georgia, and are the classic indicator species of a stream's aquatic health. Brookies, as they are sometimes called, have two distinct markings: vermiculations or worm-like patterns on their dark green backs, and white edges on their reddish pelvic and anal fins. Their underside is silver or light yellow, but during breeding periods the male's stomach or underbelly turns red or bright orange. The jawbone of a brook trout extends well past their eyes.

Brook trout spawn in the fall, laying their eggs in the redds and incubating them over the winter months. The eggs hatch in the spring and young brook trout begin to establish territories and feeding lanes.

The average length of a brook trout in the United States is 10-12 inches and weigh from several ounces up to two pounds. They are short-lived in the wild, typically only four to five years. The state record brook trout was caught in early 2014 from the Cumberland River tailwater and weighed in at 2.2 pounds.

Brooks prefer very clean, moderate flowing, cold water (50° to 64°F), and will seek cover at the slightest disturbance of the water or sight of a predator. In general, brookies are slightly less tolerant to warm water; more tolerant to acidic conditions; and require higher dissolved oxygen concentration levels as compared to rainbow and brown trout.

Consequently, the steeper-gradient Appalachian streams surrounded by rhododendron and evergreen trees provide an excellent habitat for brook trout to thrive and reproduce. Similar to other trout, brooks feed off aquatics and terrestrial insects, crayfish, worms, amphibians such as frogs and salamanders, small rodents, and other small fish.

The U.S. Fish and Wildlife Service established brook trout in two Kentucky streams from stockings in 1968, which were later expanded by KDFWR in the early 1980s. The last stocking of brook trout in Kentucky's streams was in 1990, but reproduction sustains a modest population. In 2011, annual brook trout stockings were initiated in the Cumberland River tailwater. It is doubtful if any natural reproduction occurs in the tailwater, but the trout thrive and grow there.

There are only four streams in Kentucky open to catch-and-release wild brook trout fishing, and in these only single hook flies or lures may be used. The four streams are Dog Fork and Parched Corn Creek in the Red River Gorge Geological Area (within the DBNF) and Poor Fork and Shillalah Creek in eastern Kentucky. Wild brook trout can also be found in Bad Branch and Martin's Fork, but both of these streams are closed for fishing in Kentucky.

Lake Trout

This species of trout, supplied from Canadian waters, was stocked in Dale Hollow Lake in 1980. Some lake trout were also introduced in Lake Cumberland. No additional stockings have taken place in Kentucky. Lake trout prefer very deep, cold water. In 1983 a five and one-third pounder was taken from Lake Cumberland. This was a small specimen considering the world record is 72 pounds. Lake trout are not a significant trout for Kentucky, and we will not be discussing them further.

Stocking

Why does Kentucky not have any native trout living in its streams and rivers? To simply answer that trout need cold water and most of Kentucky's streams are warm would be correct. But there are some streams in the state that are fed with cold spring water and in those streams there are no trout either. Word has spread that it takes more than just a little cold water to sustain a population of wild trout.

To hatch trout fingerlings, streams must have a yearlong, continuous flow of highly oxygenated water between 50°F and 60°F. For female trout to "fan out their redds" (a polite way of saying "laying her eggs" in trout lingo, enabling the male to release his milt—or sperm—over her eggs), a stream must contain beds of clean, small-sized gravel over which very clean, silt free water flows for a minimum of three to five months following the spawn. And of course there must be adult trout with an innate propensity to spawn in their native habitat. So what do we find in Kentucky's streams?

Unlike the cold, clean, gravel-laden streams of the Appalachian Mountains, Kentucky's low-gradient streams harbor sheets of sedimentary rock, namely limestone and sandstone, with scarcely any igneous gravel. Kentucky's stream banks are mostly clay, and when it rains they erode and the streams become torrents of muddy water filled with silt. During the hot, dry months of July, August and September stream levels fall, water temperatures rise above 75°F, oxygen concentration levels decline, and conditions for trout survival disappear. With no brown trout to spawn in the fall months and no rainbows to spawn in the spring, there can be no wild trout to carry on the species. Consequently, except for a handful of clean, cold brook trout streams in the DBNF and in the higher elevations of the eastern Appalachian Mountains, there are few prospects for any reproduction of trout in Kentucky and there probably never will be. Ultimately, whether liked or not, the federal government intervened.

During the last century, the U.S. Army Corps of Engineers oversaw the construction of a number of flood control and power generating dams across several of Kentucky's rivers. In 1952 the construction of Wolf Creek Dam across the Cumberland River was completed. The warm waters of the Cumberland were now infused with the cold water flowing from Wolf Creek Dam, pushing many of the warm-water species of fish (particularly bass, crappie and bream) further downstream. To mitigate the alteration of the river, rainbow trout were introduced into the very cold tailwaters of the Cumberland River.

Who Stocks Trout in Kentucky?

In 1975 the federal government constructed the cold water Wolf Creek National Fish Hatchery (NFH) below Lake Cumberland to rear rainbow and brown trout for stocking in the river and other federally managed waters in Kentucky and a few sites in adjacent states.

Currently the hatchery annually produces about 860,000 trout per year: 695,000 rainbows (most are about nine inches long, but a few are 6-12 inches in length); 123,000 browns (four to eight inches long); and 46,000 brook trout (all 8-12 inches long). The hatchery is not involved in any spawning activity and receives fertilized eggs overnight from other hatcheries: rainbow eggs from the NFHs in Ennis, Mont., Erwin, Tenn., and White Sulphur Spring, W. Va.; brown trout eggs from a NFH in Wyo.; and beginning in 2010, brook trout eggs were received from a state fish hatchery in Egan, Mont.

Personnel from the Wolf Creek NFH and KDFWR are responsible for stocking 115 public waters throughout Kentucky and Fort Campbell in Tennessee. A few fingerling trout are supplied to the Cherokee Indian Reservation in western North Carolina and some for mitigating waters in Indiana. The pattern for stocking by the KDFWR is adjusted to match the availability of trout from the Wolf Creek NFH, and the water levels and temperatures in the lakes and streams. Trout are transported to the various stocking sites in several thermally insulated and oxygenated trucks owned and operated by the KDFWR. In remote locations, trout are backpacked in with the help of volunteers.

When and Where are Trout Stocked in Kentucky?

Trout are stocked in streams, tailwaters and lakes across the state. While the number of streams stocked has varied little from year to year, Kentucky has slowly increased the list of lakes it stocks due to its popular "Fishing in the Neighborhood" program that targets water bodies for fish stockings in close proximity to urban areas. Public access is also an important factor and one that KDFWR is addressing through its "Voluntary Public Access" (VPA) and "Habitat Incentive Program." Unfortunately the federal funding for those programs is currently unreliable.

In general, stockings occur in the spring and fall months, when water temperatures are more conducive to trout survivability. Consequently, variation in stockings occurs throughout the year. However, stockings can and do deviate from the planned monthly stocking schedule for particular waterways. For example, heavy spring rains may delay stocking until late spring. Conversely, if water levels are too low, KDFWR may delay or even cancel monthly stockings to assure survivability of the trout. However, in the latter scenario, it is difficult to compensate for higher stockings later in the year since each stream, tailwater or lake may be limited in terms of the total fish population it is able to support.

Historically, the KDFWR used a rather complex system of stream classification to determine which waterways were stocked with what species and what numbers of trout. Streams were assessed using the following parameters: (1) trout utilization (if previously stocked), (2) fish population structure, (3) water quality, (4) habitat, (5) fishing success, and (6) aesthetics.

However, in 2013 the KDFWR devised a new, highly objective stream classification system that relies solely upon water temperature for the purpose of stocking trout. A Class I stream is categorized as "excellent" if it has fewer than five days in a year when its temperature rises above 72°F and remains below 72°F through the summer months. All of the brook trout streams and several spring-fed streams are designated Class I. If a stream's temperature rises above 75°F for fewer than 25 days and remains below 75°F through the summer months, it is designated a Class II "high quality" trout stream. If in a calendar year a stream's temperature rises above 72°F more than 25 days it is classified either Class III or IV because it is unlikely to harbor carry-over trout. A Class III stream is suited to a June stocking, whereas Class IV streams, identified as "marginal", become too warm in June to be stocked.

The stocking dates and numbers by trout species for Kentucky's lakes, ponds, streams and tailwaters can be found on KDFWR's web site: fw.ky.gov. Click on "Fish" and then select "Recreational Fishing" from the drop-down menu. Halfway down the page, under the bold heading "Stocking," click on either "Monthly Trout Stocking Schedule" or "Yearly Trout Stockings." Notably the exact dates for stocking the streams in the DBNF and the Cumberland tailwater are not published.

In recent years, about 45 creeks and streams in Kentucky were stocked with around 150,000 rainbows and of these streams, eight were also stocked with about 3,500 brown trout. The operation can begin as early as March, but for streams that begin to warm by early summer, their last stocking occurs in late May or early June. The state considers these as put-and-take (p-t) streams, i.e. they put the trout in hoping that they will all be taken out before the stream temperatures rise and oxygen levels fall making trout survival improbable.

Several streams in Kentucky are spring fed and their waters remain sufficiently cold to receive fish through the summer months. Some of these fish over-winter and grow to several pounds. These are called "put-grow-take" (p-g-t) streams. Thirteen of these streams receive rainbow trout in October and are designated as catch-and-release streams from October 1 until March 31, with the period for Swift Camp Creek extended to May 31. Only artificial lures or flies may be used during these periods.

Most of the 16 tailwaters across the state are stocked from April through November. Their temperatures hover around 55°F year-round. Annually they receive about 250,000 rainbows and four of the tailwaters received a total of about 40,000 browns. The Cumberland tailwater is the only water in the state to receive brook trout—in March it received 10,000 8-12 inch brookies. In 2010 the KDFWR began releasing sterile rainbows into the Cumberland with the expectation that they would have a greater growth rate. An additional 13,000 sterile 16-inch rainbows were released into the Cumberland in 2013 to help replenish the trophy-sized fish lost as a result of the lake's drawdown.

The 56 lakes and ponds in Kentucky receive nearly 300,000 rainbow trout, primarily in late winter and mid-fall months. No brown trout are stocked in these waters. The smaller and shallower lakes and ponds warm during the summer months and fishing in these is mostly on a put-and-take basis.

Now that the state has stocked all these waterways in Kentucky, these fish have to eat. Like the intrepid teenager, most young trout are opportunistic feeders. However, as trout mature and become more settled in their habitats, they become more specialized or picky in what they consume. The following chapter looks in more detail at feeding the Kentucky trout.

"What a tourist terms a plague of insects, the fly fisher calls a great hatch."
Patrick F. McManus

Chapter 6: Natural and Artificial Insects for Kentucky Trout

For many anglers, fly selection is the greatest challenge they face on the water. Even the names suggest the need for a magical decoder ring…Caddis, Comparadun, Scud. Or a PhD in entomology… ephemeroptera, trichoptera, plecoptera. And of course we have enough abbreviations to confuse any government employee…BWO, CDC, WD-40 (But why do you need water-displacing lubricant while fishing?).

And if the names aren't enough to befuddle the fly fisherman, you need to "match the hatch." Or choose between nymphs and streamers. And nothing comes in just one size. Which is larger: a #14 Adams or a #12?

The intent of this chapter is to demystify all these choices for you. First we'll have a short lesson in biology and talk about natural insects, some basic terminology, and the stages of aquatic insect development. Second, we'll talk about artificials and the implications for stocked trout. And lastly, we'll make some recommendations for flies that every Kentucky angler should have in their fly box.

Life Cycles of Aquatic Insects

Aquatic insects of many kinds and in various stages of development make up the dominant food supply of trout. Add to these the summer terrestrials including grasshoppers, Japanese beetles, ants and locusts, and some underwater forage of sow bugs, scuds and minnows, and their table is set. If the water temperature is above 40°F the trout will be feeding, and we need to find just the right fly to whet their appetite.

Given the importance of aquatic insects to the trout diet, let's explore this topic a little more. Only about 7 percent of all insects are considered "aquatics or semi-aquatics," meaning that during one or more stages of their life cycle they rely on water. The majority of aquatic macroinvertebrates that inhabit Kentucky's waterways are simply the juvenile form of an adult, land-dwelling insect. While there are scads of such insects, only four families are of great interest to Kentucky's trout. They are the caddisflies, midges, mayflies and stoneflies.

To understand which fly to tie to the end of your tippet, it's helpful to know just a bit about the life of an aquatic insect. In bio-lingo, these insects pass through different developmental stages, which we call the metamorphic life cycle. These cycles are classified as either complete or incomplete metamorphosis. If this is too much information, you can skip ahead to the next section. Alternately, give us a few minutes and we'll take you on a short ride through the life of a bug.

Complete Metamorphosis is when the insect begins as an egg, develops into a larva, then a pupa, and finally becomes an adult. This category of insects includes caddisflies, midges, true flies, alderflies, dobsonflies, beetles, moths and butterflies.

Egg ⇒ Larva ⇒ Pupa ⇒ Adult

For insects that develop through complete metamorphosis, the adult female deposits eggs that eventually make their way to the bottom of the water, attach to a substrate (such as sand or gravel), and hatch in one to two weeks. During the larval stage, the immature larva emerges from the egg and begins actively feeding and growing, thus requiring successive molts (or instars). The larval stage lasts for a week or up to a year for some insects, before the mature larva transforms into a pupa. The final life stage is the transformation of the pupa into a winged adult form. These adult insects typically live only a few hours or a few days before dying, which has important ramifications for what trout eat.

Incomplete Metamorphosis is when the insect begins as an egg, grows into a nymph, and finally develops into an adult. This category of insects includes mayflies, stoneflies, dragonflies, damselflies and waterbugs.

Egg ⇒ Nymph ⇒ Adult

For insects that develop through incomplete metamorphosis, the adult female deposits eggs that eventually make their way to the bottom of the water, attach to a substrate (such as sand or gravel), and hatch in one to two weeks. During the nymphal stage, the immature nymph emerges from the egg, develops an exoskeleton, grows larger and periodically sheds its exoskeleton (molting), and continues feeding and growing. The nymph stage lasts for several months or up to one to two years for some insects. During the emerger stage, the nymphs rise to the surface, shed their exoskeletons, dry their wings and fly off as adults. Again, these adult insects typically live only a few hours or a few days.

An important exception to insects that undergo incomplete metamorphosis is the mayfly nymph. After the egg hatches the nymph grows, periodically molting (shedding its skin) until it emerges to shed its last skin and becomes a winged adult form. The winged adult form that is sexually immature is known as a subimago or a "dun," the sexually mature adult form is referred to as an imago or a "spinner." Of course, many of you reading this are familiar with the common artificial flies known as Duns and Spinners, which we'll talk more about later. This knowledge might not faze your TU buddies, but might impress some of your friends at cocktail parties.

Matching the Hatch: What to Feed the Hungry Trout

Now that we know a little more about the different forms that insects take as they undergo metamorphosis, we can talk in greater detail about what trout eat. Importantly, trout like to eat aquatic insects in all stages of the metamorphic life cycle. The challenge facing the angler is to figure out exactly *what* the trout are eating at a given point in time. For example, it's not enough to simply say that the fish are feeding on caddisflies—are they feeding on the egg, larva, pupa or adult form?

The last question brings us to two more. How do we figure out what the trout are feeding on right now, given that what they were feeding on last week might not be what they are feeding on today? And short of actually tying a live nymph or a winged-adult form onto your hook, what type of artificial fly might we use to entice that big brown to come out from beneath the rock ledge or that gorgeous rainbow to snatch from the water's surface?

To begin to answer those questions, let's talk about "matching the hatch." Frequently fly anglers will want to select a fly that will match what trout are currently feeding upon. So how do you go about doing that?

First, a few anglers are misled by this well-known phrase—the hatch does not refer to the egg "hatching", but the form of the insect that is emerging from the pupa or nymph stage. Now that you understand a little about metamorphosis, it's easy to see that the "hatch" is simply the macroinvertebrate passing from the previous stage of development on its way to becoming an adult.

For most of the major rivers and more popular trout streams, there are published hatch charts indicating a week or so range of time in which a particular aquatic insect typically emerges into adult form. These charts can be purchased online or found at a local fly shop. Prior to the predicted hatch, you would want to fish with nymphs or peeking pupae of that particular aquatic insect and fish with the corresponding emerger or dry fly during the hatch itself. Of course, unusual weather patterns including rainfall and temperature changes can cause variations in predicted hatch times. You might see another problem right now. Published hatch charts for the small, local streams of Kentucky do not exist. So what should the Kentucky fly angler do?

Matching the real bugs with artificials is not as difficult as it might seem if you're willing to use your powers of observation and get your hands and feet a little wet. First, you will want to get near or on the waterway itself to identify both the type and the stage of any insects or macroinvertebrates you see both in and out of the water. Of course, it is very likely that you will find more than one type of aquatic insect and most likely will find multiple insects in more than one metamorphic stage.

61

If trout are rising, pay close attention to what the fish are sipping on. Keep your eye focused on the surface of the water, because as soon as the trout breaks the surface it is difficult to see if he took that large cream-colored insect or the small brown one. Ideally you would want to catch one of these fellows to confirm the identity of the insect and then match a dry fly with the size and color of the adult. A splashy rise suggests the trout are feeding on flies off the surface and in Kentucky most likely will be mayfly duns or spinners or dry caddisflies. The time of day can also trigger the emerging of adults—caddisflies tend to come off in the mid-afternoon, while stoneflies emerge in the evening. If the trout refuses your fly, reconfirm the identity and stage of the insect, and then make any needed adjustments in your fly type, color and size.

What if you see fish rising, but no splashes are present or there are only ripples on the water's surface? In this case, the trout are probably feeding on emerging nymphs just below the surface. Subsurface feeding suggests the use of a wet fly fished just below the surface using an emerger pattern or a floating nymph. Importantly, as we now know, the time an aquatic insect remains in the pupa or nymph stage is considerably longer than the time spent as an adult. Consequently, trout spend more time fishing below the surface and so should you. About 80 percent of what a fish eats is below the surface, so on average, only 20 percent of your fishing should be with dry flies. Of course this heavily depends on location and time of year.

So how do you go about identifying macroinvertebrates? Well, this is where you might get a little wet. Head to the stream and carefully pick up a few rocks, keeping in mind that in the process of doing so you may knock off a few of the critters you're searching for. Be on the lookout for larvae, eggs or wing cases, pupae, and nymphs. Ideally you will want to wade out into that part of the stream, pool or riffle and search for macroinvertebrates where you will be fishing (and not just next to the bank). However, given water temperatures, depths and current flows, wading out to turn up rocks may not be feasible, but do the best you can. If you catch the real thing, look at its form, size and color. Then select the closest fly pattern you can find to match it.

In summary, dry flies are typically fished on the surface of the water; emergers are fished partially submerged; and nymphs, streamers and wet flies are fished below the surface. Now that you have that straight, let's throw imitators and attractors into the mix! An imitator fly is exactly that—it's a fly that mimics certain insects or food for the awaiting fish. Generally speaking, if you can match the hatch (or the macroinvertebrate), then use an imitator.

Stimulator on a #6 hook

But if no hatch is present, no subsurface feeding is apparent, and/or the water is slightly discolored, you may want to choose an attractor, such as this #6 Stimulator. Rather than trying to imitate a particular food source, attractors use bright, flashy colors and generic patterns to attract the fish. Attractors work best when fish are complacent and the fly triggers a response, such as snatching the attractor out of the water. It's been said that trout are like people and can be difficult to figure out. We're not always sure why attractors work, but when they do we're more than grateful.

For fly anglers fishing Kentucky streams, we have another challenge in fly selection that is related to stocking. Given that Kentucky does not have any indigenous trout populations, all of our trout or their predecessors were stocked at one time or another. With the exception of our wild brook trout and some larger holdover populations in places like the Cumberland tailwater, many of our trout were not raised on a natural food supply.

Once a newly stocked trout gets hungry and it's no longer being spoon-fed on a regular basis, the stocker may jump at just about anything. But the longer the stocker lives in the wild, the wilier he or she gets. And the native brook trout and holdovers are even pickier, making fly selection and "matching the hatch" even more critical to having a good day of fishing.

Now that we have a general idea of various stages of a macroinvertebrate and the strategy behind matching the hatch, let's take a closer look at some of the more important insects in Kentucky's trout streams. For each insect we will look at the characteristics in detail and talk about artificial flies that emulate a particular macroinvertebrate. We also suggest various fly sizes—just remember, the smaller the number, the larger the hook (thus, the fly). You'll notice that many of the flies we recommend are tied onto very small hooks. Don't be misled–many trophy-size trout are caught on hooks smaller than your little finger's nail.

Artificials: Fly Selection for Kentucky Trout

Now that we've talked about what trout prefer eating in the wild, what do stocked trout in Kentucky like to eat? Once stockers are released, it takes them a few days to recover and get their bearings again. As soon as their appetite returns, a fresh stocked rainbow or brown usually isn't too particular and will go after just about anything—egg or worm patterns work wonders. But the longer the trout has survived in something close to its natural habitat, the more particular the trout will become. Like a big-city gourmand, those trout that have survived multiple seasons are increasingly difficult to fool.

Let's take a closer look at the four dominant aquatic insects that make up the Kentucky trout diet: mayflies, caddisflies, midges and stoneflies. For each insect we'll talk about how to identify their various macroinvertebrate forms and what artificial flies best imitate those forms. We've included some pictures to help you out.

Mayflies

While this species must number in the hundreds, all mayflies have some common characteristics. Where they differ are in size, color and when they emerge. As explained above, mayflies go through three stages: egg, nymph and adult. Typically when a mayfly egg hatches it is a tiny nymph that grows from 3 to 30 millimeters, eventually develops gills, grows six legs and usually three tails, and is tan to blue in color. Mayfly nymphs have mouths and most frequently reside under submerged stones and logs off of which they eat algae. If you step into a stream and pick up several stones, on the underside of one or more you may find mayfly nymphs scurrying around. As these tiny aquatics are flushed from their hideouts, hungry trout readily pick them off.

Mayfly nymphs continue to molt for one month to four years and remain active their entire lives. These nymphs develop wings in a transparent skin, rise to the surface, and shed their skin. At this point the nymph is considered a sexually immature adult and four wings emerge—two big and two small ones. Many nymphs that had three tails will have only two tails as adults. This stage is called a dun. The dun's wings are rather opaque and it will take flight and come to rest on a bush or tree branch where it will undergo a final molt resulting in transparent wings.

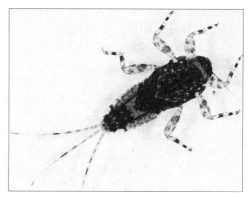

Mayfly Nymph (*Ephemerella invaria*)
Common name: Sulphur Dun

At this stage the dun has developed into a sexually mature adult and is called a spinner. The spinner mates and the female now sports a small yellow egg sack as she flies over the water where she deposits her eggs. Because her wings will no longer support flight, she falls onto the water and dies or awaits the hungry trout. Adults do not eat and their life span may be as short as 90 minutes or as long as two days.

Pods of trout will sip emerging mayflies until the hatch is over and then turn their attention to the duns as

Mayfly Dun (male) (*Ephemerella invaria*)
Common name: Sulphur Dun

they sit on the water drying their wings to ready for flight. A fluttering spinner will soon lose flight and fall to the water where it will soon disappear one way or another.

Two mayflies common to Kentucky are Blue-Winged Olives (BWO) and Sulphurs. BWOs hatch year round, but are very small and can be difficult to spot while in flight. Sulphurs hatch in midsummer, are about one centimeter long and can easily be seen as they flutter off after emerging. There are sporadic hatches of other mayflies but they can be difficult to identify without close examination.

Mayfly Spinner (male)
(*Baetis tricaudatus*)
Common name:
BWO (Blue-Winged
Olive)

What artificials are good matches for the Blue Wing Olive and the Sulphur? The answer to that depends, in part, on the stage of metamorphosis. For mayflies that are in the nymph stage, we suggest using #12 and #14 Pheasant Tails and Prince Nymphs. In the emerging stage, #14 or #16 CDC emerger mayflies would be good choices. (CDC is an abbreviation for Cul de Canard, the soft waterproof feathers of ducks.) If a lot of duns are present, try #14 and #16 BWOs and Parachute Adams, or #12 and #14 Sulphurs. We have included pictures of suggested flies at the end of the chapter.

Caddisflies

The caddisfly goes through four stages of complete metamorphosis: egg, larva, pupa and adult. In Kentucky no fewer than 180 species of caddisflies have been identified. Each has a one-year cycle.

Adults mate and drop their eggs with repeated touches on the water or even dive into the water. A mass of eggs will hatch into tiny larvae and will encase themselves with sand particles, twigs and/or leaf matter, while others will swim freely in riffles. These cases, built from silk produced by the glands of the larvae, helped distinguish the caddisfly from other macroinvertebrates. The larvae have sharp mouthparts and voracious appetites, and will build a cocoon before developing into the pupae stage.

After about 10 months the pupae will escape the cocoons, rise to the surface, shed their skins and break free as adults. The adults are about one centimeter long and have four sweptback wings, six legs, two antennae and three body parts. Mature caddisflies resemble moths with their hairy wings and long antennae, but they do not have the long siphoning mouthpart similar to moths and butterflies. Sporadic hatches of caddisflies occur from February until November in much of Kentucky's cold, clean water. The adult caddisflies can survive about a month, but soon afterward are either eaten or die.

Caddisfly Egg Cases *(Glossosomatidae)*
Common Name: Saddle-case Makers

Frequently, in May a mottled-winged caddisfly hatch can be seen on the Cumberland tailwater that is breath taking. Unfortunately it can be difficult to get a fish to take your presentation with so many real ones bouncing about the water.

Adult Caddisfly (*Glossosoma*)
Common Name: Little Brown Short-horned Sedges

What artificials are matches for the caddisfly? Bead-Head Hare's Ears and Pheasant Tails #12s and #14s are good choices for the nymph. For emergers, try a #12 or #14 CDC Caddis in olive color. Nothing is better to match the adult caddisfly than a tan Elk Hair Caddis in #12 or #14. If you see a fair number of caddis fluttering over the water of a stream or creek, do not hesitate to fish the dry Elk Hair Caddis.

Midges

These are some of the smallest aquatic insects and are considered to be part of the "true fly family." Midges have short life cycles, typically four to five weeks, and reproduce continuously throughout the year. They are extremely abundant where water temperatures remain nearly constant (like in the Cumberland tailwater), but can also thrive in very polluted and/or stagnant water. Trout will key on any one of their living stages: larva, pupa or adult. Midges are also a favorite food of damselflies and dragonflies.

Adult midges live only a few days, but before their demise the females will drop a cluster of eggs into clean water. A typical hatch will produce hundreds of ultra small tube-like larvae with about a dozen segments forming around their bodies. Midge larvae in Kentucky's cold tailwaters are about hook size #18 to #24 and are found in an assortment of colors: olive, yellow, cream and black. A few midge species produce red larvae, which are sold commercially as bloodworms.

Midge Larva (*Chironomidae*)
Common Name: Bloodworm

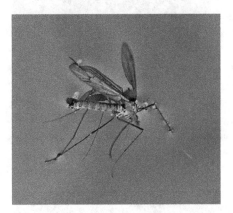

Adult Midge (*Chironomidae*)

The larvae go through several instars (molts) and eventually convert to short-lived pupae three to six millimeter in size. They have identifiable heads and wing cases. They rise to the surface, shed their skin and fly off to mate. The adults are very tiny with two short wings less than their body length.

Good representations of the midge larvae include #18 and #20 Tungsten Zebra Midges and Bead-Head WD-40s. A WD-40 midge fly uses wood duck feathers in both the wing case and tail, thus the clever WD abbreviation. Exact, drag-free drifts made with the proper size and colors are key to catching trout on imitations.

Midge adults have a propensity to skitter on the surface and, when fishing, the dry #20 Comparadun presentation doesn't have to be perfect to entice a strike. Therefore, you don't need a well-mended drift and can just skitter the dry fly across the water like the real adults do.

Stoneflies

Stoneflies are far more common out west than they are in Kentucky. On Montana, Oregon and Wyoming rivers we see salmonflies (a specie of stonefly) up to three inches long, but here in Kentucky our golden stoneflies will more likely be one inch long. Nonetheless, stoneflies remain an important food source for Kentucky trout.

Stoneflies have three stages of incomplete metamorphous development. Eggs dropped into the water mature into nymphs that grow in stages over three months to three years time. These nymphs are ferocious feeders, shredding and chewing live or decomposing plants. They have two short tails, two wing cases, two very long antennae and six legs. As the nymph nears maturity it will crawl onto land, shuck its husk and fly off. We see more stonefly nymphs than the adults because the adults land quickly after emerging. The adults are also more active at night than during the day, which may be another reason we see so few of them.

Stonefly Nymphs (*Perlidae*)
Common Name: Golden Stones

Adult stoneflies have four long, flat, hard and shiny wings. In Kentucky they range in color from yellow to dark brown, and are about one to two centimeters long. Adults mate either on the ground or in bushes. The female can drop her egg sack by flying over the water, crawling down to the water's edge, or scooting over the water.

Masses of one-centimeter-long black stonefly nymphs are common in Kentucky's streams and tailwaters. A good match is a #12 Black Stonefly Nymph and for the big golden ones try a #8 Yellow Nymph. Spotting some adults on the water's edge suggests the use of a #10 Stimulator.

In addition to these aquatic insects and their invertebrates, trout will also go after terrestrials, sow bugs and scuds. Let's take a quick look at these fast-food options.

Golden Stonefly Spinner (*Acronruria lycorias*)
Common Name: Golden Stone

Terrestrials

While not a major food source for trout, terrestrials are found along banks and hidden within vegetative growth. But a hungry trout will not pass up a terrestrial that falls on the water. Terrestrials that occasionally wind up on trout dinner plates include crayfish, grasshoppers, cicadas, Japanese beetles, salamanders and frogs. One story is an angler landed two 20-inch browns one after the other on a Dave's Hopper along some vegetative growth on the Cumberland's tailwater late one summer. That's a good time to lay black ants, grasshoppers and Japanese beetles along stream and riverbanks lined with overhanging vegetative growth. Trout will gobble up these big, tasty morsels.

Scuds and Such

There seems to be a good number of sow bugs and scuds found in the moss beds of Kentucky's streams and tailwaters. These little shrimp-like bugs are a good staple for trout and they will nose through the beds in search of these little fellows and will even consume the moss to get to them. Most sow bugs are gray in color and about three-fourths of a centimeter long.

Hellgrammites, crawfish, small shad, suckers and sculpins can also be found in many streams that have gravel bottoms. Rainbows and browns can easily out swim these little fellows and will not hesitate to slurp them up.

Artificials such as scuds, Woolly Buggers, and Clouser and Muddler Minnows are a good choice to fish if any of these critters are seen. The scuds and Woolly Buggers should be fished near the bottom. But the Clouser and Muddler Minnows should be fished retrieving the fly line with short 6-inch strips on a long leader in lakes or deep tailwaters, with a sinking or sink tip fly line.

Dream Box of Flies

This selection of three dozen dry flies, emergers, nymphs, terrestrials and streamers can be purchased for as little as $30 or as much as $100 depending upon their quality and where they are purchased. Poorly made flies can come apart with frequent use, are inclined not to follow patterns well, and are built on poorer quality hooks. But if you are a casual fisherman, spending $100 for 36 flies may not be a smart move on your part. Regardless of your investment it is a good idea to keep your flies in a small fly box that is easily accessed while wading in a stream.

The following recommended flies tend to mimic the mayflies, caddisflies, midges, stoneflies and other insects prevalent in Kentucky's streams, lakes and tailwaters and are known to catch trout on a regular basis. Two sizes and a single color are specified for almost each fly, because these seem to either be the most productive or they match the sizes and colors of the real flies. Studies indicate fish can detect color and given two flies of the same size and configuration, but different colors, fish may readily take the one and reject the other.

Dry Flies	Size #
Parachute Adams	14, 16
Elk Hair Caddis (tan)	12, 14
Blue Wing Olive (BWO)	16, 18
Sulphur	14
Stimulator	10
Comparadun	20

Emergers	
CDC Caddis (olive)	12, 14
CDC Mayfly (olive)	14, 16

Nymphs	
Bead-Head Hare's Ear	12, 14
Prince	12, 14
Pheasant Tail	12, 14
Stone Fly (black)	12
(yellow)	8
Scud (gray)	16
Copper John (green or blue)	14
San Juan Worm (red)	10
Egg (pink)	14
Tungsten Zebra Midge	18, 20
Bead-Head WD-40	18, 20

Terrestrials	
Black Ant	14
Grass Hopper	8
Japanese Beetle	12

Streamers	
Woolly Bugger (olive)	6
(brown)	6
Clouser Minnow	4
Muddler	4

Dry Flies—Row 1: Sulphur, Japanese Beetle; Row 2: Elk Hair Caddis, Blue Wing Olive; Row 3: Para Adams, Foam Black Ant; Row 4: CDC Comparadun

Emergers: CDC BWO Emerger and CDC Caddis Emerger, both tied with olive dubbing

Nymphs and Wet Flies—Row 1: San Juan Worm, Prince, Copper John;
Row 2: Bead-Head Hare's Ear, WD 40, Tungsten Zebra;
Row 3: Bead-Head Pheasant Tail, Gray Scud; Row 4: Pink Egg

Big Artificials—Row 1: Muddler Minnow, Olive Woolly Bugger;
Row 2: Clouser Minnow, Golden Stonefly Nymph;
Row 3: Dave's Hopper

If you've been reading the chapters of this book sequentially, you have all your gear, know the difference between a roll cast and single hauling, can tell a rainbow from a brookie, own a superb collection of flies specially selected for Kentucky trout, and should be all set to wet your waders. But where should you throw that first cast? The next chapter will teach you how to read water in both fast-moving streams and calm lakes, to make sure that every throw of the line is targeted to where the trout are.

"Some act and talk as though casting were the entire art of fly fishing, and grade an angler solely by the distance he can cover with his flies. This is a great mistake and pernicious in its influence. Casting is but a method of placing a fly before the trout without alarming it and within its reach. It is merely placing food before a guest. The selection of such food as will suit, and so serving it as to pleasure a fastidious and fickle taste, still remain indispensably necessarey (sic) to induce its acceptance."
Henry P Wells, "Fly-Rods and Fly Tackle" 1885

Chapter 7: Reading Water to Find Trout

Now that you know what trout like to feast upon, let's learn more about where those elusive trout are hiding so you can gently drop that irresistible fly right in front of their noses. You'll soon find out that being able to execute a basic cast with a carefully selected fly is necessary, but not always sufficient to catch trout.

Fish spend their entire lives eating, resting and hiding from predators, and in the previous chapter we talked about the use of artificials to mimic the food supply of a trout. So part of the challenge of catching fish is knowing how to get a replica of the actual food to the trout without scaring them or the fish knowing it's not the real McCoy. But just where exactly are the fish?

There is an old saying that 90 percent of the trout are caught by 10 percent of the fishermen. Whether true or not, one thing is for sure, we all want to be members of the elite top ten. But that old saying reminds us of another—90 percent of the fish are found in only 10 percent of the water. We're not sure that one's exactly true either. But if you don't know where the fish are, you certainly can't catch them, and there's no sense wasting your time fishing waters when the fish aren't there.

When you approach a trout stream, tailwater or lake, the inevitable question you should ask yourself is: Where are the trout hanging out? Reading water to find trout is essentially observing the anatomy of a waterway, understanding how that structure meets the needs of a fish, and predicting where the fish might be hanging out. While each stream, tailwater or lake is unique, there are some basic structures that give us clues as to where the trout are lying in wait. So let's talk some more about exactly where those trout are hiding and how we can get to them.

In addition to clean, cold, oxygenated water, trout need (1) an abundance of food, (2) shelter from strong currents, and (3) protection from predators. Each of these factors gives us clues as to where trout might be lounging around, waiting for that delectable morsel to come floating by while retaining their position of being the hunter, rather than the hunted.

Trout eat almost constantly, as long as the water temperature is between 40° and 72°F. If it's colder than that they're in a suppressed metabolic state and warmer than that they're probably belly-side up. But the successful trout has to be sure that the energy expended in getting the food is less than the energy obtained from eating that smidgeon of midge. As we learned from the previous chapter, trout may be scooping up eggs or crustaceans from rocky bottoms, catching nymphs as they rise through the water, or picking winged adults off the surface of the stream or lake. But all this hunting and gathering requires work and trout can't be fighting stiff currents or swirly waters in their quest for a nibble of pupa or a bite of mayfly. Consequently, trout position themselves where they find the most food while using the least amount of energy.

Trout are also fearful of predators: ospreys, herons, river otters and of course anglers. Although we have seen a brown trout threaten to snatch a small minnow from the mouth of a Great Heron, we have also witnessed a huge striped bass rip a sizable rainbow, ensnared with fly and tippet, from our clutches. But in general, trout do not expose themselves unnecessarily unless it is to feast on a hatch. So the hungry trout will work constantly keeping one eye out for food and the other eye watching for beasts of prey.

Direct sunlight is also not to a trout's liking; hence, you usually can't see trout. And if by chance you do catch a glimpse of one, they will likely see you and be gone in a flash. So finding some type of structure to hide behind is important to trout as they sit and wait for food to be delivered to their doorstep. Thus, identifying the environment in which trout like to reside is crucial to our catching them.

Of course the environment is not a static thing. Whether caused by heavy rains or changes in water release schedules, the ebb and flow of streams and tail-waters slowly alters the structure of the waterway creating riffles, high banks, pools and runs. The presence of mid-stream rocks, fallen trees and their root wads, ledges, and huge boulders add to these structures and create places where trout can be found. In the next section we will examine the structure of streams, tailwaters and lakes to learn more about where trout like to hang out.

Cold Water Streams and Rivers

In cold-water streams and rivers, trout prefer to face into the current where food will drift to them. Trout aren't just being lazy—they're being smart. They cannot stay in fast moving water indefinitely, for that would quickly exhaust them. So they seek out breaks in the swift currents and in the still waters adjacent to them. From there, the trout can tail out, pick off insects, and return to the quiet waters to rest. Find the resting spots and you have found the fish. These places are behind rocks and root wads; under and along fallen trees; close to steep banks; in deep pools beside boulders; in seams behind and in front of islands; beneath drop offs; over gravel bars and moss beds; along vegetative banks; and in washed-out depressions. Let's take a look at each of these hiding places and talk about what kinds of flies might work best to feed the hungry trout.

Obstructions

Obstructions such as big rocks, fallen trees and root wads break the natural flow of the water, induce fast-flowing seams and foam lines, and provide shelter for the trout. The water has to speed up so all of it can get around the obstruction, similar to how lift forces function on an airplane wing. Trout reside close to these obstructions because the food is more concentrated there.

Consequently, trout can be found in the quiet waters either in front of or behind big rocks, and under and along fallen trees and root wads. Basically, what you want to do is position your fly in the natural current flowing around these obstructions in order to dangle the food in front of the awaiting trout. You have several different ways to do this: dry flies placed in front of large rocks and left to drift around them can be productive. Alternately, a nymph hung below an indicator and drifted in these areas can be effective. You are also likely to bring up a nice trout using a sink tip fly line and a minnow imitation stripped along fallen trees and root wads.

Other water features to be on the lookout for are seams, riffles, tailouts, wide flats and fast runs. We admit that it takes a practiced eye to identify each of these elements, but the learning curve is quite shallow. The faster the current, the more pronounced these features tend to be; conversely the slower the current, the more difficult it may be to differentiate between them.

Seams

A seam is a water feature in which faster current is going past slack or slower moving current. Seams run nearly parallel to the stream currents. The faster flowing seam brings food to fish that are waiting and resting in the slower moving adjacent current. The difference in the velocity of the seam water and that beyond its outer edge may induce a swirl or what is called an eddy. If the slack water is moving upstream, you know the seam is at the edge of a true eddy and the seam literally forms the eddy line. Trout are known to hang out beneath the seams and large eddies.

To the untrained eye, seams can be difficult to spot. Look for bubbles, foam or debris and use these to monitor variations in the speed of the current's flow. Tailwaters frequently have foam lines coming off of fallen trees, rocks and gravel bars. These seams will likely carry insects that fish can readily pick off as they drift by.

If you cast a weighted nymph under an indicator or without an indicator at the top of a seam and let it drift completely through and out of the seam under a tight fly line, the nymph will rise to the surface and frequently at this moment a trout will strike it. It could be the trout takes it as an emerging fly. All we care is it works wonders.

Riffles

Riffles frequently form in the middle of a stream or river where the slope of the waterway has steepened somewhat, causing a short, relatively shallow stretch of moving water. Stream and river riffles are seldom more than one or two feet deep and are crammed with stones of small to moderate size. Typically the water moving through a riffle has a higher velocity and greater turbulence as compared to the water on either side of the riffle. Riffles can also be caused by an obstruction in the waterway, such as a rock or downed tree.

When looking at a riffle, typically the texture of the water's surface will mirror or mimic the texture of the stream or river bottom. Riffles formed by water flowing over small pea-sized gravel will tend to have a finer texture than water flowing over larger rocks. On bright or sunny days riffles are easier to see as the light bounces off the moving texture of the water.

Although these riffles carry lots of trout food, riffles are typically empty water (that is, water devoid of trout) because of their strong currents. But a common error in thinking is that fish will avoid hanging out in riffles altogether due to the supposed energy expended. However, it is the current flow that brings food to the fish waiting below. Directly under the riffle, along the bottom of the stream or the river, there will be small depressions and rocks holding slack water within or behind that structure. If there is a holding spot behind a big rock in the riffle, one big trout may take up there. These micro-eddies provide just enough resting space for a hungry trout awaiting his next snack. Because these micro-eddies are so small, fish will be extremely territorial and will not pod up like they do in deeper or calmer waters.

Fish usually position themselves above the riffles to one side or the other, and below the riffles in their tailouts. As fish spot a nymph floating by, they jet out, grab it and move back out of the current. You should fish a riffle by casting a dry fly or nymph above it; let the fly drift through the riffle and then out the other end of the tailout. Do not hesitate to cast to the edges of both narrow and wide riffles.

Tailouts

As discussed above, tailouts frequently form just below riffles, but they can also be found on the downstream side of any obstruction such as downed trees or large boulders. Typically, tailouts are V-shaped with the open end of the V pointing upstream and the "point" pointing downstream. Therefore, the top of the tailout tends to be wider than the bottom. Typically, slack water or even an eddy can be found on either side of a tailout, separated by an eddy line. Trout love to hang out just below the tailouts or in the adjacent waters, waiting to be fed.

To fish a tailout, cast your fly upstream into the top of the tailout. As noted above, if not too far a distance, you can also cast up above the riffle and float your fly through the tailout. This works for dry flies or for nymphs that have been set under an indicator so the nymph doesn't actually bounce along the bottom of the streambed or get hung up. Allow the fly to carry through the tailout, letting the line swing into an arc as it approaches the slack water along either side of the bottom of the V. Many strikes are made in the swing of the drift. Allow the fly to complete the drift. The nymph will rise to the surface under a tight fly line and it is then that a trout may also strike.

Pocketwater

As the name implies pocketwaters are small, partially confined parcels of quiescent water formed by protruding rocks, deadfalls, islands and such. They are moderately deep and havens for trout trying to escape the swift surrounding currents. With a short 15-20 foot cast into the pocket, trout are enticed to rise to a dry fly. Plunge a nymph into the pocket without an indicator, let it settle towards the bottom, and a trout will usually not pass it up. With the pocket guarded by rocks or dead falls, the trout are usually not easily spooked by the close proximity of the angler. The jumble of soft currents and swirly waters give the pocket a very haphazard look, but these waterways can be rich in fish food and attract many trout.

Keep in mind, that in front of, next to and behind each rock is a small amount of slack or pocketwater that can hold fish. In this scenario, short casts directed above and into the seams entering the pockets can be very productive.

Flats and Runs

Some streams will have long stretches with narrow fast runs and wide flats that are at least two or more feet deep. If covered with canopies of tree branches, these slow-flowing flats can be a haven for trout cruising around searching for nymphs holding onto rocks or pads of moss. Runs tend to be deeper than riffles, with less gradient, and larger rocks strewn along the floor, or even sandy bottoms. In the faster runs the trout will be on the bottom picking off nymphs or small crustaceans that come their way. Slowly work your way upstream if you can and downstream if you must, casting 10-15 foot sections at a time with dries on the flats and nymphs in the runs. If you see trout sipping, try an emerger.

Pools by Boulders

Some of the best fishing in Kentucky's trout streams can be found in the deep pools abutting big, limestone boulders. It is incidental, but these boulders became dislodged from the overhanging cliffs and fell into the streams a long time ago. Now torrential rainstorms producing swift currents flush sediment of all sizes from around these boulders, leaving deep, dark pools of water up to six feet deep. These pools are havens for trout seeking cooler water, shelter from sunlight and prey, and the food that passes through the pools.

To fish these pools, stand in the shallow water next to them and use the high stick method of presenting either a dry fly or a weighted nymph to the trout. With little more than a rod's length of fly line out, roll cast this upstream until your rod is nearly level, and as the fly drifts into the pool, raise the rod tip as it passes in front and then lower it as it passes out of the pool. If there are any trout in the stream, some will be in these pools, and your chance of hooking several using this method will be very good.

Plunge Pools

When water cascades over a waterfall or a big obstruction it will scar a hole in the bottom of the stream or tailwater and produce a plunge pool that will hold trout. Although big fish will hang out in deep plunge pools directly beneath waterfalls, it is unlikely they will be found upstream in front of a waterfall. Plunge pools are best fished allowing a weighted nymph without an indicator to ride from the surface all the way to the bottom. The nymph will likely exit the pool and that is when a fish is liable to strike. These pools are excellent for using a high stick method of nymph presentation. They are deep enough that even close up you are unlikely to spook the trout in them.

Banks and Bend Pools

A strong current leading directly into a dirt bank will in time wash it out and create a high bank and a bend pool in its place. In a small stream the pool may be no more than three to five feet deep and cover less than 75 square feet, but in a tailwater it may be up to 15 feet deep and extend 50-100 feet. Trout take refuge along the bottom of these pools where the fish are secure from predators and sunlight, and pick off food in the current flow above them. A high stick double presentation of a big dry fly over a deep-set nymph is suggested for fishing a bend pool in a stream. In a tailwater, drift a deep-set nymph under an indicator about three to four feet from the bank. Attractor patterns such as stimulators, hoppers, beetles and ants cast along the banks will often bring up a big brown trout.

Light and Temperature

Trout shun full sunlight, so you will not find them in thin or shallow water during the day. But in early morning hours or as the sun is going down they might move into that water if there are insects to be had there. Like us, herons and ospreys don't see well in the dark and the trout feel safe. Watch for moonlit dimples in the water, which is a good indication of feeding fish.

Warmer water tends to hold less oxygen than colder water does. In fact, several studies have indicated that it is not the warmth of the water that is positively correlated with trout mortality rates, but the oxygen-carrying capacity of the water as related to water temperature. As a stream warms in late spring or as water levels decline, fish will have a tendency to migrate towards more highly oxygenated water found in riffles, cascades or plunge pools.

Cold Water Lakes

The most striking differences between lakes, streams and tailwaters are that lakes have no currents and they are deep. The only movement of their waters is that caused either by winds, in-flows or draw-offs near dams. Because trout, particularly rainbows, thrive best in moving water they do a lot of swimming around not only to take up needed oxygen but also to search for food, including minnows and insects. Many of Kentucky's lakes are stocked with rainbows in February and again in the late fall months, October and November. In early spring you may see trout cruising near the shores and stream outlets in search of nymphs hunkered down in beds of moss or crawling over rocks. As spring wears on the trout chase the young warm water fish from recent spawns. A jerking retrieve of a minnow imitation in this water can be very productive.

As summer approaches the surface water warms and the trout move to the deeper, colder water away from the banks. The lake is now stratified with the cold, dense water down deep and the warm water up on top. The trout cruise below the thermocline where the water is cold and rich in oxygen, and can be from 10 to 30 feet below the surface. It is in these waters during daylight that trout search for small fish to feed upon. Try a Clouser Minnow appropriately weighted and trolled to catch a few big ones. See individual lake entries for more detail on how to fish a Clouser Minnow.

On cool evenings the trout may rise to the surface and feed upon surface insects. As the summer sun sets, the surface water will cool, and since it is adjacent to the air, it absorbs some oxygen, and trout will rise out of the depths to absorb it and feed on flying insects caught on the surface. Many of these will be mayflies and midges. In Kentucky's bigger lakes, bait fishermen can be seen anchored or drifting over deep water, fishing under lights extended out over the surface. The lights attract small fish, which in turn attract the trout.

In late fall, Kentucky Fish and Wildlife will stock the lakes again. Unaccustomed to the large open expanses of the water, the trout will search out moving currents and find them where small streams enter the lakes. Pods of trout will position themselves in these outflows and feed on anything that comes their way, be it nymphs, minnows or crayfish.

In early winter, the surface waters will turn much colder than those beneath them and the lakes will turn over, i.e. the much colder water will sink under the less cold water. In water less than about 40°F, trout cease to feed and will come to the surface. For a month or two you will see trout again gulping small fish particularly near shores. In water 5-10 feet deep along edges or stream entrances, the sunlight penetrates and warms the water, and insects and crustaceans thrive. Trout enter these regions and feed. Once winter has set in and the entire lake water is below 40°F, ice forms along the edges and the trout become lethargic. From late November through January their feeding drops off, and so should the fishing.

Generally speaking, bank fishing in most lakes will be unproductive unless you can position yourself near an entering stream or can reach deep water along a dam or spillway. Otherwise some type of watercraft will be required to troll in deeper waters.

Some final words: if you have made several good presentations of your fly or nymph to a likely spot and do not get a take, move on to another likely spot. When you catch a fish in one type of cover try to remember what it was like. The more you fish, the more you learn to read the water, and soon you will join that exclusive 10 percent.

"Some go to church and think about fishing, others go fishing and think about God."
Tony Blake

Chapter 8: State Licensing and Regulations

While Huck Finn never had to worry about creel limits and trout stamps, today's anglers must follow a host of rules and regulations before making that first cast. Although none of us like being overregulated or paying taxes, the laws that govern fishing in Kentucky have been carefully thought out and must be followed unless you want the officer with the state seal on the door of his truck tracking you down.

The KDFWR enforces the rules and regulations governing fishing in our state and the state's land area. KDFWR has a variety of responsibilities and operates several programs including law enforcement, fish stocking, fish and wildlife habitat improvement, conservation camps, and the maintenance of public lands and lakes.

KDFWR is funded primarily through the sale of fishing and hunting licenses and permits (50 percent), federal revenue (36 percent) and boat registration fees (6 percent). The amount of federal funding depends on the number of state hunting and fishing licensees sold in the state. Notably, KDFWR does not receive any state general fund tax dollars. Unlike many other government services, the sportsmen and women who use these programs are the ones who pay for them. In other words, we pay to play!

The following discussion pertains to the fishing of Kentucky waters. Please keep in mind that each state has its own rules and regulations. Importantly, although the information presented below was accurate at the time of publishing this book, these regulations may change from year to year. It is your responsibility to keep current, and to help you we have included contact information for the KDFWR at the end of this chapter.

Licensing and Trout Permits

All anglers 16 years of age and older must hold a current fishing license, fill out the license and carry it when fishing. There are some exceptions to who must hold a license including landowners and their immediate families when fishing on their own land; resident servicemen on furlough; those fishing on the first Saturday and Sunday in June; and those fishing in Mammoth Cave National Park. A resident sportsmen license, which includes fishing and hunting privileges, is also available.

In addition to a general fishing license, a trout permit is required for all anglers 16 years of age and older who want to keep the trout they catch. The exceptions to this requirement include landowners and their immediate families when fishing on their own land, and those anglers holding a senior or a disabled fishing license. However, all licensed anglers fishing the portion of the Cumberland River from Wolf Creek Dam to the Tennessee state line, its tributaries up to the first riffle, and all of Hatchery Creek are required to possess a trout permit. Revenue from the sale of trout permits is used to help finance the stocking of trout from Wolf Creek National Fish Hatchery into Kentucky streams and lakes.

Annual fishing licenses and trout permits are valid from the date of purchase through the last day in February. New licenses are required annually beginning March 1. Both fishing licenses and trout permits can be purchased in-person at a variety of sporting goods shops, big box stores and county court clerk offices; by phone 24 hours a day at (877) 598-2401; and via the internet at fw.ky. gov. License and permit fees increase every 5-7 years to compensate for increases in operational and infrastructure costs, such as fuel, materials, maintenance of equipment and required services. Don't complain—it's still cheaper than dinner for four at McDonald's.

Kentucky Fishing License Fees		
	Resident	**Non-Resident**
Annual Fishing	$20	$50
Joint Husband/Wife	$36	Not available
Senior Fishing	$11	Not available
Disabled Fishing	$11	Not available
3-year Fishing	$55	Not available
1-day Fishing	$7	$10
Non-resident 7-day Fishing	Not applicable	$30
Non-resident 15-day Fishing	Not applicable	$40
Trout Permit	$10	$10

Kentucky Fishing Regulations

Every sport has its own lingo, and fishing is no different. Let's cover a few phrases to help the angler navigate the regulatory waters. Some of our wording is taken verbatim from KDFWR regulations to make sure everyone has this right. For general instructions on how to properly release fish, please see special fishing techniques in Chapter 4.

Daily Limit: This is simply the number of fish of a given species that an angler is permitted to keep in one day's fishing. Notably, this is not the number of fish the angler is limited to catch. Any fish harvested that exceeds the daily limit must immediately be released. Also known as the daily creel limit.

Possession Limit: A possession limit is two times the daily creel limit for all fish species with a daily creel limit and excludes processed fish.

Minimum Size or Length Limits: Anglers are notorious for not being able to properly measure their fish. We think that's more a function of their yearning for bragging rights rather than any skill deficit. But how do you properly measure a fish? Measure all fish from the tip of the lower jaw (closed) to the tip of the tail with fish laid flat on rule with tail lobes squeezed together. Undersized fish must be returned immediately to the waters from which they were taken in the best possible physical condition.

Protective Slot Limit: For this one we need to think beyond Vegas and one-armed bandits. A protective slot limit is a management tool to reduce the number of fish harvested that falls within a certain size range. For example, there is a 15- to 20-inch protective slot limit on rainbow trout along the Cumberland tailwater from Wolf Creek Dam to the Tennessee border. Any rainbow 15 inches or longer and 20 inches or shorter in length must be immediately released. This regulation is a management tool designed to prohibit the harvesting of all trout in the slot. Slot limits also increase the number of trophy fish by decreasing the number of fish harvested within the slot.

Catch-and-Release: This is another conservation practice to ensure sustainability and overfishing of target species. In Kentucky no artificial baits may be used during this no-harvest season. You must use artificial lures or flies, but barbless hooks are not required. Any and all harvested fish are to be returned immediately to the water. See "seasonal catch-and-release" below.

Delayed Harvest Stream: This is the same thing as a catch-and-release stream. As noted above, anglers are "delaying the harvest" of fish by practicing catch-and-release of any harvested fish between the specified months.

Put-take Fisheries: Most trout-stocked streams in Kentucky are designated as put-take (p-t) fisheries. This means the KDFWR stocks the waterways with the intention that anglers can keep all the trout they catch, as long as they follow all regulations, including creel and size limitations.

Put-grow-take Fisheries: P-g-t fisheries are those waters in which trout are "put" or stocked (many as fingerlings) and conservation managers hope the fish "grow" to a desirable size before they are "taken" or harvested. Several streams and lakes in Kentucky are p-g-t fisheries. Unfortunately, overzealous fishermen turn these into p-t fisheries for themselves.

Seasonal Catch-and-Release: This is the same as "catch-and-release'" described above only that there are seasonal limitations. Many trout streams in Kentucky are designated seasonal catch-and-release streams (scr) from Oct. 1 – Mar. 31 (or May 31 in the case of Swift Camp Creek).

Culling: In its simplest terms, culling is replacing a previously caught fish with another (typically larger) fish, allowing the angler to stay within the creel limit. It makes no difference if the previously caught fish in your possession is on a stringer, in a fish basket, or in a livewell. The intent of the law is to promote trout survivability. Trout culling is prohibited on the Cumberland River tailwater. Beginning March 1, 2015, trout culling is prohibited on any Kentucky waterway.

Public Access

Kentucky state law requires obtaining landowner permission before entering or trespassing on private property. All of the trout streams, tailwaters and lakes included in this book have one or more public access points. However, some of the waters pass though private lands. If in doubt, it may be best to seek landowner permission. More information can be found at Kentucky Statute 150.092 (lrc.ky.gov/Statutes/statute.aspx?id=1953).

For more information and a complete, updated listing of all rules and regulations pertaining to fishing Kentucky's waters, please contact:

Kentucky Department of Fish and Wildlife Resources
#1 Sportsman's Lane
Frankfort, KY 40601
(800) 858-1549 or (502) 564-4336
Web: fw.ky.gov

Part II: The Best Trout Waters in Kentucky

The second half of this book covers the 36 best trout streams, lakes and tailwaters found in the Bluegrass state. As noted earlier, we defined the "best" trout waters as those having (1) top-rated water quality and trout habitat, (2) good stocking levels, (3) scenic vistas, and (4) public access with convenient parking. We fully realize there is room for a little subjectivity here and we may have omitted your favorite stream. But after conferring with several other avid anglers, we think it's a pretty darn good list.

Several people have asked us, "Did you really fly fish in all those places?" and the answer is absolutely *yes*! There is no way we could write about a stream, lake or tailwater without having actually fished it. And in many of these places we have fished more times than our spouses even know about. Fortunately neither of them will ever read this far into our book.

Realizing that fishing can be very local, we have divided the fisheries into five geographic regions scattered around the state:

- West-Central
- North-Central
- Southern
- Red River Gorge Area
- Eastern

Notably, these regions are not divided by watershed but by driving sheds. The *West-Central* region basically follows the I-65 corridor south of Elizabethtown and reaches all the way over to Hopkinsville. The *North-Central* region covers the golden triangle between Louisville, Lexington and Cincinnati, including two streams in the Ft. Knox area. The *Southern* region of the state encompasses the I-75 corridor that runs through the DBNF, extending as far west as the Cumberland River. Finally, the eastern part of the state is divided into the *Red River Gorge Area* and the far *Eastern* region, which is everything east of the Gorge.

For each entry we include a host of information that is subject to change, including trout stocking numbers, regulations and access sites. Again, please refer to the KDFRW website or publications for updates.

Within each geographic region we have organized the waterways alphabetically. If you can't remember what's where, you can always refer to the map on the next page. So load up that fishing gear, pack a lunch and leave a note for your loved ones before heading out for a great day on the water.

● West-Central Kentucky

1 Casey Creek
2 Lick Creek
3 Lynn Camp Creek
4 Nolin River Tailwater
5 Roundstone Creek
6 Sulphur Spring Creek
7 Trammel Creek

● North-Central Kentucky

1 Big Bone Creek
2 Floyds Fork
3 Herrington Lake Tailwater
4 Otter Creek
5 Royal Springs
6 Sinking Creek
7 Taylorsville Lake Tailwater

● Southern Kentucky

1 Bark Camp Creek
2 Cane Creek
3 Cumberland River Tailwater
4 Hatchery Creek
5 Laurel River Lake
6 Rock Creek
7 War Fork Creek
8 Wood Creek Lake

● Red River Gorge Area

1 Chimney Top Creek
2 Dog Fork Creek
3 East Fork of Indian Creek
4 Middle Fork of the Red River
5 Mill Creek Lake
6 Parched Corn Creek
7 Swift Camp Creek

● Eastern Kentucky

1 Big Caney Creek
2 Cave Run Lake Tailwater
3 Greenbo Lake
4 Laurel Creek
5 Paintsville Lake
6 Paintsville Lake Tailwater
7 Russell Fork

Map of Kentucky's Best Trout Waters

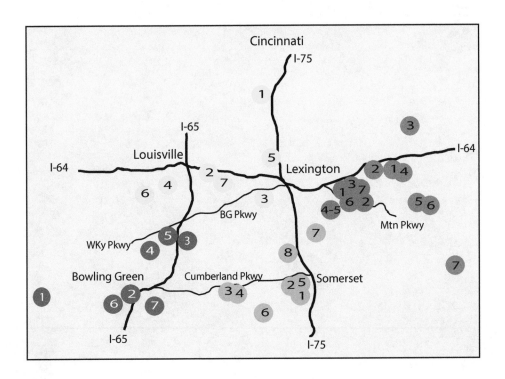

Regions:

West-Central, pg 91
North-Central, pg 109
Southern, pg 127
Red River Gorge Area, pg 157
Eastern, pg 179

FLY FISHING KENTUCKY

FLY FISHING KENTUCKY

FLY FISHING KENTUCKY

90

West-Central Kentucky

- Casey Creek
- Lick Creek
- Lynn Camp Creek
- Nolin River Tailwater
- Roundstone Creek
- Sulphur Spring Creek
- Trammel Creek

Trout streams in the western part of the state tend to have little gradient, yet are endowed with cold spring-fed waters and easy bank access.

Casey Creek

Casey Creek

A spring-fed creek stocked with a whopping 8,000 rainbow trout each year.

Ecosystem: Casey Creek cuts through the rolling landscape of western Kentucky—the never-ending land of beans and corn. When many Kentuckians think of the western part of the state they envision smoky barbeque, expansive farmland and the recreational hub of Land Between the Lakes. But locals know Casey Creek as one of the best trout fisheries in the state. Fed by countless springs, the water flows cold year-round, permitting Casey Creek to be successfully stocked through the hot summer months at the rate of 2,000 trout per mile.

The stream lies nestled within a corridor of deciduous trees that form a tall, arching canopy that stretches over this 20- to 30-foot-wide creek. While the gradient is negligible, Casey Creek produces a constant flow of oxygen-producing riffles and deep quiet pools. The occasional downed tree and root wad provides for plenty of fish cover, but does little to impede the wading angler. The water quality is excellent and the creek is abundant with aquatic invertebrates, terrestrials and small fish. Heavy rains can quickly bring the creek to the top of its banks, but the gravel-bottom stream clears quickly.

Stocking and Regulations: Casey Creek is stocked each year with 8,000 rainbows, equally distributed across the months of 3, 4, 5, 6, 7, 8, 9 and 10. There is a daily limit of 8 trout, but no minimum size required. A catch-and-release (no harvest) season applies October 1 – March 31. All other fishing regulations and permit requirements apply.

Recommendations: Kentucky Fish and Wildlife stocks Casey Creek where KY 525 crosses the stream. There is a large pool right underneath the bridge where the trout tend to pod up the first few days after being released. Although you can fish upstream or downstream of the bridge, most locals fish right at the bridge or walk the old road that goes upstream for about 300 yards (on the left side of the creek as you're looking upstream) to the first large pool. Unfortunately, this creek is fished pretty hard right after the stocking truck arrives and can be fished out within a week during the summer months. But holdovers can be had and the winter and early spring months can be productive.

You'll definitely want to bring waders to fish the best parts of Casey Creek. Upstream of the bridge it's an easy walk along the bank or across the gravel bars that connect several large pools, unless spring rains have swollen the waterway. Most of the streambed is covered with golf- and baseball-sized rocks, until you get to the first deep pool. Let us warn you loud and clear: the bottom of the first large pool is slicker than otter snot. Rather than gravel, the streambed is a slippery rock slab, covered with moss, fine silt and soggy leaves. From early fall until late winter, this pool averages about three to four feet deep. But after a good rain, the pool can easily be over your head with a stiff current running though it. Be sure to fish this pool, as many of the newly stocked trout head this way.

Further upstream of the pool, the creek meanders from gravel bar to riffle and back to gravel bar again. There are a few more pools, but mostly the water only deepens next to the steep embankments. The canopy is high here, easily allowing overhead or side-arm casts. Be sure to fish the deep waters along the banks, around the root wads, and below the tailouts.

Downstream of the KY 525 bridge are multiple deep pools. However, the landowner on the right bank (as you are facing downstream) has not taken too kindly to anglers and has vigorously posted several signs discouraging bank access. Again be sure to bring your waders along and wade the stream, unless heavy rains have swollen the creek. Just below the bridge you can wade through several deep pools until you reach a small set of 20- to 25-foot limestone cliffs on the right-hand side of the creek. Here the creek makes a slight bend to the left and the water has cut a deep trench that runs 40-50 yards underneath the cliffs (pictured here). Be sure to fish the tailout at the top of the trench and all along the trench itself.

Prince Nymphs, Pheasant Tails, Copper Johns and Hare's Ear nymphs all fish well here. Tie an indicator 18-24 inches above the fly and cast into the shadows along the seam lines, through the tailouts, and along the deep embankments. As the nymph drifts through the currents, strip in line to keep the fly at the edges of the root wads and occasional downed trees. Dry flies such as an Adams or Elk Hair Caddis can also be productive in the deep pools and tailouts. The chubs are abundant throughout Casey Creek and are never bashful at taking your fly.

Directions: From the Western Kentucky Parkway, take exit 38A for the Pennyrile Parkway towards Hopkinsville. Drive 22.8 miles. Take exit 11 for Dr. ML King Way, also towards Hopkinsville. Turn left onto KY 1682 West, towards Lake Barkley State Resort Park. Drive 6.1 miles. Turn right onto KY 272 West. Drive 0.5 miles. Turn left onto KY 164 West. Drive 12.8 miles. Turn right onto KY 525 North. Drive 2.5 miles until the road crosses Casey Creek. Just upstream of the bridge on your left is a great little parking area that can easily hold five or six vehicles.

Lick Creek

Just six miles from the Tennessee border, Lick Creek is a small spit of a stream, unknown to most anglers.

Ecosystem: Lick Creek flows with clear water over a bed of small stones and averages 20-25 feet wide in most places. Little to no gradient and shallow pools make this an easy-wading stream. The clearly posted "No Trespassing" signs on either side of the creek suggest the land owners do not want you in their cornfields, and we encourage you to stay clear of them.

At low water levels, the creek bed can become moss and grass covered, providing safe harbor for a multitude of nymphs. You'll also want to be on the lookout for tan caddis and yellow sulphurs flying about, and logs covered with small black stoneflies. A variety of deciduous trees, including large sycamores, come right to the water's edge, interrupted by the occasional small gravel bar. Higher water levels have eroded the base of many of the creek-side trees, creating lots of root wads under which trout hide.

Stocking and Regulations: Lick Creek is stocked with 1,250 rainbows, in the months 4, 5, 6, 7 and 10. Standard regulations apply: 8 rainbows per day, with no minimum size limit, and a valid fishing license and trout permit are required. There is no closed season and no catch-and-release period. The creek had previously been classified as a put-take, seasonal catch-and-release stream, but those restrictions have been lifted. Trout are released from the KY 585 bridge. Lick Creek is known to be a holdover stream.

Recommendations: Fishing can be had by wading both upstream and downstream of the bridge, but better luck is found below the bridge. Again, wading is highly recommended and easily accomplished. The creek remains shallow, with lots of overhead canopy and close quarters for those relying on an overhead cast. You may want to rely on a combination pull-and-roll cast.

Looking downstream, you can see where the creek curves around, forming the boundary of a large field. Most anglers begin fishing downstream and work their way back upstream to the bridge. Be sure not to miss the riffle area right by the parking pull-off. Locals like using small Bead-Head Woolly Buggers (size 8, olive or brown). An across and downstream pull cast next to a bank will feed your fly down along the bank and allow it to swing out into the main channel. Work both banks as you move your way upstream. You will thoroughly cover lots of water with this technique and should attract some strikes. Look for nymphs under some rocks in the stream, and if you find several, try to match them in size with your artificials and the same technique.

Directions: Just outside of Franklin, Ky., take exit 6 off of I-65 (yes, you'll be 6 miles from the Tennessee border.) Turn west on KY 100 towards Scottsville/Franklin. Drive 1.1 miles. Turn right on KY 73 (with signs to KY 585.) You will shortly come to a stop sign. Turn right on KY 585. Drive 3.6 miles, crossing over I-65 once again. You will soon cross a small bridge that spans Lick Creek. There is a small pull-off on the right side of the road.

Lynn Camp Creek

Located just 35 minutes south of Elizabethtown, Lynn Camp Creek is easily accessible for most anglers in central Kentucky.

Ecosystem: Lynn Camp Creek is a wide, shallow stream, perfect for wading and open enough for overhead casting. It is an ideal stream for the novice to try that new fly rod. The bottom of the stream is covered with small stones, sand and silt, with several small spring-fed waterfalls coming in just upstream of the bridge.

Fishing is permitted 0.4 miles above the bridge and 1.35 miles below the bridge (pictured below); both upper and lower boundaries are well marked. Despite the tempting large grassy field and wood tables found here, no camping is permitted.

Stocking and Regulations: Lynn Camp Creek is stocked with 2,500 rainbows in the months 4, 5, 6, 7 and 10. There is no minimum size limit; the daily limit is 8 trout.

Recommendations: Fishing the steep banks near the waterfalls can be productive, as the waters run cold and clear here. A weighted nymph such as a #14 Bead-Head Hare's Ear cast below the falls and along the nearby steep banks will likely bring a hookup. It helps to do away with using an indicator; just watch the end of your fly line.

Most of the larger fish can be found below the bridge, tucked into the occasional deep pool. While most trout caught are stockers, it is rumored that from time to time holdover fish can be caught, although we have yet to catch one of these.

Trout also like to hang out above, along and below the sand and gravel bars that have formed both upstream and downstream of the bridge. A down-stream pull cast followed by line feed with either a dry fly or nymph may prove successful in these areas. If you feel compelled to fish the long thin slicks, do so with lots of line out as the fish spook easily in these waters.

Directions: Lynn Camp Creek is near the intersection of US 31E and KY 569 (Powder Mills Road), just 30 miles south of Elizabethtown. If coming off I-65, take exit 71. Turn left (east) on KY 728 and drive 5.8 miles. Turn right (south) on KY 357 and drive 2.1 miles. Turn left (east) on KY 936 and drive another 2.2 miles. Turn right (south) on US 31E and drive 2.8 miles. Finally, turn left on KY 569 and drive 2.8 miles to where the bridge crosses the creek. The upstream left bank and downstream right bank is the VPA site.

Nolin River Tailwater

Sandwiched between Nolin Lake State Park to the north and Mammoth Cave National Park to the south, easy access and good stocking levels make this tailwater a regional favorite for many anglers.

Ecosystem: In the hot summer months, the waters in this narrow tailwater below Nolin Lake will begin to warm less than 1.5 miles from the dam. Nevertheless, there are two easily accessible spots that can be waded and provide good casting room and some fine nymph fishing year round. There are occasional reports of holdover trout and some fish do disperse downstream.

Generally speaking the Nolin River tailwater is primarily slow moving flat water, with the occasional riffle. Bank fishing works just fine here or launching a small craft is also a good option. There are deciduous trees and other vegetation along both banks as you move downstream from the dam.

Before making a trip to fish this tailwater, check the water release schedule; anything in excess of 150 cubic feet per second (cfs) and there is no wading, and at 250 cfs the tailrace becomes a torrent of foaming water. Water levels for Nolin Lake can be found at tinyurl.com/lbacp76.

Stockings and Regulations: The Nolin River tailwater is stocked with 14,000 rainbows in the months 4, 5, 6, 7, 8, 9, 10 and 11. In addition, 1,000 brown trout will be stocked beginning 2014. There is no minimum size limit; the daily and possession limit is 8 trout, of which no more than 3 may be browns no less than 12 inches.

Recommendations: From the parking lot (see directions below), a 120-yard walk across an open field will bring you to a point where a small creek enters the tailwater. A few steps down and you are wading in a shoal. On the far side below a high rock formation (known as Dismal Rock, pictured here), there is a deep run that usually holds some frisky rainbows. Nymphs such as #10 and #12 Bead-Head Hare's Ears, Tellicos and Pheasant Tails hung below an indicator and drifted near the wall will be all that are needed to bring some fish to hand.

Just beyond the shoal there should be some quiet water. At the edge of this spot and the run, try using a dry #14 or #16 Adams to bring up a fish or two.

At low water release rates, you can wade down along the right side and beyond the run the water tails out. Here both nymphs and dry flies should bring a take. The tailrace just below the dam holds rainbows, but this section is usually crowded with bait fishermen.

Back at the parking lot you can walk further down the road towards the well-maintained boat ramp. A small stream enters the tailwater between the dam and the boat ramp, on the parking lot side of the river. Just downstream of the boat ramp there is a small wadeable shoal that usually holds fish.

A small (3-5 horsepower) motorized boat will allow anglers access to the water along the banks and cliffs of the tailwater to be fished with either nymphs or streamers for about one mile. After this the channel narrows and the water warms up in the summer. The current can be stiff at times and, as there is no downstream takeout, one must motor back to the ramp.

Directions: Take exit 107 on the Western Kentucky Parkway near Leitchfield and drive south on KY 259 for 17.1 miles to KY 728 (Nolin Dam Road). Turn left (west) and drive another 2.9 miles. Before crossing the dam, veer to the right and drive down Nolin Tailwater Road to the bottom of the dam and a paved parking lot.

The tailwater can also be reached off I-65, by following signs to Mammoth Cave National Park and KY 728.

Roundstone Creek

One creek, multiple access points and hours of good fun. Regular stockings and the occasional deep pool make this a favorite amongst anglers.

Ecosystem: The water in Roundstone Creek comes from rain runoff and the Blue Hole Spring that originates at its head. Unfortunately, flow from the spring is not uniform and in the dry summer months is little more than a trickle. However, moderate to heavy rains can muddy the stream and raise water levels, making wading and fishing all but impossible. But once the stream has cleared, wading is not difficult and it is a joy to fish.

Roundstone Creek averages about 25 feet across, with moderate amounts of low overhanging tree branches. Keep your roll cast handy in your front pocket, as you may want to drag it out periodically.

In general, the creek bottom is sandy and silt-covered, sprinkled with the occasional large rock or gravel bar. The moss beds of Roundstone Creek hold scuds and the nymphs of mayflies and stoneflies, but the long shallow runs are not productive for trout fishing. Kingfishers like this creek, which is a good indicator for the fly angler.

Fortunately, stream access points are abundant, as Roundstone Creek is difficult to bank fish. For the most part the banks are steep and thickly covered with river cane, and can get quite overgrown during the growing season. In the summer months, the swarms of gnats and mosquitoes can keep you swatting.

There are two main access points to Roundstone Creek available on the Nancy Priddy Nature Preserve, which is located on a private farm. Ample parking is available at both sites. The stream is open for fishing from just below the Blue Hole Spring and downstream to KY 1140. Below KY 1140 there is only intermittent fishing.

Stocking and Regulations: Roundstone is stocked with 2,800 8-10 inch rainbows, in the months 4, 5, 6, 7, 8, 9 and 10. There is no closed season and no catch-and-release period. In addition, 300 browns will be stocked beginning in 2014. Stockings have been much higher in previous years (up to 3,600 rainbows). In addition to the stockings, there are some holdover trout. The daily limit is 8 trout per day, of which only 3 may be browns of at least 12 inches or more. There is no size limit specified for kept rainbows.

Recommendations: The upstream access point (#1 below) leads you to the portion of the stream just below the Blue Hole. After parking, follow the old farm road down the hill. The trail is adequately marked with yellow fishing access signs. Continue through the woods, cross a second field, then a second patch of woods, and out into a third field. From this vantage point, Roundstone Creek makes a large concave bow in front of you, forming the boundary of the far side of the field at the bottom of the hill.

From this field you can see the three short trails leading to fishing access sites. Looking far left at 9 o'clock, a narrow trail leads to small rocky overhangs overlooking a large, deep pool just below Blue Hole Spring. Here the creek bed is mostly sandy, with occasional large rocks. Alternately, if you look straight ahead at 12 o'clock, at the opposite end of the field, a small wooden dock extends out in the creek. Just upstream, another small stream enters Roundstone Creek, dumping its tailout right in front of the dock. Finally, at the 3 o'clock position, downstream of the dock, a large rootball blocks the creek before the water flows into yet another deep pool, impounded with large rocks on one side.

Some anglers think the second site (#2 below) is the better one to fish. Adjacent to the parking area there is a very large and deep pool. Fish the big pool and upstream in and below the several tailouts. Use #12-16 nymphs such as Pheasant Tails and Hare's Ears two feet below a strike indicator. Eight fish a day is good in this stream.

In summer, fish have been seen sipping small Mayfly spinners in the center of the pool noted above. On a well-mended cast of a #16 Adams, a 16-inch rainbow was brought to net by one of the authors. This strongly suggests that trout overwinter in this stream. Upstream of this pool can be found several riffles in and below which fish are known to hang out. Recommended flies include sizes #14 or #16 Pheasant Tails, Bead-Head Hare's Ears or dark Stone Fly nymphs to produce strikes. Fishing a #14 or #16 Adams in several of the smaller pools can also bring up fish from the moss beds in Roundstone Creek.

You can also fish Roundstone where the KY 1140 bridge crosses the creek, downstream of both access points described above. South of the concrete bridge on a narrow gravel shoulder is a small pull-off. Steps go down to the stream, just next to the abutment. Locals use this spot a lot for fishing and as a summer swimming hole, so you may want to fish here only in early spring and late fall months.

A small riffle passes under the bridge, leading to a large, deep pool just downstream. Here the creek is about 30-40 feet across, its sandy banks lined with cane and a few large trees at the waters edge to cast near. You can walk 50-100 yards downstream on creek left (the left side of the creek, as you are facing downstream), where there are a few more riffles and some shallow pools. Alternately, if you walk upstream about 50 yards, there is a large pool about 50-60 feet wide, just below a small Class I rapid. Again, locals fish this out pretty quickly due to easy access.

Directions: As noted above, Roundstone Creek has two primary access points. Access #1 is upstream (east) of access #2. These two access points can easily be fished in the same day. Take N. Pleasant Hill Rd., KY 224, or KY 728 to reach the other end of the stream.

Access #1: From I-65 exit #76, go west on KY 224 for 0.5 miles and then turn right on US 31W/KY 224. Go another 3.9 miles on KY 224 and then turn left on KY 1391. Travel 2.6 miles to site on right. Just past the driveway leading to a small white house and mailbox, look to your right and you can see an old VPA sign at the top of a small pasture road. Park at the sign, close to the three-board fence. After parking, pass through the gate and follow the old farm road approximately 0.3 miles through three fields before reaching the stream. VPA signs mark the way.

Access #2: Take exit #76 off I-65 between Elizabethtown and Bowling Green. At the end of the ramp, turn west on KY 224 toward Upton. After 0.4 miles turn right onto US 31W and in the town of Upton turn left back onto SR 224. Go about 7.4 miles on KY 224 from the interstate. Turn left (south) on Copelin Valley Road and then left again on Raider Hollow Road. (KY 1140). Drive 1.7 miles until you come to Riders Mill and the road crosses Roundstone Creek. Turn left after crossing the bridge into the Nancy Priddy Nature Preserve. Drive less than 200 feet, and then park off the roadway. The stream is next to the road. The stream can be entered at several slightly obscured sites on the left.

Sulphur Spring Creek

A spring-fed creek, south of Bowling Green, west of Franklin, and almost in the Volunteer State.

Ecosystem: While not particularly scenic, Sulphur Spring Creek is blessed with cool waters that flow year round, allowing KDFWR to stock the stream during the summer months through July. Although the creek is quite a haul for most Kentucky anglers, it may be worth the drive to complete a trifecta of trout fishing, with added fishing opportunities in both Lick and Trammel Creeks located close by.

The stocking site (directions below) is heavily used by local fishermen, who always seem to know when the hatchery truck is about to pull up. The stream forms a nice little pool right next to the parking area, where another small creek enters Sulphur Spring, emptying more cool water and food for the hungry trout waiting just below. Downstream of this pool, Sulphur Spring Creek is relatively narrow, running about 20 foot wide in most places, with a combination of mud banks and the occasional gravel shoal.

Small trails run alongside the creek, but the steep banks and heavy vegetation make bank fishing difficult. However, the creek is very wadeable, except after heavy rains when the current can become quite swift. The gravel road continues to parallel the creek for about 100 yards past the stocking site until it crosses an old wooden bridge and heads away from the creek.

A second access point is at a new concrete bridge on Bracken Price Mill Road downstream of the stocking site, where the road crosses Sulphur Spring Creek. Multiple trails lead both upstream and downstream from the bridge area. Here the creek widens into several channels (depending on water levels) and the stream bottom is quite rocky, making wading a little more difficult. However, bank fishing is a good option as the deciduous trees form a large canopy overhead.

One of the oldest access sites is just beyond Neosheo, a tiny hamlet on Sulphur Springs Church Road where the road passes over the stream. Parking and access are available here on the left side of the road. The better fishing is downstream from this site.

Stocking and Regulations: This is a put-grow-take stream, stocked with 2,500 rainbows in the months of 4, 5, 6, 7 and 10. In addition, 100 brown trout will be stocked beginning 2014. There is a daily limit of eight trout per day, with no minimum size specified for the rainbows. However, of the 8 trout, only 3 browns may be kept, of which each must be at least 12 inches or more in length.

Recommendations: If the waters in the stream are running clear, #14 or #16 size nymphs work just fine; however, if the waters are murky try a #12 nymph or a Woolly Bugger. In the long runs use a pull cast and feed additional line out slowly. If you can detect a strike without using an indicator, do so. Fish these near the bottom, even if with the smaller flies that means adding a split shot above the nymph. Fish these along the banks and in any deeper slots that may be located in the middle of the stream. Some fish will hold up off and just downstream of the shoals—so, don't pass up that water. Bead-Head Hare's Ears, Prince Nymphs and Pheasant Tails are good selections for this stream.

During the late summer months an errant grasshopper may find itself in the stream and a trout is not likely to pass up such a big morsel. For that reason, under vegetation and around root wads a big dry fly like a Stimulator or Hopper may bring up a nice rainbow.

There is a scarcity of deep pools in this stream, but if you come upon one, give a #12 or #14 Adams a go at it. These rainbows are not to too selective, but they spook easily.

Directions: Heading south on I-65, just above the Kentucky/Tennessee border, take exit 6 towards Franklin, Ky. Turn right (west) on KY 100, following it through the town of Franklin. One mile west of Franklin, turn south on McLendon Road (KY 1321 on some maps). Drive 0.6 miles and then bear right (heading southwest) on KY 383 (W. Madison Street). Drive 2.3 miles. Take a slight right on Sulphur Springs Church Road. Drive 2.6 miles. Turn left onto Neosheo Price Mill Road. Drive 1.4 miles. Turn right onto a small gravel farm lane, known as DB Burr Road (which may or may not be marked). The stocking site and parking area are just ahead, about 0.1 miles down this road.

To reach the new bridge off Bracken Price Mill Road, head back to Neosheo Price Mill Road and turn right (southwest). Drive 1.9 miles on Neosheo (KY 1885). Turn right on Bracken Price Mill Road. Drive 0.3 miles to the bridge. Several pull-offs can be found.

The third site is located 2.4 miles after making the slight right turn onto Sulphur Springs Church Road and is at the bridge near the Neosheo hamlet.

Trammel Creek

Hands down, one of the best trout streams in southwestern Kentucky.

Ecosystem: A pretty spring-fed creek. Generous stocking schedule throughout the summer. Holds rainbows and browns. Stream restoration work by KDFWR. Need we say more? If you've not fished Trammel Creek, be sure to put this one on your short list.

Trammel Creek is widely considered one of the best holdover trout streams in the state, including the over-wintering of a number of 18- to 20-inch brown trout. The cold waters stay in the mid-60 degrees, even in the dog days of summer. Generally speaking, the stream is a pool-riffle with occasional gravel beds, root wads, large rocks and some undercut banks. Some of the pools are up to seven feet deep.

Fishing access along Trammel Creek is excellent, with two streamside-parking areas less than a mile apart by road, providing anglers access to almost two miles of bank fishing and wading. Anglers can easily bank fish at either location, or you can park at one and fish your way to the other. If you're interested in the latter, we suggest you park at access #1 (the downstream location described in the directions below), and then fish your way upstream to access #2. Of course this will require you to fish your way back downstream again, but if it's a beautiful day and the fish are biting, you'll be hard-pressed to find a better way to spend your time.

Access point #1 comes equipped with a nice little picnic shelter and table (compliments of the local church), and a large pool and gravel shoals both upstream and downstream of the bridge. While there are some trails along the creek, simply wading in the stream may be your best bet. The creek is quite wide here, averaging 30-40 feet across in most places, with several shoals punctuated by the occasional large pool. Multiple tailouts and a high canopy provide several inviting spots to cast a line. There are a few root wads here and there, but mostly the streambed is gravel and silt. Excellent fishing can be had both upstream and downstream of the bridge.

Access #2 has a different character than that described above, but the fishing is just as good, if not better. There is a nice parking area on the downstream side of the bridge that will hold several vehicles. Just on the upstream side of the bridge is a large pool that always holds trout, regardless of the time of year. A small trail starting behind the guard rail leads to the pool, which has been deepened with the strategic placement of several large stones that funnel the water through one of the most natural-looking, man-made sluices you've ever seen. Here the water runs cold and swift, before lazily filling the pool and dumping particles of food into the piscatorial mouths patiently waiting below.

About 200 yards from the parking lot, downstream of the bridge, Trammel Creek makes an S-turn along a floodplain on the right and a hillside on the left. The state has been working diligently to repair damage done by a flood in May of 2010. Improvements to the riparian zone include the planting of a host of swamp and white oak, red maple, tulip popular, river birch and other deciduous trees, which will help keep the banks from eroding. Along the flood plain the creek widens to about 40 feet before flowing through yet another man-made sluice of natural stone and then falling into yet another deep pool. Again, holdovers are often prevalent. Obviously the state is making a significant investment in improving the trout habitat along Trammel Creek. In time, the trees will provide much-needed shade along this section of the creek and will help stabilize the bank during spring rains.

Stocking and Regulations: This stream is stocked with 8,750 rainbows in the months of 4, 5, 6, 7, 8, 9 and 10. The rainbows are put-take, and seasonal catch-and-release from Oct. 1 until March 31. In addition, 400 8-inch browns are stocked annually, usually in the month of March, although the timing is not announced. The browns are also put-grow-take and seasonal catch-and-release. There is a daily limit of 8 trout, although only 1 may be a brown trout, and it must be 16 inches or longer. During the scr period, all trout caught must be immediately released and only artificial baits may be used.

Recommendations: The longer trout survive in a stream, the more persnickety they get. So if you want to catch one other than recent stockers, presentation and fly selection become all-important. In Trammel Creek you will come upon the occasional deep pool adjacent to a large boulder. Be on the sharp look-out for flies overhead and dimple rises; if you see some, gauge their size, match it and drift a similar artificial downstream into the pool without disturbing it. It's a good bet you will get a take. Both mayflies and caddis can be found in this stream, so Adams, BWOs or dry Caddis should work.

Absent any rises, try using a #14 Pheasant Tail or Prince Nymph without an indicator. Simply watch the end of your floating fly line, and if it makes an abrupt move, set the hook.

Avoid the long slicks, as they seldom hold fish, but the long deep pools are worth fishing either up or downstream with both dries and nymphs. These deep pools frequently have tailouts; don't pass up fishing these as they almost always hold feeding fish. Through the late summer and early fall months, float a Hopper through these, and during other times try a Woolly Bugger without an indicator.

This stream does not have a lot of overhanging vegetation, but if you come upon some, do not hesitate to drift a dry fly under it. On sunny days trout take cover under these shady enclaves, and you might bring a nice one up.

There are many ways to fish this gem of a stream and it's hard to fish Trammel Creek without catching fish. If the creek has received heavy rain, let it clear out for a day and you'll be back in business.

Directions: Access #1 (downstream access point): From I-65, take exit 38 and turn left (south) onto KY 101 towards Scottsville. Drive about 21 miles. In the middle of Scottsville, KY 101 becomes KY 100. Drive 0.2 miles. Turn left (south) on KY 2160 (Old Hartsville Road). Drive 5.5 miles. Turn right (west) onto Concord Church Road. Parking is available on the other side of the stream, in a small gravel lot on your right.

Access #2 (upstream access point): From I-65, take exit 38 and turn left (south) onto KY 101 towards Scottsville. Drive about 21 miles. In the middle of Scottsville, KY 101 becomes KY 100. Drive 0.2 miles. Turn left (south) on KY 2160 (Old Hartsville Road). Drive 6.1 miles. Turn right (west) onto Blankenship Road. Parking is available on the other side of the stream, in a small gravel lot on your right.

North-Central Kentucky

- Big Bone Creek
- Floyds Fork
- Herrington Lake Tailwater
- Otter Creek
- Royal Springs
- Sinking Creek
- Taylorsville Lake Tailwater

Five streams and two tailwaters, all within a short drive from the metropolitan areas of Louisville, Lexington and Cincinnati.

Floyds Fork

Big Bone Creek

The mastodons are gone, but their bones still surround this little stream, with its many access points and nice pools.

Ecosystem: Long ago mastodons inhabited this area and may have drunk from this stream. Many of their bones have been found in the vicinity and some are on display in Big Bone Lick State Park, through which the 2.1-mile fishable portion of the stream passes. Studies indicate the mastodons were attracted to the site for its salt licks from which the park gets its name.

Big Bone Creek, never more than 20-feet wide, meanders through the park under a canopy of big deciduous trees: black locusts, hackberries and a few sycamores. Wide swaths of heavy brush and reeds encroach on several sections of the stream, but anglers have pushed these aside creating multiple paths to the stream. However there are many places with easier, more open access to the water. Nearly the entire stream is accessible to wading, but there are several sites that are more likely to hold the 8- to 12-inch rainbows.

Wading Big Bone is not difficult, as it is filled with a considerable amount of gravel; however there are a few sections that have big rocks and pods of mud. Avoid these areas, as it is easy to get stuck in the mud or find your waders filled with water. The trout like to hang out in the centers of the deep pools and out of the sunlight as opposed to near the muddy banks.

The stream is a pleasure to fish and the canopies of big trees bordering the stream present no problems casting. Short overhead and roll casts of 30 feet are adequate. As summer approaches, the stream warms and the fish become stressed, so the months of April through June and October and November are the best fishing times. Much of the stream can freeze over in the winter.

Stocking and Regulations: The stream is stocked with 1,200 rainbows during the months 4, 5 and 10. The daily possession limit is 8 fish, with no size restrictions; however, from Oct. 1 until March 31 all fishing is artificial flies and lures, and catch-and-release.

Recommendations: As you enter the park, and before you drive across the bridge over Big Bone Creek, turn left and park anywhere off the gravel road. It is best to cross the bridge on foot and enter the water downstream of the bridge. Barring rainfall of one-half inch or more, which can muddy the stream for a week, Big Bone is fully wadeable for a half-mile. Immediately upstream of the bridge, trout are stocked in a very long pool. This pool and the numerous riffles with intervening pockets of water harbor lots of trout.

If Big Bone Creek is running clear, cast into the pool and pocket water using dries of #14 Adams and Caddis. You may also find success in this pool, below the tailouts and in the pocket waters with #12 and #14 Bead-Head Hare's Ear and Pheasant Tail nymphs tied about three feet under an indicator.

Having fished this section, you can drive across the bridge and up the hill, before turning right and pulling off in the second parking lot adjacent to the picnic area. Walk down the hill across the dry creek branch to reach the stream. Here you will find numerous points of access down to the water. Use care, as the banks can be slippery. There are no fewer than 10 pools in this stretch, all holding trout. Some pools are very deep, so do not attempt to wade through them. There will be no trout in the thin water, so wade through it.

A second way of reaching this section is to drive back towards the highway, and before exiting the park turn left and park in the big lot. You can't miss the recently renovated footbridge across the stream. As you cross the bridge, look down and to your right to spot a nice site to enter the stream.

There is a third section you might also want to fish at the end the roadway past the park museum and the bison yard. This roadway is closed to vehicles, so you must trek about 300 yards to reach this section. The stream is very shallow here and strewn with shoebox-sized rocks. A few fish may be found behind the bigger rocks and out of the sunlight.

Directions: Traveling to the park is straightforward. If you are driving north on I-75 take exit 171, just south of the I-75/71 interchange and turn west at the top of the ramp. After crossing over I-75, immediately turn right (north) onto KY 1292 or Beaver Road. Remain on KY 1292 for 7.8 miles until you reach the state park, which is clearly identified by signage on the left.

From northern Kentucky, if traveling south on I-75 take exit 175 towards Richwood. Turn west on KY 338. Stay on KY 338 for 7.7 miles until you reach the park entrance. In the park there are numerous paved parking lots in close proximity to the fishing.

Floyds Fork

Located just east of Louisville, this stream traverses four interconnected urban parks known collectively as The Parklands of Floyds Fork.

Ecosystem: If 10 years ago you had asked most of the residents of Louisville if they had ever heard of Floyds Fork they might have answered: "Whose fork?" Ask them now, and they will reply: "You mean the stream that flows through the Parklands?" The Parklands is reported to be the newest, largest urban greenspace in the US and with 4,000 acres is five times the size of Central Park in New York. Supported by 21st Century Parks, a private non-profit organization, all four of the major parks will be completed by 2015. Floyds Fork, a 62-mile-long tributary of the Salt River just outside the Gene Snyder Freeway, is within easy reach of much of central Kentucky.

But to call Floyds Fork an ideal trout fishery is stretching it a bit. It is a warm water stream that in early spring, late fall and winter carries enough cold water to support stockings of rainbow trout on a put-take basis. But by mid-July of 2013 we found the stream temperature had risen to 84°F. To survive those waters a rainbow what have to be packing ice water and an oxygen tank.

If you wade or float this stream you will find its ecosystem astonishing. The streambed alternates between long stretches of gravel, flat shelves of limestone, and meandering islands of silvergrass and reeds. If there are any pockets of mud, they are few. In some places the stream may be 10 feet wide and 10 feet deep, and in others 40 feet wide and 3 feet deep. Prolonged heavy rains turn the stream into a torrent of muddy water that tears at the banks, exposing tree roots and covering the islands. In a few days it clears and returns to a graceful stream with canoeists and kayakers paddling beneath the gracious canopies of huge deciduous trees, some of which may be several hundred years old, including 6-foot-diameter sycamores, towering oaks, arching maples and river willows.

Along the trails you will find an assortment of native plants and wildflowers. In the spring, Solomon's seal, spring beauty and hepatica are prolific, while in summer and fall the goldenrod, pink meadow phlox, black-eyed Susan and English asters abound. The Parklands attracts many users, but it is so expansive that there is space for all.

Stocking and Regulations: Floyds Fork was first stocked with rainbow trout in 2013. The 2014 schedule calls for a total of 3,600 9-12 inch rainbows to be stocked in the months 3, 4, and 10 on a put-take, seasonal catch-and-release basis. As stream temperatures rise into the 80s by midsummer, the spring stockers do not survive. The October stocking allows for late fall and early winter fishing before periods of stream iceovers. The trout are released both north and south of the crossover of I-64 and the Beckley Creek Parkway. All other creel limits and licensing regulations apply to the stream.

Recommendations: When Floyds Fork received its very first spring stocking of rainbows, we were debating whether to include it in these writings and time did not allowed us to fish it before all the trout were gone. Several friends using nymphs under small indicators had good success, and we listened to their tales.

That July we walked the stream when the water was hot, low and clear, and no trout were found. No surprise there. Under these conditions the stream produces numerous riffles, long slicks, deep pools, multiple grassy islands and tangles of tree branches. The undersides of some wetted rocks revealed many mayfly nymphs and a few cases of live caddisflies. With no other insight than this, we surmised that Bead-Head Hare's Ears, Prince Nymphs and Woolly Buggers fished in the pools and through the riffles and tailouts in both spring and fall shortly after it has been stocked would be our best recommendation.

In early November, following the fall stocking of 750 rainbows, we donned our waders and took to casting nymphs below indicators, which to our displeasure landed on droves of floating sycamore leaves. But between these episodes a #14 Bead-Head Hare's Ears brought several nice rainbows to hand.

You can enter the stream near the North Beckley Paddling Access and off the Sycamore Trail that parallels the stream. Under low to moderate water levels, wade fishing in the gravel stretches should bring success, but with elevated water levels you should stick to fishing from a water craft launched and taken out at the paddling access points. Don't forget those life preservers and paddles.

Directions: From the intersection of the Gene Snyder Parkway (I-265) and Shelbyville Road (US 60), drive east on US 60 for 1.9 miles to the entrance of Beckley Creek Park in the Parklands of Floyds Fork. Hopefully, you will see the brown sign on your right marking the park entrance; it is erected slightly back from the highway. From the entrance drive 0.5 miles on the Beckley Creek Parkway to the "North Beckley Paddling Access." This is clearly marked on your right. Turn right and you will see a 20-slot parking area. From here it is but a very short walk over a paved path to several points of stream access for either wading or launching non-motorized watercraft. Be aware that the gate to this area opens at dawn and closes at dusk.

If you return to your vehicle, drive back up to the parkway and turn right. Exactly 1 mile after passing under I-64 you will come to a 'T" in the road. Turn left and after 0.1 mile pull into the parking area on your right. Across the parkway you will see a paved path that after 100 yards will put you at the "Gravel Bar Overlook." Here the Sycamore Trail parallels the stream both left and right. There are numerous points of stream access along the trail. If you have launched watercraft upstream, you can take it out here, but you will have to carry it 100 yards back to the parking lot. A better choice would be to drift downstream in your watercraft and take out at the "Creekside Paddling Access" located about 0.25 miles downstream.

Herrington Lake Tailwater

When a hydroelectric dam was first built across the Dix River in 1925, it was the oldest earth-filled dam in the world. But it was more than a half-century later before trout were stocked in the tailwaters.

Ecosystem: Ask a Kentucky angler about the Herrington Lake tailwater and the quick comeback will be: "You mean the Dix?" Less than 100 feet in width, the Dix River meanders from the dam for about two miles before it enters the Kentucky River at High Bridge, a 275-foot-high railroad trestle constructed in 1876. Interestingly, High Bridge was the highest railroad bridge in the world until the early 20th century. We're not sure the trout care, but we find little anecdotes like this quite interesting.

While it's not easy to get to the tailwater, the determined angler will be rewarded with some excellent, albeit inconsistent, trout-fishing waters. Kentucky Utilities owns both the dam and the power generating station, and for reasons of liability, fishermen are not allowed to enter the tailrace from their property. Consequently, to reach the trout fishery section of the river, you must launch a boat at the old VPA boat ramp on the east side of the Kentucky River, motor up the Kentucky, pass un-

der High Bridge, and immediately on the west side of the river enter the Dix. Vigorous anglers may opt to kayak or canoe, but that makes for a very long day. The going will be slow, as there are numerous tree falls, root wads and low overhangs. Here the river can be a bit murky, as the dirt banks have muddied the water.

While the fish population along this section of the Dix can be quite plentiful, keep on motoring, as the trout will be found closer to the tailrace. After about one and one-half miles, you will see a big sign on the right bank posting fishing regulations. It is at this point you will feel a change in the air temperature; you have entered cold water and good trout habitat. Upriver, the cold water released from the dam slowly slips under the warm water of the Dix.

Further upstream, 100-foot-high limestone cliffs or palisades will appear on your left. Along this section of the Dix, the river continues to narrow, and large rocks line the waters edge. Interspersed with deeper channels, you'll have to maneuver through some shallow spots, which are only problematic in late summer and early fall when the water levels drop.

Continue up to the dam and the concrete spillway. In the summer months, birds of prey nest in the outcrops of the cliffs and some feed their hatchlings on trout lifted from the Dix. But the birds have left a few for anglers who have ventured up the river. Just below the dam, you will find the river bottom rather rocky and the water quite clear.

Stocking and Regulations: The annual stocking for the Dix is 4,800 rainbows and 1,000 browns distributed across January to August, plus November. All of the trout are introduced just below the dam from KU's property. The creel limit is 8 fish, of which only 3 may be browns and these must be at least 12 inches in length. This two-mile-long fishery has a special regulation that only artificial flies and lures may be used. It is strongly enforced.

Recommendations: The only time to fish the Dix is when there are no generating turbines running. If you phone the E.W. Brown Station (859-748-5607) they will tell you if they are currently or are planning to release water and when. But you should understand they could change their schedule without any notice and frequently do so. So count on their information about 80 percent of the time.

Current water level data can also be obtained from the USGS at tinyurl.com/mkpb6w8. This data is updated hourly, but only shows current discharge rates at the dam and does not provide predicted water levels.

As you come into sight of the dam you will be approaching a sizable gravel bar on your left and a big riffle. The best fishing in the Dix is from the dam down to about 200 yards below this gravel bar. On rare occasions a big brown is taken on a spinning or casting lure below this section. If you are in a small johnboat or a canoe you might be able to walk it through the riffle. There are at least five areas that give up trout in this section of the Dix.

- If the river has been recently stocked, you will find 8- to 10-inch fish in the pool just below the dam in foam lines and next to the tailrace wall on the left. If they are rising, try a #14 Adams or Blue Wing Olive; otherwise use a #12 Bead-Head Hare's Ear or Pheasant Tail set three feet below an indicator. After a water release, the smaller stocked fish scatter downstream.

- Along the steep bank, opposite the big, shallow pool formed by outflow from the spillway, there is a deep, hidden channel with a swift flow. Rainbows inhabit this run and feed on every morsel that comes their way.

A long 50-foot cast above the run with both dries, and nymphs four feet under an indicator with a mended line and a natural drift will bring strikes.

• The narrow channel above the riffle frequently will yield some nice fish. Fish this section standing out of the water on the rocks on the right bank. The water is swift in the channel and a high stick presentation of a #14 weighted nymph is often needed.

• Rainbows, some 16 to 18 inches, are frequently taken out of the riffle and below it. Nymphs without an indicator work best in this water.

• Below the riffle and down to and including the gravel bar is brown trout water. Fish up to 20 inches are taken on streamers such as a Muddler or Clouser Minnow when worked in 6-inch jerks, or big stone fly nymphs naturally drifted with the flow.

There are years the Dix fishes very well, but for an assortment of reasons there are years the fishing is very slow and anglers want to know where all the fish have gone. Some opine that when the Kentucky River floods, it backs up into the Dix, warming and depleting the water of oxygen, causing an inhospitable environment for trout.

Directions: One of the criteria for including a particular trout water in this book was ease of access to the waterway. Clearly, we have disregarded that criterion in including the Dix. Easy access, no! But the beauty of the Dix and the size of the trout have convinced us to encourage you to fish these waters.

From the intersection of Lexington's Man-a-War Boulevard and US 68, drive west on US 68 for 9.2 miles, before veering off to your left onto KY 29 (Lexington Road). There is a service station at this juncture. Stay on KY 29 straight through the town of Wilmore (which becomes High Bridge Road), and after 6.4 miles you will enter the Kentucky River palisades area and the crossroads of the "town" High Bridge. Veer right on Pleasant Hill Road for another 0.3 miles.

Make a very sharp 120-degree right turn onto Lock No. 7 Road (this road is unmarked.) After 0.4 miles avoid the left turn, drive through the two stone pillars, and immediately on your left you will see the very well paved VPA boat ramp and parking area. From Man-a-War /US 68 to the dam will take all of one and one-half hours of motorized vehicle and boat time. Be sure to return back down the Dix with at least one hour of good light left in the day, or you'll need to turn on the running lights of your boat. Or if you are canoeing, trade off your fishing cap for a miner's cap. Either way, plan on a full day of adventure.

Otter Creek

Nestled in the reaches of the Ohio River Valley, just southwest of Louisville, Otter Creek provides an angler's respite only minutes from the state's largest urban area.

Ecosystem: The National Park Service opened Otter Creek Park in 1937 to serve as a recreational area for the citizens of Louisville and nearby communities. Since that time, Otter Creek and its forested surroundings have had a rather tumultuous history. Over the last 75 years, some of the land was leased to the YMCA to create Camp Piomingo, while the park was enlarged via transferred land holdings from Fort Knox. Ownership of the park has passed from the federal government to the City of Louisville, and finally in 2010 to the KDFWR, when the agency changed the park's name to the Otter Creek Outdoor Recreation Area (ORA).

Otter Creek encompasses 2,600 acres of forest with marked trails, picnic tables, pavilions and, of course, the creek. The area is home to deer, turkey, small mammals and numerous species of songbirds. Bald Eagles and Great Blue Herons can be found hanging out near the northern boundary of the park, formed by the Ohio River. Activities include hiking, horseback and mountain bike riding, disc golf, camping, controlled hunting, and fishing for trout, bass and sauger in Otter Creek. The stream is 20 to 40-feet-wide, five miles long and seldom more than three to four feet deep. It's a great place to strap on your waders and wander downstream as you lose time and add tranquility back into your life.

Otter Creek flows out of the Fort Knox Military Reservation and several miles later flows into the Ohio River. The creek's shoreline is strewn with wide bars of golf ball-sized rocks, intermittent limestone cliffs, and towering canopies of tulip poplar, oak and maple trees that make for unobstructed fly casting. Heavy rains can muddy the waters and raise their levels, and it takes three to four days to flush them clear. But once the creek levels fall, great stretches of the stream can be waded for several miles and the fishing improves.

Stocking and Regulations: The ORA portion of the stream is stocked with 7,500 rainbows in the months 2, 3, 4, 5, 10 and 11. There are no browns stocked in the ORA section, but 500 browns and 4,000 rainbows are released in the section of Otter Creek flowing through the Fort Knox Reservation, and some of these migrate down into the ORA. The daily creel limit within ORA is 8 trout and only 3 may be browns, of which the latter must be 12 inches or longer. If you should claim to have caught three browns in one day, we'd chalk that up as a fishing tale. From Oct. 1 to Mar. 31 all fishing for trout is catch-and-release with flies and lures only. In addition to the daily fee (described below), a KY fishing license and trout stamp is needed to fish.

Those cleared to fish the military reservation may not enter the ORA without a KY license and trout stamp, and those fishing the ORA may not enter the reservation under the KY 1638 bridge at any time, without proper authorization. Trust us – you do not want to be caught illegally fishing on Fort Knox, as access is "strictly controlled and rigidly enforced." If caught, you may miss more than supper.

If you are interested in fishing the upstream section of Otter Creek that flows through Fort Knox, special fishing regulations apply and a "post" fishing permit is required in addition to a valid KY fishing license and trout permit. For more information contact the Hunt Control Office, Fort Knox, (502) 624-2712.

Recommendations: Trout fishing in the Otter is best from late fall through late spring. In the summer the stream warms to above 75°F and then you are more likely to catch smallmouths and small children rather than cold-blooded trout. On warm, sultry days your first access site, just below the KY 1638 bridge identified as the Garnettsville Picnic Area, is overrun with swimmers and tubers. But if you choose a crisp autumn or inspiring spring day during the week, you are likely to have the place to yourself. Note: ORA is closed Monday and Tuesday, as we too frequently forget.

After passing through the guardhouse at the park entrance, bear right to find the picnic area and large parking lot. From here, Otter Creek flows north for several miles before emptying into the Ohio River. Upstream from this area, the stream flows out of Fort Knox. Most anglers begin at this first access point, and many spend their entire day wading downstream casting for rainbows and the elusive brown.

119

A second access point is known colloquially as the Blue Hole, which can be reached by wading downstream from the Garnettsville Picnic Area, or using the hiking/mountain biking trail which parallels the stream from the picnic area to Blue Hole. Alternately, you can also drive to Blue Hole and follow a short hiking trail to reach the creek using the directions given below.

With low to moderate flow you will find easy wading from below the bridge to beyond the Blue Hole as your footing will find only clean, small rocks. Turn over several of these stones and you will discover abundant mayfly nymphs and some caddis cases. This should clue you to fish #14 and #16 Pheasant Tails and Hare's Ears nymphs. Otherwise, if you see mayflies above the water and see trout sipping, try a #14 or #16 Adams. At times, #20 WD40s and Zebra midges also work well.

The stream has numerous long, three to four-feet-deep pools and some shallow riffles with tailouts; avoid wading into these as the trout concentrate in them. Dead drift your nymph on a tight line downstream through the pools while slowly feeding out line. There are a few drop offs, so watch your footing. Slowly work downstream covering all the water. Where you see a riffle, drift your nymph or an olive Woolly Bugger through it and its tailout. At times a sizable trout may take residence behind a big stone in the riffle. On occasion you may catch a brown that has moved down from the Fort Knox Reservation where they are stocked, but most fish are 8- to 12-inch rainbows.

Directions: At the intersection of US 31W/US 60 and KY 1638 in the town of Muldraugh, take KY 1638 west for 2.7 miles. After crossing the Otter Creek bridge, turn right at the brown and yellow Otter Creek Outdoor Recreation Area sign and be prepared to pay the entrance fee at the gate. Ask the gate attendant for the two-sided map showing the trails and the directions to the two access sites—the one at the Garnettsville Picnic Area and the other at Blue Hole. To reach the latter you must drive 1.7 miles from the gate down Otter Creek Road and turn right on dilapidated Lick Skillet Road, at the sign indicating the way to the Blue Hole. The paved and gravel road will end at a parking area. From there you must hike 0.5 miles down an abandoned road to an easy access into the stream.

To offset maintenance costs, the agency charges a daily fee of $3 for hiking and fishing (or an annual permit fee of $30). For those using the rifle and bow ranges, horseback, and/or bike trails, expect to pay an additional $7. Children under 12 are admitted free. The ORA is open from daylight to sunset and closed on Mondays and Tuesdays, except holidays.

Royal Springs

A small urban fishery continually submerged in cold spring water.

Ecosystem: This very narrow, 0.7-mile trout stream originates from the discarded waters of the Georgetown Water Treatment Plant, which receives its water from the underground Royal Springs. John Floyd discovered the spring in 1774, and Baptist Preacher Elijah Craig used its waters in bourbon whiskey making. The spring itself is surrounded by very old and beautiful stonework. The surrounding property and log cabin have been turned into a small city park and museum.

The springs flow cold year-round, and the lower section of the stream has produced some fish up to 20 inches. From the park, the stream flows along a small canal before emptying into Elkhorn Creek. The flow of the current can wane during dry periods, but the stream depths seem to hold at about two to  four feet. The bottom of the stream has patches of moss, which harbor a myriad of insects. One would think that flowing through the heart of Georgetown that Royal Springs would be heavily fished; it is not and that is inexplicable.

Stockings and Regulations: A total of 1,600 rainbows are released into Royal Springs annually, spread out over the months of 6, 7, 8 and 10. The daily limit is 8 trout, with no minimum size limit. Trout are released directly into the springs.

Recommendations: The best place to fish is in the little civic park that abuts the stream. For those who may be wheelchair bound or are mobility impaired, this is an ideal place to cast a line. There is a guardrail-protected deck that extends from the paved parking area up to the edge of the stream from which one can easily make simple casts. This is not a stream to wade, but off the deck there is an additional 50-yard stretch of water that is accessible along the bank down to the iron rail fence that blocks further access. The opposite bank is off limits as it houses some of the water treatment facilities.

After the rainbows are stocked some trout can be seen nosing insects out of the moss or rising to feed on periodic hatches of little mayflies. Soon these trout become wary, but a #16 Adams, #16 BWO or a Bead-Head Hare's Ear might bring some strikes. The best fishing is in the summer months.

Another place to fish Royal Springs is at the mouth of the stream where it enters Elkhorn Creek. Following the driving directions below, from the parking area you can wade downstream in Elkhorn Creek for about 20 yards, before crossing the creek. Here you will see Royal Springs entering the Elkhorn. In the downstream plume the waters will be cold and rainbows reside here, plucking food from the Elkhorn. Standing upstream cast #12s Prince or Hare's Ears Nymphs ahead of the plume and let them drift into the plume. You will likely get strikes.

Directions: To access the stream from the intersection of US 25 and US 460 in downtown Georgetown, turn west on 460 and at the very next street, less than 0.1 mile, turn left onto S. Water Street. Immediately you will see the civic park on your right and ample parking.

On the other side of US 460 along N. Water Street and adjacent to an industrial complex, there is a small green with a park bench and some room to cast. One-tenth mile further along N. Water Street there is a gravel pull off near a 24-inch pipe traversing the stream. To the right of this pipe one can walk down to the stream and flip several casts into the stream. Further downstream is all private land.

To reach the mouth of Royal Springs where it enters Elkhorn Creek, drive 0.7 miles north of U.S. 460 on U.S. 25. Immediately after crossing Elkhorn Creek, take the next right into Richard Winder Park. Park and walk under the bridge. Follow the pavement and on the other side of the bridge veer off to the left on a gravel path that ends where you can enter Elkhorn Creek. Wade down and across stream about 20 yards and you will see Royal Springs entering the Elkhorn.

Sinking Creek

The Dents Road covered bridge, built across Sinking Creek in 1858, had its wood planking raddled by stagecoaches running from Hardinsburg to Bewleyville for over 50 years and by autos for another 50 before it was replaced by a concrete bridge.

Ecosystem: A second bridge crosses Sinking Creek further upstream at the intersection of Dents Bridge Rosetta Road and Rosetta Corner Road. It is below this bridge and into a pool behind a small makeshift dam (pictured below), that the KDFWR annually releases 1,200 rainbows. Local residents hightail it to this stocking site soon after with their live bait and canned corn. But the close proximity of Sinking Creek to the greater Louisville metropolitan area has made this creek a popular one.

Sinking Creek meanders through open farmland with grazing cattle, fields of corn and a few stands of timber. The stream holds to its name and in the dry summer months parts of its headwaters may go underground. Most of the creek

is 20-30 feet wide and 2-3 feet deep, except following moderate to heavy rains when the stream can become 10 feet deep and a torrent of log-infested muddy water. It can take several days for the stream to clear and revert back to its normal flow of long, lazy runs with sporadic stretches of riffles.

Navigating the steep, muddy slopes that border this stream might send you sliding on your rear end. The better choice is to trek or drive along the gravel Dents Bridge Rosetta Road that parallels over half of this section and look for the several access spots that have more comforting admissions. Of course getting out of the stream can also present a problem, so be prepared to dirty your hands and waders. The stream has very few boulders or deep holes, and except for the occasional patch of slippery limestone, the gravel streambed makes for easy wading. A canopy of deciduous trees, none of them remarkable in diameter, set along the top edges of the steep banks clears the way for up and downstream casting.

Stocking and Regulations: The stream is stocked with 1,200 9- to 12-inch rainbows across the months of 4, 5, and 6. Standard regulations apply.

Recommendations: Avoid fishing this stream after a big rainfall; let the waters recede and clear. Then fish the pool at the stocking point below the Rosetta Corner Road Bridge and work downstream with moderately long casts using #12 or #14 Adams or BWOs with a natural drift. Don't rush it—the drift will be slow. Above and below the riffles fish a Nymph, such as a #14 Bead-Head Hare's Ears, Pheasant Tail or an olive-colored Woolly Bugger. Use an indicator if that helps you see the strikes. If you see rises in the long runs, drift a fly into them. If you don't get a take, try a different fly, a different size or an emerger. After wading a tenth of a mile and you don't frighten up some trout, the stream has likely been fished out. Anyway you look at it, wading along this beautiful stream sure beats working.

Directions: From the town of Muldraugh, Ky. drive south on US 31W for 1.5 miles and then turn right onto US 60. Drive 7.1 miles toward the town of Irvington and turn left onto KY 144, Joe Prather Highway. Drive another 0.4 miles and then turn right onto KY 333. Drive this winding narrow road for 11.5 miles. When you come to a hamlet called Corners, continue straight onto Rosetta Corners Road for 2.4 miles. As you approach the bridge over Sinking Creek, turn right onto the gravel Dents Bridge Rosetta Road and pull off and park. A small path provides stream access. Alternately, walk the gravel road and look for the several other access sites. At the far end of this road, a left turn and 100 yards of walking leads you to the second bridge.

Taylorsville Lake Tailwater

Located less than 20 miles from the greater Louisville area, this is Kentucky's newest tailwater to be stocked with trout.

Ecosystem: The tailwaters of Taylorsville Lake are not the pristine trout environment of which many anglers dream. But with adequate stocking levels and its close proximity to Louisville, the tailwaters have attracted many local fishermen.

One would think that with a 150-foot-deep, 3,000-acre, clear water reservoir behind the Taylorsville Lake dam, that there would be lots of cold, clear water to sustain a year-round population of rainbow trout. Think that and you'll be wrong. The banks of the tailwater are muddy slopes with protruding root wads and fallen deciduous trees. With alternating fluctuations in water releases from the dam, there is a near constant wash of mud into the waters. With little more than two feet variation between the summer and winter pool elevations, the summer months find warm water entering the tailwater. The trout quickly succumb to the tepid temperatures, unless caught by the bait fishermen that line the shore.

For nearly its entire length, from the dam to where it enters the town of Taylorville, the 50- to 100-foot-wide tailwater is lined with 10- to 15-foot-high muddy slopes. The water is so off-colored that one cannot see the bottom of the channel. Except for a few stretches of graveled riffles, the tailwater is mud bottom the whole way, creating inhospitable conditions for the wading, fly fishing angler.

The area below the dam is very user friendly. Here there are restroom facilities, picnic tables, a shelter, benches and ample parking slots. On both sides of the 100-foot-long tailrace there are sets of steps leading to three-foot-wide walkways from which most of the fishing occurs. The tailrace channel is filled with big stones, making wading impossible. On any given day there will be bait and lure fishermen lining the walkways reeling in sauger, perch, crappie, bass, bluegill, strippers and rainbows. For every one trout caught there will be a dozen warmwater species landed. There is room for everyone, and a fly-line wheeling angler should have no problem staying clear of the bait fishermen, although the latter may lodge some verbal jabs at the former.

About 0.6 miles downstream from the dam there is a concrete boat ramp. As there is no downstream takeout ramp, only motorized crafts should be launched here as they will have to motor back to the ramp.

Beginning near the bridge in Taylorville, the E. River Road parallels the tailwater. There are several points of access to the tailwater from the road, but they lead to very murky water and a muddy bottom tailwater.

Stocking and Regulations: During April and May, the tailwater receives a stocking of 1,000 rainbows each month; an additional 500 rainbows are stocked in June and November. The 3,000 trout are released into the tailwater near the dam. There are no brown trout released in these waters. There is a standard daily limit of 8 trout of any size.

Recommendations: Since we have not fished this tailwater from a boat, we can only offer a few suggestions as how to fish it with flies and a fly rod. In our one outing, fishing from the tailrace walkway we hooked two modest-sized fish on a #14 Bead-Head Hare's Ear and landed neither. Given more time, we might have tried a Woolly Bugger under an indicator. As the bait fishermen use minnows as their preferred bait, fly anglers might want to try a flashy, brightly colored Clouser Minnow in these murky waters.

Directions: Take exit 23 on I-265, the Gene Snyder Parkway. Drive east on KY 155, Taylorsville Lake Road, for 15.1 miles to the town of Taylorsville. At a stoplight near the village of Elk Creek, KY 155 picks up KY 55 before they enter Taylorsville together. Remain on KY 55 as it passes through town. Just before KY 55 crosses Salt River Bridge, turn left onto E. River Road. This narrow, paved road parallels the tailwater for about 1 mile before it dead ends. Along this road there are one or two places to enter the water. At the end of the road there is a large shoal and riffle, but accessing this is impossible except at low water and before you enter private, posted land.

The more accessible portion of the tailwater is near the dam. As you approach Taylorsville, turn left onto the divided highway KY 44, Briar Ridge Road, and drive 2.2 miles. Turn right onto CR 2239, Overlook Road. At the intersection of CR 2239 and Tailwater Road, turn right and drive 1.4 miles to the parking lot overlooking the Salt River tailrace . There are several sets of steps down to the concrete walkway along the tailrace. If you wish to launch a boat, there is a wide concrete ramp 0.6 miles back up Tailwater Road on your left with over a dozen parking slots for trailers.

The tailwater can also be reached off of I-64 at exit 32. Drive south on SR 55 for 8.5 miles and at the stoplight turn left, remaining on KY 55. Drive 4.6 miles. Where KY 55 and SR 44 intersect, turn left onto SR 44 and drive 2.2 miles. On your right you will see a sign indicating the 1.4-mile road to the dam and tailwater. The total distance from I-64 to the dam is 16.9 miles.

Southern Kentucky

- Bark Camp Creek
- Cane Creek
- Cumberland River Tailwater
- Hatchery Creek
- Laurel River Lake
- Rock Creek
- War Fork Creek
- Wood Creek Lake

Southern Kentucky offers a huge variety of fly fishing, including one of the top 50 best tailwaters in the United States, gorgeous backwoods angling and clear, cold water.

Cumberland River Tailwater Rainbow

Bark Camp Creek

A gorgeous hiking trail provides easy access to this classic woodland stream in the heart of the Daniel Boone National Forest.

Ecosystem: Hiking along Bark Camp Creek is so delightful that you might forget you actually came to fish. Daniel Boone Forest Trail #413 parallels the stream for 2.6 miles as it runs downstream from the parking area to where the creek tumbles into the Cumberland River. Slowly working your way down the hiking trail you'll find yourself sandwiched between the creek on your left and a towering rock wall on your right. Several rock houses overhang the trail, providing shelter for many of the renegade campsites found along the creek.

The spring-fed stream gently flows under stately hemlock trees, rhododendrons and mountain laurel. Anglers will be privy to a spectacular wildflower display in the spring. And in the fall, maples, sassafras and tulip poplars provide splashes of yellow and red, while the leaves from the bigleaf and umbrella magnolias litter the forest floor.

The creek itself varies between 20 and 40 feet wide and alternates between pool-drop and riffle-pool. In many spots, large boulders and root wads have barricaded the stream, resulting in slack water above and small plunge pools below.

Further downstream, close to where the trail joins the Sheltowee Trace at the Cumberland River, the boulders are the size of small log cabins. Along this section, Bark Camp Creek forms a series of cascading waterfalls and the plunge pools only deepen (as seen on the cover of this book). With the exception of a few flat rock slides, the bottom of the creek is scattered with baseball- and football-sized rocks, sprinkled with quartz pebbles and sand. After heavy spring rains, the creek only needs a day or two to clear.

Stocking and Regulations: Bark Camp Creek is stocked each year with 3,750 rainbows, equally distributed across the months of 3, 4, 5, 6 and 10, with an additional 500 8-inch brown trout stocked annually. A catch-and-release season applies Oct. 1 to March 31, during which only artificial lures and flies may be used. At other times 8 trout may be kept, but only 3 may be browns and these must be 12 inches or longer.

Recommendations: Fish and Wildlife stocks Bark Camp Creek where Forest Service Road 193 crosses the creek. On the downstream side of the road there is a large, deep pool with relatively easy access. Anglers can wade upstream for quite a bit, although bank fishing is somewhat difficult due to rhododendron thickets and overhanging vegetation. Just below the stocking pool, the creek begins a series of riffles and slack water, alternating with small plunge pools. Try fishing below the riffles with a Copper John or something with a little flash or color, as the stream is quite shady in many places and the water stained almost a dark brown.

The hiking trail provides easy access to many of the large pools downstream. Diptera (midges) thrive in Bark Camp Creek and #20 midges should work well. But be forewarned, such an accessible, well-stocked and beautiful creek attracts a lot of other fisherman and competition can be fierce. These pools can be fished out all-too quickly.

In the deeper plunge pools located further downstream, any nymph fishing requires getting the fly down to where the fish hang out. This may require either a weighted nymph or a BB split shot attached about 12 inches above the nymph. Use an indicator and adjust as needed.

Directions: From I-75 south, take Exit #25 at Corbin. Turn right on US 25W. Drive 4.7 miles. Turn right onto KY 1193. Drive another 4.6 miles. Stay straight on KY 1277 where KY 1193 bears to the right. (KY 1277 is known as Bee Creek Road on some maps, but is not physically marked as such.) Drive 1.2 miles. You will see a slightly misleading brown Forest Service sign for FS 88 and State Hwy 90 on your right. Immediately past the sign, turn left onto Forest Service Road 193, a gravel road lightly pocked with potholes. In 1.7 miles the road will cross Bark Camp Creek. Shoulder parking is available for two or three cars.

Cane Creek

Cane Creek is a challenging stream to access and a challenging stream to fish, but some might find the scenery and the possibility of hooking a 16-inch rainbow well worth the effort.

Ecosystem: Cane Creek flows through the heart of the Cane Creek Wildlife Management Area (WMA) in the DBNF, just west of London, Ky. The creek is pristine and abundant with life. Beaver have dammed several upper stretches of the stream above the stocking point, a bounty of macroinvertebrates provide ample trout fare, and the well-aerated waters run clear and cold. It's no wonder Fish and Wildlife stocks this incredible trout habitat. But fishing Cane Creek is not for the weak of heart or those without waders. Even locals leave this one alone and rarely go after the 3,750 rainbows stocked here.

The headwaters of Cane Creek begin north of KY 192, before slowly making their way down to the stocking point off Rooks Road. The gradient of upper Cane Creek is relatively flat as the water picks its way through deciduous forests and the banks, occasionally broken with rock overhangs, and can become rather muddy. Downstream of the stocking point, the creek becomes increasingly choked with rhododendron thickets and downed trees before giving way to clear riffles and larger pools.

Below the stocking point, Cane Creek enters the Cane Creek WMA and access is severely restricted. The next good access point is several miles downstream and is gained by hiking into the mid-section of the stream via a 2-mile hike along the Sheltowee Trace or a 1.6-mile walk along Forest Service Road #109, both of which originate off KY 192. The mid-section of the stream probably has the best fishing and certainly is the easiest to wade when water levels are right.

Lower Cane Creek can be accessed via Bee Rock Campground, just upstream of where the stream joins the Rockcastle River. In this section of Cane Creek there are some winter holdovers up to 16 inches in length found in the deep pools next to the big boulders. Although the trout habitat here is ideal and the scenery first class, the lower section of the creek is impossible to wade and trail access is extremely limited. However, if you can get in and out of the stream and fish it at low flows, the lower section has some very good fishing.

Stocking and Regulations: Cane Creek is stocked annually with 3,750 rainbows, equally distributed across the months of 3, 4, 5, 6 and 10. A catch-and-release (artificial flies and lures only) season applies Oct. 1 – March 31. All other fishing regulations and permit requirements apply.

Recommendations: We'll discuss fishing Cane Creek at three points: at the point of stocking, at mid-point where the Sheltowee Trace Trail intersects the creek, and lower Cane Creek.

At the stocking site off Rooks Road (directions below), Cane Creek is relatively narrow, averaging only 20-25 foot across. Rhododendron and mountain laurel form dense thickets along the creek and no trails exist on either side. Bank fishing is all but impossible. But if you're up for some adventure and don't mind climbing over a strainer or two (formed by downed trees and collected debris that have blocked the creek), pull on your waders and wade either upstream or downstream of the stocking point. The gradient is negligible and the stream floor is an easy-wading combination of small rocks, sand and some silt. In the fall the stream is extremely shallow, but after a heavy spring rain it can be too difficult to wade.

Better fishing can be found in the mid-section of Cane Creek by hiking in either on the Sheltowee Trace Trail #100 or FSR #109 (directions given below). Choosing FSR #109 is about 0.4 miles shorter one-way, but not nearly as scenic. The Sheltowee (or 'Big Turtle," named for Mr. Boone) is a gorgeous hike, but dragging along your gear can wear you down, particularly on the way home. Either way, both hikes end up at the same wooden footbridge that spans Cane Creek. Be sure to bring your waders, boots, fishing gear, and plenty of drinking water and snacks for the day.

Fishing below this footbridge is nearly impossible as the creek quickly picks up gradient, small rocks become large boulders, no trail access is available, and the resident mink have cleaned out the deeper pools. We suggest you pull on your waders and boots and work your way upstream from the bridge. Cast into the deep pools flowing beneath the shaded, rocky overhangs and below the riffles. Mid-stream boulders have left downstream microeddies and seam lines to either side. Given the remoteness of this stream, we guarantee you won't see another person and the creek will be yours.

Other than the hike in and out, another difficulty of fishing the mid-section of Cane Creek is water levels. Stream wading is an absolute must, as no trails are available. However, in the spring swift currents can make this a cold and dangerous proposition, yet in the fall the water levels are so low you have to search for the deeper pools where the trout like to hang out.

Your last option is to follow the directions to lower Cane Creek, but we recommend this section with some reservation. As noted, due to the steep gradient this section of the creek is impossible to wade and bank access is extremely limited. But many of the larger trout hold out in this lower section and the scenery along the creek is stunning. Follow the driving directions below and then hike east along Rockcastle Narrows Trail #401, which roughly parallels the stream. Do your best to get in and out of the stream wherever possible, and for safety only fish at low water flows. Fish weighted nymphs next to the large boulders and below the plunge pools. Fishing is also excellent at the mouth of Cane Creek where it enters the Rockcastle River. In the spring the banks of the river are full of bait fishermen and it may be just as easy to join them there.

Directions: From I-75 South, take exit #38 for London. Turn right onto KY 192 West. From here we provide directions for four different ways to access Cane Creek:

Stocking Access: After turning right onto KY 192 West, drive 10.0 miles to Rooks Road (FSR #761). Rooks Road is 0.4 miles past the Bald Rock Picnic Area and immediately past the white concrete block building on your right with the large Ashland sign and the two dilapidated gas pumps. Turn right onto Rooks Road and drive 2.4 miles to where it basically dead-ends into Cane Creek. Rooks Road begins as a paved road (the first 1.8 miles), before turning into a gravel road (the last 0.6 miles).

Access mid-point via hiking Sheltowee Trace Trail #100: After turning right onto KY 192 West, drive 14 miles to the intersection of KY 192 W and KY 1193 S. A large gravel parking lot will be on your left. Park here and carefully cross back over KY 192 to the north side of the road. Hike along Sheltowee Trace Trail #100 for approximately 2 miles until you reach the footbridge at Cane Creek.

Access mid-point via hiking FSR #109: After turning right onto KY 192 West, drive 16.2 miles to Forest Service Road #109. This is a gated road. Park on the gravel pull-off. Hike along FSR #109 for approximately 1.6 miles until you reach the footbridge at Cane Creek. (The first mile of FSR #109 is an old logging road. The road then ends where a clearly marked single-track hiking trail descends for 0.35 miles before reaching Sheltowee Trace Trail #100. Turn left or east on Trail #100 and hike the last 0.25 miles. The first bridge you cross goes over Pounder Branch; the second bridge crosses Cane Creek. Both are well marked.)

Access lower Cane Creek: After turning right onto KY 192 West, drive 18.0 miles to Bee Rock Campground. Turn right into the campground. Hike the Rockcastle Narrows Connector Trail #401A for approximately 1 mile until you reach Cane Creek upstream of where it flows into the Rockcastle River. To continue on Rockcastle Narrows Trail #401, you must cross Cane Creek. Do NOT attempt to cross the creek in high water. Hiking Trail #401 east will take you along the lower reaches of Cane Creek, but access is very limited.

A map of the Cane Creek Wilderness Management Area can be found at tinyurl.com/CaneCreekWMA. Although the trails are marked but not identified, both Rooks Road and FSR#109 are clearly labeled.

Cumberland River Tailwater

Rated one of the 50 best trout tailwaters in the U.S., there is little doubt that the Lake Cumberland Tailwater is the best trout fishery in Kentucky.

Ecosystem: The tailwater of the Cumberland River extends for 75 miles, beginning at Wolf Creek Dam and running all the way to the Tennessee border. Water coming out from the dam tends to be very cold, typically 54 +/- 6°F, but in the heart of winter when there are few anglers on the water, the river's temperature can dip to 40°F. In summer, the water warms as it flows southwest towards the Volunteer state, but because of daily releases, it remains cool enough to support trout throughout the Kentucky portion of the tailwater. However, in winter, the tailwater can actually cool as it flows downstream since the ambient air temperature and the inflowing creeks are colder than the water being released from the dam.

Scattered along the tailwater are 10 islands and over 50 in-coming streams, creating constantly converging and diverging water, a large number of shoals, and a multitude of plummeting holes. The river averages about 200 feet wide and along its course are numerous deadfalls, drop offs, tree wads, rocky banks, steep cliffs, moss beds and other structures that create an ideal aquatic habitat for fish. Access along the tailwater is easy via nine boat ramps and at least 15 walk-ins sites.

The river conditions noted above provide an excellent forage base for trout habitat, including many types of mayflies, stoneflies, caddisflies, midges, scuds and sow bugs. In the summer months the terrestrials appear, including Japanese beetles, grasshoppers, cicadas and black ants. An in-depth study of the fauna in the tailwater was conducted several years ago and revealed that the section of the river known as Rainbow Run has the highest concentration of macroinvertebrates in the entire tailwater. The number and variety of aquatic macroinvertebrates are key indicators of stream quality and include animals such as crayfish, mussels, aquatic snails, aquatic worms and the larvae of aquatic insects. The section of tailwater from the dam down to Rainbow Run has mostly Diptera (two-winged insects). Clearly, the variety of habitat and the abundance of food make the Cumberland River tailwater an ideal trout habitat.

As a result, the tailwater of the Cumberland is known for its trophy-size trout, including a 21-pound brown and a 14-pound 6-ounce rainbow (both Kentucky records) having been pulled from its waters. For the reasons noted above, we will concentrate on the upstream portion of the river from the dam down to Winfrey's Landing (see the map on the accompanying page.)

It is worthwhile to note that prior to 2013 Wolf Creek Dam underwent major repairs for several years. Water flowing through the karsts below the earth-filled portion of the dam had been slowly washing away the fill, leaks were developing, and the integrity of the dam was at risk. During the repair period the water level in the lake was substantially reduced and held at near constant levels by periodically releasing low to modest volumes of water following rains. While this did not significantly alter the structure of the riverbanks, it had some effect on the fishing. Importantly, the warmer waters being released from the dam significantly reduced the quality of trout habitat in the tailwater and encouraged other species (bass, catfish, bluegill and others) to migrate further upstream toward the dam. Periods of on-again, off-again fishing occurred and average fish size seemed to decline, although a few trophy fish were still being caught. As this book was being drafted, the lake was being returned to its normal pool level, and most anglers are confident the tailwater will return to its former glory.

Finally, at the time of publication, US Highway 127 between Jamestown and Albany, Ky. is being rerouted. The new section of US 127 will cross Blackfish Creek, northeast of Wolf Creek Dam. The highway will no longer cross the dam itself, although public road access will remain. At this point it is not clear what impact the new bridge will have on the structure of the Cumberland River tailwater.

Stockings and Regulations: The tailwater of the Cumberland was the first waterway where KDFWR began earnestly stocking rainbow trout in Kentucky, beginning in 1952. Stockings of brown trout began in 1982 and have been stocked annually since that time. Brook trout were added to the list in 2011. The Cumberland receives the largest stockings of any waterway in the state and is now listed as one of the 50 top tailwaters in the U.S. according to "50 Best Tailwaters to Fly Fish" published in 2013 by Stonefly Press.

On average, about 160,000 rainbows are stocked annually, from April through November. About 40 percent of these rainbows are sterile, in an effort to improve the growth, survival and quality of the population. In addition, the Cumberland tailwater receives 38,000 browns, averaging 8 inches, and 40,000 8- to 12-inch brook trout annually via a one-time stocking in February or March. There have been some supplemental stockings in recent years to help alleviate the deleterious effects of previous drawdowns, but the opportunity for similar stockings in the future are unknown.

Currently there is a daily limit of 5 rainbows, of which each must be less than 15 inches in length, except one rainbow may be longer than 20 inches in length. One brown trout 20 inches or greater may be kept. Only 1 brook trout can be kept and it must be 15 inches or more. Culling (returning a fish in possession for a more recent catch) is prohibited. All licensed anglers fishing the portion of the Cumberland River from Wolf Creek Dam to the Tennessee state line, its tributaries up to the first riffle, and all of Hatchery Creek are required to possess a trout permit. Please check signage at access points and KDFWR for updates in these regulations.

Recommendations

Water Levels

As is the case with most tailwater fisheries, the Cumberland can be fished year-round. However, the volume of water released through the turbines and oxygenating sluice gates greatly influences the quality of the fishing. Before making the trip one should always check the water release schedule. Daily generation release information for Wolf Creek Dam can be obtained through the Tennessee Valley Authority at tva.gov/lakes/wch_r.htm. You can also phone the Lake Cumberland Fishing Information number operated by the US Army Corps of Engineers at (606) 678-8697. For more detailed information, especially more than one day in advance, you can call the Nashville Corps Water Management office at (615) 736-5635 or explore the US Army Corps of Engineers website for the Cumberland River at Burkesville (tinyurl.com/mocpg8h) or Rowena (tinyurl.com/k9csstu).

Let's take a closer look at the amount of water released into the tailwater from these turbines and the six sluice gates. A listing of 3,800 cfs (cubic feet per second) indicates that one generator is running at full capacity; each additional turbine will release approximately an extra 3,500 cfs into the river. Importantly, the actual lake level at the time of release can impact these numbers. However, with the flow of two turbines approaching (anything much greater than 7,000 cfs), you do not want to be wading in the river in the stretches above Winfrey's Ferry. Of course, the distance you are from the dam can also impact wading safety, as discussed below.

In addition to the water being released from the turbines, the sluice gates also release water into the Cumberland tailwater. Each of the four of the six sluice gates can release roughly 1,500-1,700 cfs apiece. The other two sluice gates have been modified with a metal restrictor plate (known as "orifice gates") and the outflow from these is about 260 cfs each. Again the actual lake level at the time of release can influence actual release rates, but since the sluice gates are deeper than the turbines the impact is not as great.

At 5 to 15 percent of the maximum flow of 22,000 cfs, fishing can be very good. For about 30 minutes after the water level begins to rise, the fish go on a feeding frenzy and then feeding falls off.

The quantity of water released through the dam's turbines directly affects the water levels downstream and the delay times before those levels are achieved. The table below provides estimates as to how long it takes for the water being released from Wolf Creek Dam to travel downstream, assuming various numbers of generators have been turned on.

Estimated Arrival Time from Dam (0.1 hour = 6 minutes) All information is approximate				
Location	River Miles from Dam	Water Speed in MPH		
		4 mph or less (1-3 turbines)	5 mph (4 turbines)	6 mph or greater (6 turbines)
Helms	4.25	1.1 hours	0.9 hours	0.7 hours
Rock House	10.75	2.7 hours	2.2 hours	1.8 hours
Rainbow Run	12.5	3.1 hours	2.5 hours	2.1 hours
Big Willis	21.25	5.3 hours	4.3 hours	3.5 hours

Adjacent to the dam the rise is immediate; however, as indicated in the table the number of turbines or generators in operation will result in water level rising at various times and locations along the tailwater. Frequently there will be hydropower generation every day, but typically during the summer and fall fishing season, there is a period overnight when they don't generate. Such release patterns allow you to continue to fish downstream for some time even after the turbines have been turned on at the dam. For example, with four turbines in operation you could continue to fish at the Rock House for approximately two hours and 12 minutes before the water level begins to rise there. The times are not precise and are affected slightly by the water depth behind the dam.

If you are wade fishing, it is a good idea to place a big stone adjacent to the edge of the water where you can see it. Glance at it occasionally and if you see water rising around it, and you are wading, you should get out; however, if you are fishing from a power boat you might elect to move downstream to fish a while longer. Alternately, you may want to stop at Hatchery Creek and try your luck there.

Access Points

There are nine public access walk-in sites between the dam and Winfrey's Ferry. Eight of these sites are shown on the accompanying map: the ninth will be the new Hatchery Creek fishing site. There are other private access points, but you must have permission from the property owners to use them.

KDFWR has bought two parcels of land downstream from the dam for anglers to gain wading access to two islands: Long Bar (with drive-up bank access and wading) and Rainbow Run shoal (currently with boat-only access). About 75 percent of the purchase price of these two properties was made using federal monies from the Sportfish Restoration Fund. Long Bar is located upstream of Rainbow Run, with Rock House almost equidistant between the two. Rock House is a gigantic sandstone arch lying between the parking area off KY 379 and the river. Canoeists, kayakers and float tubers frequently access the river through this arch. Fishing from these crafts with life vests on has recently become more popular.

Several Cumberland tailwater guides believe that some of the best fishing can be found in those parts of the river that become shallow (but not exposed) in the lowest water; but, in high water conditions these same areas don't receive excessive cfs flows because of bottom structure or gradient decreases. One such area is Long Bar, which has some of the most extensive moss beds and highest fish numbers per mile.

To reach Long Bar, known locally as Snow Island, park in the gravel lot (see directions below) and follow the dirt trail that leads to a small overlook of the half-mile island. At low water, waders can cross the 2- to 3-feet-deep narrow channel to reach the island. The main river channel is on the opposite side of Long Bar.

If fishing Long Bar at low water levels, anglers can walk directly to the head of the island by wading the channel between the bank and the island. On the upstream edge of Long Bar, the shoal flows directly into a large hole. Good fishing can be found in this gravel–covered shoal where trout feed on the mayflies and stoneflies found here.

If fishing Long Bar at moderate water levels (at high water levels you should not be wading in the stream), there is a scour hole on river–left, just downstream of the island. A scour hole is formed in a fast-moving stream in which the current has washed away sediment from the river bottom, and the corrosive action has left a "hole" in the floor. The submerged trees caught in the hole provide protection for the trout and large striped bass that sometimes congregate here.

Many of the trout that inhabit the Cumberland prefer abrupt depth changes like those found below shelves or ledges, and along cuts in the river bottom. While trout like shallow riffles during prolific hatches and other highly oxygenated areas, they also like to hang out towards the center of the river or along banks with access to deep water. Frequently trout will be found at each depth change; but rather than continually adjusting the depth of your rig (such as changing your indicator), you may want to simply move on to match the water to the depth of your rig.

Cumberland River Below Wolf Creek Dam

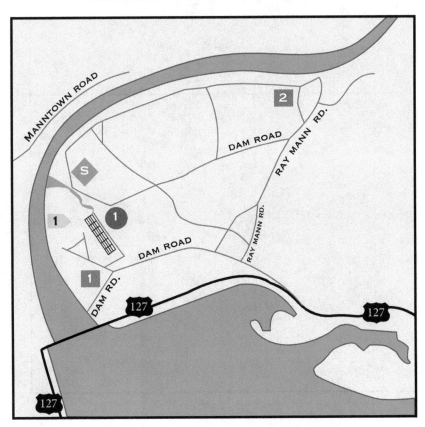

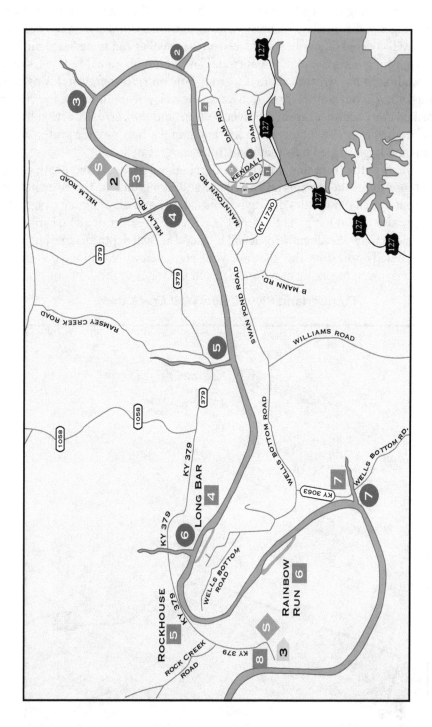

Cumberland River Tailwater Maps

Fishing Sites	Creeks	Boat Ramps
1 Substation Pool	1 Hatchery Creek	1 Kendall Boat Ramp
2 Long Bottom Pool	2 Little Indian Creek	2 Helm's Landing Boat Ramp
3 Helm's Landing Ledge	3 Blackfish Creek	3 Winfrey's Ferry Boat Ramp
4 Long Bar (Snow Island)	4 Coe Creek	
5 Rock House Banks	5 Ramsey Creek	S Stocking Sites
6 Rainbow Run	6 Sycamore Creek	
7 Tearcoat Shelf	7 Tearcoat Creek	
8 Winfrey's Ferry Ledge		

Fly Selection

The Cumberland River tailwater is widely viewed as a nymph fishing stream. Bead-Head Midges #18 to #22 (such as WD40s and Zebras) and other weighted nymphs #14 to #16 (for example Copper Johns, Prince Nymphs or Pheasant Tails) dropped three to six feet below a small white or yellow Styrofoam indicator will work just fine. Brassies, a generic nymph pattern that imitates midges and caddisflies, also works well as it sinks quickly and stays deep. You want the nymph in a natural drift just off the bottom of the river where the fish tend to hang out. If the water is off-color, you can use slightly larger flies. These should be cast across and upstream under a 9-foot, 6X leader and two to three feet of fluorocarbon tippet, and allowed to drift with periodic mending until they are directly downstream. A 40- or 50-foot cast is adequate, but mending is important. Strikes can occur at any time and frequently as the nymph begins to rise to the surface at the end of the drift. This can be repeated along any of the other bars that dot the tailwater. Fish seem to congregate mostly at the heads and ends of these bars, along foam lines, and seams separating the fast water from the slow.

If fish are seen breaking water taking spinners or duns, or sipping emergers, see if you can identify what they are taking. Try to match it in size and color maybe with a BWO (Blue Wing Olive) or a CDC Emerger. Before leaving this bar you might try 6-inch strips of a Clouser Minnow or Woolly Bugger along the dead falls above the scour hole.

If you opt for fishing the island in Rainbow Run, you must access it by boat. The two-thirds-mile island encompasses nearly 10 acres at low water, but that can easily be covered with swift water when two generators are running. Otherwise, anglers can beach their boats at the head of the island and wade fish.

While Rainbow Run is known for the high numbers of trophy-sized rainbows caught here, it is equally touted for its brown trout. Browns up to 28 inches and rainbows up to 25 inches are regularly taken from this river section. Brown trout also tend to be more heat-tolerant, as compared to the rainbows and brookies. Fall sampling by KDFWR personnel continues to confirm the inordinate number and quality of trout found here.

Fishing from either a drift boat or 14- to 18-foot motorized craft can bring you to the best water. There are three very good launching ramps between the dam and Winfrey's Ferry. Their locations are identified on the map. If using a drift boat, you must have someone shuttle your vehicle and trailer to your take-out point. Any motorized craft with less than a 10 horsepower motor will find it impossible to move upstream when more than two generators are operating; the boat would be unable to make any headway.

If fishing from a boat and using the above-mentioned flies, tie the smaller nymph as a dropper one to two feet below a second larger nymph, and both below an adjustable indicator. These should be fished along rocky shores, close to root wads and fallen trees, through runs adjacent to bars, above patches of moss, and over drop offs. The latter may be in the center of the river. The indicator should be adjusted so the bottom fly rides just above the bottom of the river where the fish search for sow bugs and midges.

Looking in a fly shop or a sportsman's catalog to find an artificial wet fly that matches a sow bug is almost impossible. One alternative is to trim the dangling legs from a #16 gray, artificial scud. Although this will not give an exact match to a sow bug, the modified scud in terms of size, color and configuration will look quite similar to the sow bug. This replica should be fished over and downstream of the moss beds frequently found in the Cumberland's shallow waters.

On occasion the underside of a stone in the river will reveal some nymphs. Small, one-inch black stonefly nymphs and cases of caddis flies are common, which may give you some guidance in fly selection.

Dry fly fishing can be very productive at times. Anglers often see trout sipping at the surface and a #22 cream or black midge may produce strikes. Periodically pods of fish can be found feeding on emergers, as well as duns and spinners on the surface. Without disturbing the pod, if you can gather up a few of these aquatic insects, you might be able to match them. Otherwise anglers can try a #14 - #18 BWO or Adams. Cast above the pod, mend and let it drift into the pod to increase your odds of a strike.

In May and early June the river can produce an afternoon of hatching

mottled-winged caddis. Elk Hair Caddis in #12 - #14 can be productive. Later in the summer there may be hatches of sulphurs and at times Japanese beetles. Matching these with artificials can bring some big fish to nets.

Streamer fishing can also bring success to the net. The Cumberland has a good population of crawfish and sculpins, providing an important high protein diet for trout. Typically anglers should drag the streamers across the bottom, using full sinking lines with short leaders.

As summer fades, large brown trout can frequently be seen feeding on grasshoppers along banks of vegetation. A Dave's Hopper (pictured on the previous page) tossed along the bank may well bring a trophy brown up. Entering the fall months, many browns move up to Hatchery creek and attempt to spawn there. An egg pattern may get results. Down near Cloyds Landing and Bear Creek, big brown trout are known to be spawning with some success. Little brown trout under four inches have been seen in the river here. Big stonefly nymphs are a favorite at this time and place.

Hearty souls brave enough to try some winter fishing will find #12 and #14 Copper Johns, Bead Head Hare's Ears and Pheasant Tails tied on 5X or 6X fluorocarbon tippet under an adjustable indicator can entice big fish to strike. If the water is off color, a brighter and bigger fly is called for. During the winter months of January and early February, the water temperature cools to the low 40s and feeding falls off significantly.

Due to the importance and the complexity of fly selection for the Cumberland Tailwater, we have developed a table indicating the active periods for various insects prevalent in this trout fishery. Please see the following page. Be aware that variations in rainfall, temperature, release levels and so forth can alter these periods.

The invasive algae Didymo, which harms plants and native insects, has been discovered in the Cumberland tailwaters. It cannot be over-emphasized that all fishermen leaving the waters of the Cumberland should thoroughly disinfect their waders, boots, and the sides and live wells of their boats with a 2 percent bleach solution to kill the algae and then allowed to dry for several days.

Downstream of Winfrey's Ferry

Although the section of tailwater from the dam to Winfrey's Ferry is regarded as the richest in aquatic life and the most heavily fished, other fishing opportunities can be found further downstream. Several miles downriver from Winfrey's, Crocus Creek enters the river and anglers can find parking for three cars, walk-in access with easy wading at low water levels, and some good fishing. Prince Nymphs and midges in a natural drift off the bottom will be productive here.

Further downriver, the town of Burkesville borders the tailwater, providing anglers excellent overnight accommodations and a very good boat ramp. During the summer months hatches of light Cahills might be spotted coming off the river. If you are fortunate enough to have a matching dry in your box, give it a go along this section of the tailwater.

Some of the best shoals in the river are to be found below Burkesville at Cloyd's Landing. In the fall, hefty brown trout will commence spawning in the shoals. In the evening, look for hatches of golden stoneflies, tie on a matching nymph, and if trout are surface feeding, try a #8 Stimulator. A Muddler Minnow, fished with long strips along the bottom, is known to bring a big trout to net in these waters.

Directions: There are lots of places to wade fish along the 75-mile Cumberland River tailwaters. Unfortunately, access to these areas is very limited because much of the bordering land is private or otherwise lined with steep cliffs. However in addition to Long Bar, there are several walk-in sites that are located at the boat ramps and some adjacent to the inlet streams. These frequently have gravel shoals from which you can fish.

To reach Long Bar from Jamestown, follow US 127 south about 12 miles to Wolf Creek Dam. Once across the dam, take the first right turn onto CR 1730. Drive north for 1.5 miles. CR 1730 Ts into Manntown Road. Turn left (west) on Manntown Road, which becomes Wells Bottom Road. Drive almost 3 miles. Stay on Wells Bottom Road (which veers right or north), rather than taking Desda-Wells Bottom Road / CR 3063 (which bears left or south). Drive 0.9 miles. Take the small road on your right that heads towards the river. Follow the KDFWR signs to a 15-slot gravel parking lot. It is then a short trek through a narrow wet or dry run to the water's edge.

Active Periods for Cumberland Tailwater Insects

Insects and Artificials	Jan	Feb	Mar	Apr	May	Jun	Jul	Aug	Sep	Oct	Nov	Dec
Blue-Winged Olives #14-18 BWO, CDC BWO Emerger, Copper John			X	X	X					X	X	X
Midges #18-20 WD40, Tungsten Zebra	X	X	X	X	X	X	X	X	X	X	X	X
Caddis #12-14 Elk Hair Caddis, CDC Emerger, Prince, BH Hare's Ear				X	X							
Sulphurs #14 Sulphur, CDC Emerger, CDC Comparadun						X	X					
Black Stonefly Early Black Stonefly Nymph, #12 Black Stonefly		X	X									
Yellow Stonefly #12 Prince, #8 Yellow Stonefly Nymph, #10 Stimulator						X	X	X				
Crustaceans #16 Sow Bug, #6 Woolly Bugger	X	X	X	X	X	X	X	X	X	X	X	X
Terrestrials #8 Dave's Hopper, #12 Japanese Beetle, #14 Black Ant,						X	X	X	X	X		
Minnows #4 Muddler and Clouser Minnows	X	X	X	X	X	X	X	X	X	X	X	X

Hatchery Creek

Most of Kentucky's streams have been around for centuries, if not millennia, but this "new" creek is just hatching out.

Ecosystem: If you're a little confused by our last sentence, you probably aren't alone. But in early summer of 2014, as this book was rolling off the press, the new Hatchery Creek was under development. It was an imaginary stream, an aggregation of ideas, calculations and illustrations compiled into a detailed proposal with the hopes of constructing a new 1.1-mile-long stream. Confident this enterprise would be completed by late 2014, we met with KDFWR personnel to gain additional insight into the design. But before we continue, let's take a quick look at the "old" Hatchery Creek.

The original creek brought cold, oxygen-rich water from the Wolf Creek National Fish Hatchery and emptied into the Cumberland River tailwater just below the dam. The stream was about 15-foot wide and 75-yards long; wide open along the banks, with no wading possible; and had concrete walls that ran the length of the sluice to a steep drop-off. The creek was basically a 3- to 4-foot-deep ditch and ran straight as a poker. Needless to say, there were no visual aesthetics to the old Hatchery Creek.

However, the old Hatchery Creek did have some desirable amenities and was popular amongst fishermen and their families. The 27,000 put-take rainbows stocked annually were a definite attention-grabber and many anglers appreciated the handicap access. Further, the drop off to the tailwater was in two sections: The first drop off ran about 10 feet before landing in a 4x4 foot pool, and the second included a 25- to 30-foot cascade that fell to a steep run and then into the tailwater. So the fishing was not bad here and could be quite good. But for many fly anglers the old Hatchery Creek rated a zero in sex appeal and romance.

Fortunately, the Feds and KDFWR felt the same way and proposed radically restructuring Hatchery Creek into a man-made, world-class trout stream. The $1.95 million project will be funded through Kentucky's Wetland and Stream Mitigation Fund. A nationally known company was contracted to design and build a 6,000-foot-long, 25-foot-wide braided stream, similar to what is found in the western United States. Right before the drop-off point the water of the "old" Hatchery Creek will be diverted to the new stream. The stream will slide out of the cold-water trout races of the Wolf Creek Hatchery and fall over 45 vertical feet before entering the tailwaters of the Cumberland River. That's over a mile of fishable water.

The upper section of the new stream will have very modest riffles intermixed with shallow runs and pocket water, flowing over pea-sized river gravel much like the streams in our country's western plains. Narrow braids, some only several feet wide, will branch off from the main channel and reunite with it downstream. A wetland, meadow and pond will reside off to the sides. In the lower stretch before entering the tailwater, a fish ladder is planned for the stream using a series of step pools. The ladder system will allow browns, rainbows and brooks to move into and out of the tailwater to spawn in the gravel bars. However, spawning will be modest and only a trifle of what would be needed to support the river's robust trout population.

Near the stream's mid-section a culvert will carry the stream under a roadway. There will be ample parking and access to the stream, restroom facilities, and for those anglers who want to get an early morning start on the fishing, the Kendall Campground will provide overnight stays. The old Hatchery Creek will be reworked and its handicap access retained.

Stocking and Regulations: Stocking levels have not been fully specified but are likely to follow those for the old creek, which had been 27,000 rainbows, distributed across all months. The "old" portion of Hatchery Creek will remain put-take and will maintain standard regulations and creel limits. Importantly, the new Hatchery Creek will be year-round catch-and-release fishing only. Although regulations for lures and bait are yet to be specified, KDFWR does not anticipate anything different from other c-and-r streams in Kentucky. Wading in this new section will be permitted and there will be no closed season.

Recommendations: Only a fly fishing wizard would dare to make specific recommendations for fishing an imaginary, man-made stream. But lacking a wizard, we conjured up memories of fishing the braided, spring streams out west and applied those to this new Hatchery Creek and came up with a few ideas.

Most of the trout introduced into Hatchery Creek will either be caught within a few days or find their way downstream into the river. For a stream no more than 25-feet wide, fishing with a low profile off the banks seems a better idea than slouching through the gravel beds and scaring off the game. Small nymphs fished above, through and below the riffles without an indicator, and small dries and nymphs in the pools and pocket water should work fine. If you have egg or worm patterns hidden in your fly box, break one out; it's time to use it. And if the tailwater is blown out, the new Hatchery Creek may provide an excellent alternative for a day of fishing.

Directions: To reach Hatchery Creek from north of Jamestown, follow US 127 South using the town's bypass and travel 12 miles to the dam. Prior to crossing the dam veer right and follow the paved road. Specific directions to parking for the new creek are currently unavailable but before creek construction is completed, there should be good signage for parking and stream access.

Map: A close-up map of the Cumberland River tailwater was provided in the previous entry. Although the new Hatchery Creek will be rerouted from the drop-off mentioned above, please see the map on page 140 for other details, including stocking and other fishing sites.

Laurel River Lake

Covering 6,000 acres, Laurel River Lake is the largest trout-stocked lake in Kentucky. Impounded in 1977, it has a maximum depth of 280 feet and an average depth of 50 feet.

Ecosystem: Laurel River Lake is set in the wild beauty of the DBNF. Its pristine waters are surrounded by forested hillsides that roll down to gravel shorelines, scattered with white stone cliffs harboring birds of prey. The area abounds in wildlife: deer grazing along its shores, Bald Eagles soaring overhead, and gaggles of Canada geese setting up permanent residence near the water. Occasionally you will see an osprey swoop down to snatch a fish off the lake's surface. The lake has a multitude of secluded coves, gravel bars and several small islands. Fishing for its rainbow trout, bass, walleye, crappie, catfish and bluegill is touted as excellent.

The Corps of Engineers operates the 280-foot-high earth and rock-filled dam, as well as its hydroelectric power plant and the swimming and recreational facilities above the spillway. The only man-made structures surrounding the lake are the six boat ramps, and the two boat-in and two drive-in campgrounds that are the mutual responsibility of the Corps of Engineers and the US Forest Service. Thousands of visitors visit this lake annually and find it a place for adventure, relaxation and reflection.

Stocking and Regulations: In January the lake receives a total stocking of 45,000 8- to 12-inch rainbows. The KDFWR's standard fishing regulations apply, including a daily creel limit of 8 trout, with no minimum size specified.

Recommendations: The rainbows in Laurel Lake over-winter, feeding on both small fish and insects, and many reach upwards of five pounds. Use less than eight-pound line and you may be deeply disappointed when that big one breaks off.

The most productive trout fishing is had in the cool spring and fall months. Since the trout favor clean, cold oxygenated water, they find the deep, clear water near the dam to their liking, particularly in the hot summer months. The best bet for the fly rod angler is to slowly troll a Muddler Minnow (pictured), Clouser Minnow, or similar imitation near the dam, set well below the lake's surface—preferably 15-20 feet deep. This may require you to use a sink tip fly line with 30 feet of no less than eight-pound monofilament attached to a treble swivel. To the second swivel you should attach a short, five-foot segment of monofilament line dragging a bullet-shaped weight, and to the third a five-foot segment of monofilament and your minnow imitation. It is best to use a trolling motor set at a slow speed with at least 70-100 feet of line out, and your rod set to either side of your boat and held high.

Fly fishing from the shoreline or in the summer months will not be that successful. There are several gravel bars to which you can hike off of Forest Service Roads 611A and 611B, but fly fishing from the water's edge is probably not worth the effort. Fishing in the hot summer months is usually not as productive and is best confined to the late evenings using the same line and fishing methods described above. It is at this time that you will see bait anglers fishing at night anchored off the dam with live minnows under lights.

Directions: To reach the popular Holly Bay Marina, campground and boat ramp, take Exit 38 off I-75, just south of London. Drive west on West Laurel Road / KY 192 for 14.1 miles. Bear left on Laurel Lake Road / KY 1193 south and drive for 2.4 miles. At the Holly Bay signage, make a left turn and drive 0.2 miles along Holly Bay Marina Road to reach the recreation compound.

Rock Creek

Rock Creek, a designated Kentucky Wild River, is undoubtedly the best and longest free flowing trout stream in Kentucky, providing more than 18 miles of fishable water from White Oak Junction to the Tennessee border.

Ecosystem: We won't lie—Rock Creek is not easy to get to. But once there, you might not want to leave. Hands down, Rock Creek has to be the most beautiful trout stream in all of Caintuck. With lots of water to fish and a long drive to get to it, you should consider using one of the fine campgrounds bordering this stream for an overnight stay.

Rock Creek originates in Tennessee's Pickett State Forest where several springs and tributaries provide the streams year-round flow of cold water. For years, acid mine drainage from an abandoned coalmine was sterilizing water below the junction. However, in 2000 the Rock Creek Task Force, working with state and federal agencies and Trout Unlimited, began to make progress in significantly reducing the acidity of this section of the stream. The following year a fish survey documented some trout in this once-sterile watershed. Since then, Rock Creek has continued to make strides in water quality, leading to increases in stockings and more trout overwintering. The stream has been known to give up three-pound rainbows on more than one occasion.

As Kentucky streams go, Rock Creek is wide, varying from 20 feet to as much as 40 feet across. And some of the pools are not only big, but can easily run over your waders. A 12-foot-deep pool may be up to 30 feet in diameter with no wading around it. There are long vegetation-free sections of the stream where the angler can let out some fly line, but other sections may encumber the open cast. Rock Creek's modest gradient and gravel beds means that even after a good rain it will clear out in a day or two.

Forest Service roads 137 and 566 closely parallel the stream for much of its length, and the Sheltowee Trace parallels FR 137 for a small stretch around the campgrounds. Hemlock Grove and Great Meadows are two full-facilities campgrounds with several dozen tent sites and mini-home pads with electrical hookups. The campgrounds are within one-half mile of one another, within a stone's throw of the stream and just a short drive from the state's border.

Stocking and Regulations: If there is any natural reproduction of trout in Rock Creek, it is not sufficient to support the fishing pressure this stream receives, and an annual stocking of 15,600 rainbows is provided. This stocking rate is the second highest of all streams in the state, only after Hatchery Creek. These trout are released during each month except January and February. The standard creel limit of 8 rainbows per day and no size restrictions are enforced, but there is a catch-and-release period from Oct. 1 until March 31 with only artificial flies and lures allowed. This applies to the 9.8-mile section downstream from the state's border.

Recommendations: The section of Rock Creek around the campgrounds is heavily fished, but the sections above and below the campgrounds hold equally good

fishing. There are numerous short-access paths along FR 137 into the stream. With its stretches of gravel, pocket water, runs, slicks, riffles and deep pools adjacent to giant boulders overlooking the stream, the angler must resort to a variety of fishing techniques to entice these trout to strike. Rainbows can be taken from all of these areas, but they spook easily so approach your casting spots with care and mend your casts. Presentation will be more important than the choice of the fly.

Rock Creek has good current flow and nymph fishing requires getting the fly down to where the fish hang out. This may require either a weighted nymph or a BB split shot attached 12 inches above the nymph. Fish will avoid high riding nymphs. If you see some air borne flies try to match them with an artificial. At dusk if you can tear yourself away from that warm campfire, you may see some spinners of Mayflies loosing flight over the big pools. You should try a #14 Adams to match these. Above the campgrounds towards the state border there are several very deep pools with overhanging low cliffs that have yielded some big fish.

Several macroinvertebrate studies have turned up nymphs and pupa of stoneflies, caddisflies and mayflies. Mayflies and an assortment of diptera (midges) thrive in Rock Creek. The usual assortment of dries and nymphs (#12, 14 and 16) and midges (#20) should be all that are needed.

Directions: The stream lies in the DBNF, about one and one-half hours south of Somerset, and is only accessible by a series of paved and gravel roads. Off US 27, 2.4 miles south of Whitley City turn right (west) onto KY 92 toward the town of Stearns. Stay on KY 92 for 6.6 miles until you reach Yamacraw. Drive over the South Fork of the Cumberland River and immediately turn left (south) onto CR 1363 (Yamacraw-Bell Farm Road on some maps). Drive 11.0 miles until you reach Bell Farm-Lonesome Creek Road. You may see some horseback riders along the stretch, so be cautious. Turn right onto FR 564 and drive 1.1 mile before turning onto FR 137. Drive 6.9 miles to the US Forest Service's Hemlock Campground or one-half mile further to Great Meadows Campground. Both of these have excellent bathhouse facilities and electrical hookups. FR 137 and the Sheltowee Trace hiking trail parallels Rock Creek all the way to and beyond the Kentucky/Tennessee border.

War Fork Creek

Now you see it, now you don't...War Fork Creek appears and disappears as it makes its way downstream and down under the ground, before popping up again.

Ecosystem: This has to be one of the darnest streams you might have fished. The karst geology of the region has created myriad underground caverns into which the creek waters flow above and below ground, depending on the season. During the early part of the year, the spring rains rush through this streambed, babbling across small rocks and rumbling around large boulders. The beauty of this geology is that the water returning above ground remains aerated and a cool mid-60 degrees or less, perfect for the rainbows that are stocked here.

But when the weather dries out, so does the creek as it disappears deep underground. While War Fork stays nice and shady throughout the summer, when the water levels drop the streambed goes dry and only a few large pools of tepid water remain, making it difficult for trout to survive the dog days of summer.

The rest of the topography is classic DBNF with a hodgepodge of hemlocks, oaks, tulip poplars, maples and more. The autumn colors make for beautiful fall fishing. A portion of the Sheltowee Trace, a hiking trail over 300 miles in length, that runs the length of the DBNF before ending in northern Tennessee, borders this section of the creek.

Fish and Wildlife stock War Fork Creek at the bridge as you enter Turkey Foot Campground. There is a large pool here—several actually, depending on how you count—about three to six feet deep each, just below the bridge. Below the concrete culverts that carry water under the bridge, large cut stones line one side of the creek and a natural stone and earthen embankment lines the opposite side. The trout love to hang out here in the shady pools, waiting for food to flush through the culverts. While the stream is rocky in most places, the pools retain a sandy bottom running amuck with crawfish. The high overhead canopy makes casting a breeze.

153

With the creek adjacent to the parking area, access is about as easy as it gets. But these same conditions attract lots of locals who rely on word of mouth to know when the stocking truck has arrived. Half-empty cans of corn and plastic containers holding leftover mealy bugs and worms frequently adorn the creek sides.

The concrete culverts make it difficult, if not impossible, for the trout to move upstream. However, as summer moves on we have heard stories of trout migrating downstream to some of the large scour holes below the campground. Unfortunately we have not been able to confirm these local tales. Beginning in early summer the water downstream of the campground moves underground and does not reappear for almost two miles until it comes gushing out of Resurgence Cave where the Sheltowee Trace crosses War Fork Creek. If you happen to hike down here in the summer, cool breezes coming out of the ground blow nonstop. This is truly Mother Earth's natural air conditioning.

Stocking and Regulations: War Fork Creek is stocked with 2,500 rainbows in the months 3, 4, 5, 6 and 10. There is a daily limit of 8 trout and no minimum size limit. A word of caution: Occasionally a really dry spring leaves War Fork Creek with inadequate water flow and KDFWR is forced to delay or even cancel the stocking until conditions improve. In that situation, they will not increase subsequent stockings to make up for missed stockings.

Recommendations: The best fishing is early in the spring, before the locals get too excited about the season, or late fall. In June, usually right before Father's Day, a fishing derby is held at the campground. The creek is stocked the evening before, access is closed off, and only seniors and children are allowed to fish the following morning.

Fish the pools right below the culvert, using nymphs and an indicator. The trout quickly wise up to what you're up to and the clear water and lack of bank vegetation leaves little to their imagination. There are a couple of large boulders, tree trunks and rock overhangs on the opposite bank. Cast over into the shadows and be patient. Later in the spring, move down to some of the large holes below the campground.

Directions: Head south on I-75 and take Berea exit #76. Turn left (east) on KY 21, traveling 1.5 miles to downtown Berea. Continue straight on KY 21 for another 5 miles until it dead ends into US 421. Turn right on 421. Stay on US 421 for 18.5 miles, passing through the small towns of Big Hill, Sand Gap and Waneta, until you get to McKee. Take a left on KY 89 and travel another 3.1 miles. Make a right on Macedonia Road. Drive another half-mile, then make a left on Turkey Foot Road (also known as Pilgrim's Rest Road or FR 4). You should see a sign for Turkey Foot National Forest Recreation Area. In about a mile, the paved road turns to gravel. Drive an additional two miles and turn left just prior to the bridge. This is Elsam Fork Road or Forest Development Road 345. Heed the flood prone area signs, as you must cross a small creek bed. Turn right onto Girl Scout Road, which takes you into the campground. Park in one of the gravel lots or pull-offs. Whew. Despite these lengthy directions, War Fork Creek is slightly over one-hour from Lexington and relatively easy to find.

154

Wood Creek Lake

The dam for this lake is also the highway fill for a small section of I-75, and the spillway runs under the interstate.

Ecosystem: How many times have you driven south on I-75 and noticed a quaint little lake right next to the interstate, just north of London? It seems like we always see a fishing boat or two floating its waters. But one would never suspect that this long and twisting 625-acre lake has almost 30 miles of shoreline and a maximum depth of 127 feet.

Although the northern half of Wood Creek Lake is situated within the DBNF, most of the land surrounding the lake is private and not accessible to the general public. Much of the land has been developed into residential lots, including some with very nice houses and cabins on them. Thick deciduous forests run down to the shore, shrouding many homes, and giving the lake its pristine, wilderness appearance.

The lake is owned by the Wood Creek Water District, which operates a five-million-gallon-per-day water treatment plant nearby. The district also manages a boat dock, boat ramp, bait shop and boat slip rental operation out of a 20 x 20 foot shanty. We can only imagine the low overhead costs of such an operation and wish more municipalities were so budget-conscious. The maintenance and operating costs of this little complex are pretty much covered by the $3 boat launch and $1 bank fishing fees, and the boat slip rentals.

The ramp is fully paved and can handle three trailers at a time, but the unpaved parking lot gets very crowded on weekends and holidays. There is one other paved public ramp on the lake, but that's it. The majority of the slips are filled with pontoon boats and there are a zillion of these. Water skiing, swimming and jet boats

155

are prohibited. In fact, a careful reading of the "rules" sign also dictates "No Alcohol Below 1030 Elevation." It has to make you smile.

Rental of powered boats was discontinued in 2014, so lake access is limited to those who own their own boats. From mid October until the first of April, the shanty operation is closed; however, boats may still be launched through the winter and early spring months. There are no restroom facilities other than what Mother Nature has provided.

Because the lake has sections of deep water that remain cool through the summer months, some of the rainbows survive and overwinter. Reports of trout up to five pounds being landed each year are not without foundation. Fishing for bass, crappie, walleye and catfish is extremely popular, and in 1984 the state record largemouth bass was taken from the lake, weighing a hefty 13 pounds, 10.4 ounces.

Stocking and Regulations: Wood Creek Lake receives 8,000 rainbows, averaging 8-12 inches in length, distributed across the months of February and October. The daily creel limit is 8 trout with no size restrictions. A valid license and trout permit are required to fish the lake.

Recommendations: Some of the bass anglers will turn to trout fishing after the fall and late winter stockings. From late October until stiff winter winds set in, trout can be found pooled up close to sunny shorelines and in estuaries. The locals will fish with minnow imitations, spinners and jigs of an assortment of different colors. Those who fly fish will strip Clouser Minnows (pictured) through these pods of fish. If you are unsuccessful in one spot move on to another that looks more promising. Most catches are the recently stocked 8-to 12-inch fish, but upon occasion a hefty three- or four-pound trout will be landed. When the lake turns over, put your rod away and head for the warmth of your fireplace and tie a few flies.

After the late winter stocking in February, the recommendations above can be repeated right up to the hot summer months. Then the trout seek out the cool confines of deeper water. Trolling a minnow imitation at a depth of 12 to 15 feet in the evening hours will be your best opportunity to catch a few rainbows. The stocking density in this lake is a modest 15 fish per acre, but if you have a boat, fishing this lake for trout can be a nice way to spend a day or an evening.

Directions: Just north of London, take exit 41 on I-75. Turn right (west) on US 80. Drive 4.8 miles and watch for a sign on your right for Wood Creek Lake indicating a right turn (heading north) onto Hawks Creek Road. Drive 1.9 miles, passing through several stop signs. At the fork in the road, veer right onto Moriah Road and drive an additional 0.9 miles down a winding, paved road to the boat dock.

Red River Gorge Area

- Chimney Top Creek
- Dog Fork Creek
- East Fork of Indian Creek
- Middle Fork of the Red River
- Mill Creek Lake
- Parched Corn Creek
- Swift Camp Creek

The Red River Gorge area offers cool mountain streams, stately hemlocks, lush rhododendron and the opportunity to get lost in time.

Chimney Top Creek

Chimney Top Creek, traversing the heart of the Red River Gorge Geological Area, provides stunning scenery and challenging brown trout fly fishing.

Ecosystem: The brown trout that reside in Chimney Top Creek are living la buena vida—the good life. And what is there not to like about this creek? The cascading stream falls over 200 feet in less than 3.3 miles, creating an ecological masterpiece. Rising out of rivulets near the Mountain Parkway, Chimney Top dumps its cold, clear water into the frequently muddy Red River. The stream stays cold year–round and with its steep gradient the creek flushes clean in quick fashion. Chimney Top Creek varies in width from a few feet to several yards and displays an assortment of riffles, boulder-sheltered deep pools, dead falls, undercut banks and short slicks.

Over the centuries decaying leaf matter has produced a rich soil for sustaining the flora of the valley. Chimney Top Creek is straddled by both hardwood

and evergreen trees, some with diameters up to three and four feet that tower over 100 feet in height. The canopy formed by the giant oaks, sycamores, poplars, hickories, hemlocks and pines allows even rooky anglers the opportunity for the perfect overhead cast. Even if you fail to catch one of the elusive browns that inhabit this stream, you will enjoy having fished in one of the few waterways in the state where trout survive the hot summer months and grow to keeper size.

Chimney Top Creek can be accessed at two points—at the confluence with the Red River, or further upstream by hiking in from Chimney Top Road. Starting at the confluence, Chimney Top Creek is paralleled by the famous Sheltowee Trace (Trail #100), where the path crosses the Red River on a long suspension bridge, strung high above the water. Anglers can enter the downstream section of the stream at a number of sites along this trail.

However, the best access to the upper drainage of Chimney Top Creek might be gained from hiking in a short distance from the gravel road that leads to Chimney Top Rock (see directions below). A half-mile hike west on Rough Trail (#221) leads you to the intersection with Koomer Ridge Trail (#220). Bear north here, by turning right to stay on the merged #220/221 trails. Another 3/8-mile of walking will lead you to the intersection of Sheltowee Trace (#100) and Rough Trail (#221). While this may sound confusing, it's actually quite simple. However, we recommend obtaining a good topographical trail map of the area before you set out.

(Note: A third approach is the Koomer Ridge Trail #220 which runs 2.3 miles from Koomer Ridge Road (and Campground) to join Rough Trail #221. Some anglers prefer this route, but we feel it only adds mileage to your day.)

The above-mentioned trails meet just to the southeast of where the upper drainage of Chimney Top Creek and its tributary, Right Fork, join together. However, there is some inconsistency across maps as to which is the main stem and which is the feeder creek, so the actual name on your map might differ from other maps. It's always good to bring your sense of adventure.

Follow the trail downstream along the smaller feeder creek. At the intersection of Sheltowee Trace (#100) and Rough Trail (#221), bear left (now walking west) on #221/100 to cross first the smaller feeder creek and then the larger tributary. It is the larger tributary that you will want to fish, on the west side of Koomer Ridge.

The valley is somewhat open here and a half-dozen primitive campsites have been established through repeated usage. If you elect to try a little camping, responsibly select a site that is at least 300 feet from any developed trail. Also be aware that food storage restrictions are in effect and overnight camping permits are required in the Gorge.

Alternately, at the intersection of Sheltowee Trace (#100) and Rough Trail (#221) you can continue walking north on the #100 as the Sheltowee Trace parallels Chimney Top Creek downstream for over 2.5 miles, before reaching the confluence with Red River. Again, the fishing is good here and worth spending time along this beautiful mountain stream.

One caveat: It is unfortunate but the Pine Bark Beetles are having a field day in this area, and along and across the stream you will find fallen pines by the dozens. Where they have fallen across the trails the Forest Service has power-sawed openings. On the plus side, the loss of pines has increased the available sunlight, encouraging the growth of other tree species.

Stocking and Regulations: Chimney Top Creek and its Right Fork receive one annual stocking of 450 4- to 6-inch browns in the month of June. There are two special fishing regulations: (1) if you are skilled enough to catch one of these browns, it must be 16 inches for you to keep it, with a one-fish creel limit per day (all others must be returned); and (2) only single hook flies and artificial lures may be used in this stream.

Recommendations: You would think that with an annual stocking of 450 browns into this tiny creek, and with few fly fishermen venturing into the valley to pursue them, catching one would not be that difficult. Think again. These fish are wild, wary and smart. They hide under outcropped rocks along the banks, in the deep pools near boulders, beneath the overhanging vegetation, and in the plunge pools and dead falls in the stream. If you are to have any hope of catching one of these browns you are going to have to locate likely holding spots and present a dry fly with a natural drift without revealing yourself. Stationing yourself upstream and using a downstream pull cast might be your best technique. Or keeping a low profile behind a rock and dropping a fly over the rock into a likely pool might also work. Good luck!

The midsection of the Right Fork might be your best opportunity to catch one of these wary brownies. Walk around the pools and not through them, even if that means getting out of the stream. A #16 or smaller Adams might do the trick, or a big morsel like a #8 Stimulator might bring them out. Presentation is more important than the fly or its size in this clear, small stream and using a 9-foot 6X fluorocarbon leader will increase your chances. Remember, if the trout sees your fly line you are doomed; so, just move on.

Suppose you have managed to fool a brownie and it takes your fly—getting it landed will be your final challenge. In a creek this small and with a light tippet anything can happen, and it probably will. There are rumors floating around that there are some browns up to 20 inches in this little creek but we have yet to catch, let alone see one. Catch a 16-incher in this stream and you have bragging rights.

Directions: From Exit 33 on the Mountain Parkway, turn left on KY 11 (Natural Bridge Road.) Drive back under the Parkway and turn left again onto KY 11. Drive 1.5 miles. Turn right onto KY 77 (Nada Tunnel Road.) Continue on KY 77 for 4.3 miles, passing through the Nada Tunnel in which you must turn on your headlights to stay alive. Do not enter the tunnel if you see oncoming headlights, as the tunnel will not accommodate cars moving in opposite directions. This is no place to play chicken.

After crossing the Red River Bridge, continue on KY 77 for another 2.4 miles, bearing to your right onto KY 715 until you see a sign on your left reading "Sheltowee Trail and Suspension Bridge." You will see a gravel road descending on your right that leads to a good parking area. Park and lock up your vehicle.

You now have two choices to cross the Red River to reach Chimney Top Creek: (1) if the river is low, as it is in late summer and wadeable, trek a very short distance down to its edge and wade across and the mouth of Chimney Top Creek will be to your left; (2) if the river is running high, you must hike the clearly marked, but un-numbered trail on the north side of the Red River for 0.4 miles to reach the suspension bridge and the Sheltowee Trace Trail (#100). The Sheltowee runs up Chimney Top Valley and parallels the stream. After about 1.5 miles the trail will cross a small creek where the Right Fork of Chimney Top veers left. You should fish up the Right Fork. This is a rather open area with a number of frequently used primitive campsites.

The alternative approach requires a little hike down a clearly marked but moderately difficult trail to reach the Right Fork. Drive east on the Mountain Parkway, take Exit 40 at Pine Ridge and turn right (north) onto KY 15. After 1.1 miles, turn right onto KY 715. There is a wood-framed outfitter store at the corner whose proprietor will be more than happy to answer questions about the Gorge area and sell you a cold beer. Back on KY 715, you quickly crossover the parkway and enter the DBNF. Drive 2.1 miles until you see a Forest Service sign on your right: "Chimney Rock Road"; veer left onto FR 10. Drive this gravel road 1.6 miles and do so carefully as it is filled with potholes. You will see signage on your right indicating a parking lot for Rough Trail #221. Pull in and park. A sign will direct you to #221. Follow the hiking directions given above. It will take you all of 40 minutes to reach the Right Fork of Chimney Top Creek.

The Sheltowee Trail (#100) and Rough Trail (#221) are well marked with a turtle and a white diamond, respectively; however, there are sections of both that can be a little difficult to navigate. We suggest you carry your rod unassembled, and waders and wading shoes, if you choose to wear them, in a backpack. Again, don't forget that topo map.

Dog Fork Creek

One of the few places in Kentucky to try your hand at catching a wild brook trout.

Ecosystem: If you like your angling days mixed with a heavy-dose of hiking and backwoods swashbuckling, you'll like fishing Dog Fork. No one said that the pursuit of wild brook trout would be easy. And we're not sure it should be. Located deep in the confines of the Red River Gorge Geological Area, this little stream is about as remote as they come.

Dog Fork creek is one of only six wild brook trout streams in Kentucky, and one of only four that can be fished (the others being Parched Corn Creek, also described in this book; Shillalah Creek, outside Cumberland Gap National Historic Park; and Poor Fork, also located in Letcher County). For some anglers, catching a brookie, a rainbow, and a brown completes the trifecta of trout fishing in the Bluegrass state. But again, we must stress it won't be easy scoring a wild brook trout at Dog Fork Creek.

The stream tumbles down a steep, rhododendron-choked terrain as it makes its way to Swift Camp Creek. The brook trout are located in the one-mile stretch beginning just below where the headwaters begin to just above a small waterfall. Dog Fork averages about 16 inches in depth, with a maximum of about 30 inches in the deepest pools. In several places the stream narrows so significantly you could easily jump across and is only about 12 feet at its widest. In general, the streambed is rocky with generous amounts of sand and decaying matter, crisscrossed with intermittent deadfall.

And we've not even talked about getting to the stream yet. Access can only be gained by hiking in several miles, with gear in tow. The most scenic hike into Dog Fork is off the parking area at the end of Rock Bridge Road (directions below). Rock Bridge Loop (trail #207) is a 1.4-mile loop that starts at the parking lot and leads to Swift Camp Creek. The shortest half of the loop is the northern-most section, which is an easy 0.5-mile hike downhill to intersect with Swift Camp Creek Trail (#219). At this intersection, turn left and begin hiking downstream atop a small ridge overlooking the creek.

You will cross several small tributaries that flow into Swift Camp Creek. Hike approximately 3.3 miles from the parking lot to reach Dog Fork Creek. Keep in mind that you now have a 1-mile wade up Dog Fork, a 1-mile wade back down the creek, and then a 3.3-mile hike back to your vehicle. What would possess you to do this?

A wild brook trout is probably one of the most challenging fish to catch in Kentucky. They are shy. They are elusive. And they are cunningly smart. But the hike into Dog Fork is beautiful. Fish and Wildlife rates the creek a Class I stream, with waters that never exceed 68 degrees, no roads within a half-mile, the entire area is in silviculture, and the brook trout reproduce year after year. If you enjoy being alone with only the sound of bubbling water and the maniacal cry of pileated woodpeckers, this is about as good as it gets.

Hikers can also enjoy the pink blooms of lady slippers in late spring and the shimmering white magnolias flowers in the summer, protected under a canopy of giant hemlocks and the occasional deciduous tree. Spring and fall months reveal the countless rock houses that can be seen along Swift Camp Creek Trail and a short hike to Rock Bridge showcases the only "waterfall arch" in Kentucky, where Swift Camp Creek flows under the gorgeous rock formation.

An alternative hike into Dog Fork is using the Wildcat Creek Trail (#228) off of KY 715. Park at the Wildcat Creek Trailhead (past the Rock Bridge Road turn off described in the directions below). Hike east on the trail for 1.8 miles until is dead ends into Swift Camp Creek Trail (#229). Turn right and hike south (upstream) for about one mile. This access route is about a 0.5-mile shorter one-way than the Rock Bridge access description above, but we don't think it's quite as scenic.

So if you think of Dog Fork as a hiking trip with a rod and reel thrown in for grins, this stream might be for you.

Stocking and Regulations: This is a catch-and-release stream only year-round. Only artificial flies and lures with a single hook may be used. No live bait. No stocking is done. The brook trout are naturally reproducing.

Recommendations: Unlike Parched Corn Creek, we have yet to catch a brookie out of Dog Fork, but that doesn't mean we haven't tried. We know they are there. These little fellows are elusive, and it is not a stream we are inclined to hike into on a whim. Brook trout are very skittish and they will scurry to cover at the sight of any predator whether man or fowl.

As noted above, the trout live secluded between the falls and the headwater. If you hike in from Swift Camp Creek Trail, you must then hike up Dog Fork until you reach a small waterfall. Fish upstream of the falls.

We have tried our luck fishing deep pools next to boulders, overhanging ledges with rhododendron cover, and around fallen trees. In future efforts we would stick to these simple basics: keep a low profile and drop a small dry fly upstream and secure a natural drift to the selected sites. In other streams both in and out of our state, brook trout seem to be attracted to the colors red or dark orange. A #14 or #16 Royal Coachman might be a good bet. Hope you have better luck than we have had.

Directions: Traveling east on the Mountain Parkway, take Exit 40. Turn right onto KY 15 North. After driving 0.7 miles you will pass the Dessie Scott Children's Home and come upon KY 715, sometimes called Sky Bridge Road. Turn right and drive 0.4 miles. You will cross back over the Parkway and enter the clearly marked DBNF. Take the first right onto Rock Bridge Road. This is a 3.5-mile gravel road scattered with potholes guaranteed to knock both your wheels and your teeth out of alignment.

East Fork of Indian Creek

This beautiful little stream comes generously stocked with rainbows and browns, glorious wildflowers in the spring and magnificent colors in the fall.

Ecosystem: The East Fork of Indian Creek lies in the DBNF, just outside the Red River Gorge Geological Area. The 10-mile stream varies in width from 10-30 feet as it meanders through a wide valley, yet remains easily accessible as it parallels Forest Road 9B for over three miles. The valley is heavily forested with stands of deciduous trees and an abundance of spring and summer wildflowers grow along the stream banks, valley flats and steep roadsides. In April and May, white bent and red sessile trillium, yellow trout-lily, dwarf iris, Celandine poppy, bloodroot and May apple appear along FR 9B, and if you look hard you'll find Jack-in-the-pulpits and occasionally yellow lady slippers. In the summer Joe-pye and ironweed bloom in the open flats.

Canopies of mature trees overhang the stream, keeping its waters fairly cool even through the hot summer months. In the late summer, the flow of the East Fork wanes but the waters remain cool and trout are known to hold over in the deeper pools. In August 2013 the stream's temperature was a refreshing 65°F.

There are at least 11 creeks, some spring-fed, that feed the upper drainage of the East Fork: Little and Big Amos, Hall Sink, and Laurel Spring, to name a few.

To reach its headwaters one must hike the abandoned road and an old trail that fords the stream in several places. Numerous big boulders with abutting deep pools have formed along the stream. Long bars of fine silt and gravel are common, a by-product of heavy spring flooding. Occasional deadfall impedes the streams flow, while riffles abound.

A bridge and three culverts that ran under FR 9B were planned to be removed in Fall 2014, allowing the stream to flow more freely, creating additional riffles and deeper pools, adding to the quality of fish habitat and fishing opportunities. Additional stream work is underway. To reach the upper stretches of the East Fork and Big Amos now requires some additional hiking, for which the ambitious angler can be well rewarded.

Recreation permits are needed to use the overnight campsites scattered along the stream. The area has been designated an official Archaeological Site by the US Forest Service and removal of any artifacts is prohibited.

Stocking and Regulations: The East Fork is stocked with 4,500 rainbows in months 3, 4, 5 and 10; and a one-time stocking of 400 8-inch browns during some undisclosed month. The daily creel limit is 8 trout with no more than three being browns, of which the latter must be 12 inches or longer. In addition to a valid license you must have a trout permit if you keep your trout. From Oct. 1 until March 31 the stream fishes catch-and-release and artificial flies and lures only.

Recommendations: As you drive along FR 9B you will encounter numerous pull-offs. This is a good indication that there is easy access to the stream nearby and probably excellent fishing there. Mayfly, caddisfly and small stonefly nymphs abound the East Fork. Look for dark green shaded water and deep pools adjacent to the big boulders and deadfall. While trout are not stocked in this stream during the summer months, you can catch recent stockers and holdovers that reside in these deep pools year-round.

Drifting a #14 or #16 Prince Nymph or a Bead-Head Hare's Ear will get you a hookup. If possible use a high stick presentation and a small indicator. If trout are rising do not hesitate to switch to a small dry fly; a #14 Adams or Caddis, or #16 BWO is worth trying. The tailouts from large riffles frequently will hold rainbows, and drifting a big nymph or Woolly Bugger through them can be productive. Frequently, a downstream pull cast of a #14 or #16 dry Adams left to drift into long moderately deep pools can bring up fish.

The browns stocked in this stream prefer to hang out under deadfalls. If you are game to try it, drift a Woolly Bugger under these trees and large branches. You will find most of them upstream from the end of FR 9B. During the hot summer months stick to fishing the deep pools. Staying out of occupied campsites and their adjacent fishing holes is good courtesy.

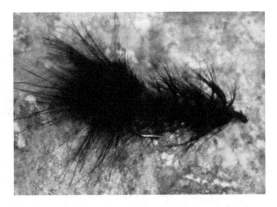

Directions: Driving east on the Bert T. Combs Mountain Parkway, take Exit 33 and turn left (north) on KY 11 and drive back under the parkway. Turn left onto KY 11/15. Drive 1.5 miles and turn right (heading east) onto KY 77, Nada Tunnel Road. Drive 4.3 miles. After crossing the Red River Bridge turn left onto FR 23, a gravel road. All these gravel roads are filled with bomb craters. Cautious words are drive slowly and avoid the potholes, as they can be tie-rod breakers. After 1.5 miles FR 23 becomes SR 613, a paved road. In a short drive of 0.9 miles you will see a sign on your left indicating the entrance to the Indian Creek Archaeological Sites. Turn right onto FR 9. Drive another 1.1 miles. After crossing the bridge, the creek forks; turn right onto FR 9B. The East Fork of Indian Creek parallels FR 9B with multiple pull-offs on the right side.

Middle Fork of the Red River

At the turn of the last century, the Lexington and Eastern Railway ran weekend excursion trains bringing tourists to Slade, Ky., promoting what eventually became Natural Bridge State Park and the Red River Gorge Geological Area. That was long before there were any roads into the area and trout fishing the Red was only wishful thinking.

Ecosystem: The KDFWR releases rainbow trout in two different sections along the Middle Fork of the Red River. The downstream location is just below Hoedown Lake, within the boundaries of Natural Bridge State Resort Park, and the second stocking site is further upstream of Mill Creek Lake, along KY 11.

    The downstream section of this trout-stocked tributary of the Red River lies in the heart of Natural Bridge State Resort Park. After passing through the park's campgrounds, the Middle Fork of the Red feeds Hoedown Lake, a small, non-fishable lake lying below Hemlock Lodge. Water spilling over the lake's concrete dam forms a moderately deep pool before riffling into a 200-yard long slick. Here the stream picks up some width and depth as it creeps through the park's picnic area. With cliff-covered scrubby vegetation along one side and fully open on the other, the now 40-foot-wide stream makes for easy fly-casting. Fishing is good along this short section of the Mid-

dle Fork between the concrete dam and the picnic area located just downstream of Hoedown Lake, although locals can fish it out pretty quickly.

    The upstream section of the trout-stocked Middle Fork lies south of the state park, and is eventu-

ally joined by spill water from Mill Creek Lake, just above Middle Fork Campground. You can fish the stream for at least a mile above this lake and all the way down to the picnic area just above Hoedown Lake. In the summer the water from the Mill Creek Lake is very warm, and any trout remaining in the stream become stressed. The Forest Service has planted protected species of perennial ornamental grasses along KY 11 and other highways in this region. In the autumn their tan-colored grass plumes graciously sway in the breeze. Patches of gravel, firm silt, sand and occasional pools of decaying leaves make for easy wading in the stream all the way through the campground and picnic area.

However, parts of the Middle Fork of the Red River upstream of Natural Bridge State Park are totally different in character from the downstream section. Along the upper section, the Middle Fork weaves its way through thick undergrowth and downed trees, and around large boulders. In many places you can easily leap across the one- or two-foot-deep stream, although after a heavy rain you may get more than your boots wet. The stream is never more than a hop, skip or jump off KY 11, off which there are several good pull-offs. At places the tree canopy may be less than 10 feet high, but these stretches provide some excellent trout habitat. There is an abundance of aquatic insects in this stretch of the stream, both mayflies and caddis flies.

Stocking and Regulations: There is an annual stocking of 3,000 rainbow trout in the Middle Fork in the months 3, 4, 5 and 10. In the 2.2 miles of the stream that lie in Natural Bridge State Park, there is a catch-and-release period from Oct. 1 until March 31 during which only artificial lures and flies may be used. Other times 8 trout of any size may be kept per day.

Recommendations: How you fish the Middle Fork will depend upon when and where you fish it. If you fish the upstream section, about 220 yards upstream of the park boundary and down to the edge of Middle Fork Campground, the pools around the boulders and tree falls should be fished with #12 and #14 Bead Head Hare's Ears, Prince Nymphs and Pheasant Tails in natural drifts with or without an indicator.

The spring and late fall months will be the most fruitful. Because of the tight vegetation along the stream here, you may need very short roll and high stick casts. Fishing dries in the autumn may prove difficult with heavy leaf falls on the water. But in the spring months tie a dry fly to your tippet, such as a #12 Adams or Elk Hair Caddis, and float it along the edges of the boulders and through the pools. It's best to stick to 18- or 24-inch 6X tippets.

Through the campgrounds and below Hoedown Lake, the stream opens up for some back casts. Use the same flies suggested above, but fish them downstream with pull casts above the lake, and up and across stream casts near the far bank below the lake's dam. Keep to natural drifts and mend your line along the far bank below the dam. The riffle just below the dam's pool is known to hold both rainbows and smallmouth bass. Don't be surprised if you catch one of the latter.

From the middle of June until October, this stream warms up and it will be time for you to find other places to fish.

169

Directions: Traveling east on the Mountain Parkway, take Exit 33 at Slade and turn right onto KY 11 toward Natural Bridge State Resort Park. Drive 4.1 miles. Past the entrance to Hemlock Lodge on your right and Mill Creek Lake on your left, you will see a small graveled pull-off area on your right. This pull-off is not marked but it is quite obvious. The stream is just 20 feet from this spot. You can enter the stream here or walk 50 yards back towards Mill Creek Lake and you will see a very large boulder between the road and the stream. You can walk down and into the stream from either side of this boulder. Trout habitat along this stretch of the stream is excellent.

There are a number of other pull-offs along KY 11 that allow for easy access to the stream including the picnic area below Hemlock Lodge. The sign to this parking area is posted on your right as you drive down KY 11. Sheltered picnic tables, clean restrooms and numbered hiking trails are some of the amenities of the area.

Mill Creek Lake

Heading over to fish the Middle Fork of the Red? Don't miss this little lake and the 6,000 rainbows stocked here.

Ecosystem: The Red River Gorge Geological Area has some terrific little mountain streams home to native brookies and other creeks stocked with rainbows and browns. If you're heading that way, you may want to add one more fishing hole to your list. Mill Creek Lake is located just outside the Gorge in Natural Bridge State Resort Park.

The lake was created in 1963 by damming up Mill Creek just upstream of where it flows into the Middle Fork of the Red River. The lake supports a good population of largemouth bass, bluegill, crappie, sunfish, catfish and stocked rainbow trout. Most of the shoreline of the lake is heavily forested right down to the water's edge, providing limited open sites for bank fishing. Consequently those without a boat typically fish from the shoreline along the dam and around the boat ramp.

A very overgrown trail, elevated some 25-50 feet above the northern shoreline, can be reached by walking across the dam towards the sign that reads "No Camping." The trail terminates halfway down the left side of the lake, into a pile of fallen trees. Poison ivy is abundant, so be prepared.

There is also a very short trail on the southern side of the lake, but to reach it you must slosh through the waters running down the spillway. From the opposite side of the spillway, climb a set of steps cut into a small boulder to begin your hike.

Canoes, kayaks and boats with electric trolling motors are permitted on the lake, but all gasoline-powered boats are prohibited. But running a bass boat on this 41-acre body of water would be overkill as Mill Creek Lake is only about three-fourths of a mile long and less than 1,000 feet wide. But the lake is moderately deep, about 50 feet near the dam, and averages 26 feet in depth overall.

Natural Bridge State Resort Park offers overnight accommodations at Hemlock Lodge, 11 cottages and 2 campgrounds. The lodge overlooks Hoedown Lake, a damned section of the Middle Fork of the Red River (no fishing permitted). Several hiking trails leave from near the lodge including the famous "Original Trail," 0.75 miles one-way, which leads to Natural Bridge.

Stocking and Regulations: There is an annual stocking of 6,000 rainbows distributed across the months 1, 4, 5, and 10. These stockers average 8-12 inches in length. Because the water near the dam is deep and remains cold even through the heart of summer, there are many holdover trout, and fish up to 3 pounds are not uncommon. Trout anglers may keep 8 trout per day, with no size minimum. But if you land a largemouth bass it must be at least 15 inches, with a daily creel limit of 3. We mention this because you just might tie into a bass and want to keep it.

Recommendations: Limited shoreline access around the lake compels you to fish from some type of watercraft, and a johnboat fitted with an electric trolling motor is ideal. After lake turnover in the spring, and before fall turnover but after stocking, your chance of catching these silver-sided rainbows is excellent. Why these fish take on a silvery-sided appearance in this lake befuddles us, but they do.

The trout cruise the deeper waters near the dam to about halfway towards the headwaters. Trolling a #6 or #8 Clouser Minnow with a treble swivel in this region of the lake will bring strikes. Attached to one swivel use five feet of six-pound monofilament and a bullet shaped 1/4 oz. weight. To the second swivel attach 10 feet of the same weight monofilament and the Minnow imitation. To the third swivel attach your fly line's leader, a #4 or 5.

Troll this rig off the side of the boat so that the minnow moves slowly about 15 -20 feet deep and about 100 feet behind the boat. Your motor speed should be about 6 feet per second (or 4 miles per hour). If you do not get a strike after 30 minutes increase or decrease your trolling speed and/or the bullet's weight. With some heavy minnow imitations you may not need the treble swivel and bullet weight.

In the spring, warm water species will have spawned and their fry (juvenile fish) will be near the shore; casting your Clouser Minnow in close might bring up a rainbow. If you see trout rising off the shoreline, switch to a #14 Adams or #16 BWO.

If you must fish in the summer months, it is best to troll deep in late evening into darkness. In August the surface temperature in the lake can easily reach into the high 70s°F. Remember the bait fishermen will be on the lake with their lanterns and buckets of minnows then.

If dinner is on your mind, head over to Hemlock Lodge. Alternately, if you have a hankering for pizza, try Miguel's (off KY 11 as you head back to the parkway). Miguel's has a strong following both locally and nationally amongst the rock-climbing crowd, and they make the best pies around.

Directions: Access to and parking at Mill Creek Lake is a snap. Traveling east on the Bert T. Combs Mountain Parkway, turn right off exit 33 and follow KY 11 south for 3.6 miles. On your right you will see a sign marking the drive up a short paved road to 50 slots for car and trailer parking. The parking lot abuts the lake.

Parched Corn Creek

The name of this creek may come from the way American Indians parched their corn over hot coals to secure a stable food for their long travels.

Ecosystem: Measuring no more than three or four feet wide in most places, Parched Corn Creek gathers waters from rivulets draining the left and right slopes off Wildcat Ridge in the Red River Gorge of the DBNF. The tiny stream cascades over 500 feet down a steep valley before entering the Red River. Parched Corn is one of only four creeks in Kentucky with a sustaining population of wild brook trout that is open to fishing.

Albeit very narrow, the creek carries cool (less than 70°F), clear water year-round over gravel beds, through shallow pools abutting boulders, and under fallen trees—many being giant pines that have succumbed to the pine bark beetle. The stream flows through a heavily shaded forest of hemlocks, pines, tulip poplars, and a few oaks and beech. Rhododendrons continually line the banks of Parched Corn Creek, with only occasional openings for slipping a rod through.

Access to Parched Corn Creek is found by hiking west along Rough Trail #221, which originates off KY 715 (see directions below). The trail drops 300 feet in 0.5 miles before crossing the creek on a 30-foot-long doublewide, split log bridge, at one of the few sunlit openings along the stream. In late summer you will find bright red cardinal flowers blooming here. Beyond the bridge, the trail bears left and runs upstream along the creek for about 100 yards, before rising out of the valley heading west to intersect FR 10 (Chimney Top Road). This intersection provides another access route to Parched Corn Creek, but involves a longer hike.

At the log bridge spanning Parched Corn Creek, multiple rogue trails head downstream along the creek and lead to several nice campsites. Most anglers use these trails to gain access to the creek. Turning over stones in the stream, one will find some cases of caddis flies and a few mayfly nymphs racing around. These aquatics and the minnows in the stream provide the food necessary to sustain the wild brook trout.

Stocking and Regulations: A modest population of three- to four-inch brook trout was released in this creek in either 1980 or 1981. No stockings have taken place since then. The clean, cold water and gravel have made reproduction possible and sustained a modest population for catch-and-release fishing only with single hook lures and flies.

Recommendations: Brook trout are very skittish and you must see them before they see you; otherwise, they are prone to scurry to the nearest cover. They spawn in fanned out redds in gravel beds in the fall.

We have caught several small four- to six-inch brookies out of Parched Corn over the years and so have several fellow anglers we know, but it has been a challenge. To be successful we recommend finding some deep pools next to boulders, overhanging ledges with rhododendron cover, and fallen trees in the creek. Keep a low profile and drop a small dry fly upstream and secure a natural drift to these selected sites. We have caught numerous brook trout in other streams using the Royal Coachman dry—they seem to strike at flies that have a little red color to them. If you plan to seek out some Parched Corn's brookies, we recommend you latch onto a #14 or #16 Royal Coachman dry and give it a go. Good luck.

Directions: Traveling east on the Mountain Parkway, take Exit 40. Turn right onto KY 15 north. After driving 0.7 miles you will pass the Dessie Scott Children's Home and come upon KY 715, sometimes called Sky Bridge Road. Turn right and after you cross back over the Parkway you will enter the clearly marked DBNF. The road is paved but curved. After 4.1 miles you will see a sign on your right: "Rough Trail #221." You can park your vehicle in the gravel lot on your left and begin the 0.5-mile hike on #221 to the stream. It is best not to wear waders or wading boots, and carry your rod with great care. The trail is well traveled but matches its name perfectly.

Swift Camp Creek

This stream gets its name from an old abandoned camp that lay in the designated Clifty Wilderness area of the Red River Geological Area, which in turn is encompassed by the Daniel Boone National Forest.

Ecosystem: Quite honestly, you would be hard-pressed to find a more beautiful place to fly fish in all of Kentucky. A steep and rugged terrain, complete with dense hemlocks, towering hardwoods and rhododendron thickets, characterizes the Clifty Wilderness Area. Swift Camp Creek is a tributary of the Red River, the latter classified as a Wild and Scenic River. Both streams are filled with house-size boulders, clear running waters, and plenty of shade for elusive fish. The surrounding wilderness area contains a wide variety of flora and fauna, and is a delight to all the senses.

A well-used trail originates at the small access parking area before dropping down to the stream, paralleling it upstream for about a mile, rising up and down, crossing it, and then narrowing before quickly petering out. If you look hard on your right (creek left), you may be able to detect where the purported silver camp use to be located. Most of the camp's remnants are now hidden out of sight, buried beneath decades of fallen trees and leaf litter. On the far side of the stream, the land slopes sharply upward, and in springtime hosts numerous wildflowers including trillium, Jack-in-the pulpit, May apple, Solomon seal and others.

When the water is in casual flow, you will detect deep, clear pools beside huge boulders, lightly moving riffles, promising pocket water and a few slicks. If you wade upstream, you will have to leave the creek on several occasions because the pools will stretch from one side of the stream to the other. In some places trees have fallen across the stream, and you may have to either crawl under or over them. All this structure makes for good habitat for the trout.

Stockings and Regulations: Before this section of the DBNF was declared a wilderness area, the stream was heavily stocked with trout. Were it not for a law that states: "... if a stream was once stocked with trout before it was declared a wilderness area, stocking of the same species may continue..." there would be no stocking. Such is the case for this stream and some stocking continues.

Currently, Swift Camp Creek receives an annual stocking of only 1,000 rainbows across April and October. One may ask why this idyllic stream receives such a meager stocking? Simply put, all those trout must be backpacked into the wilderness area. Members of Trout Unlimited, a cold water conservation organization, and other interested fishermen volunteer with KDFWR and carry about 20 loads of 25 trout each and distribute them along a 1.5-mile course of the stream. This is a special catch-and-release stream using artificials only that runs from Oct. 1 to May 31. Notably, most catch-and-release streams only run to March 31. The normal regulations apply all other times. The daily limit is 8, with no minimum size limit.

Recommendations: High sticking Bead Head Hare's Ear and Pheasant Tail nymphs with or without an indicator through the pools very close to the boulders should be very productive. Trout will also hang out below riffles and near submerged tree trunks. If you find fish, they will not be too picky. However, if you see trout rising to either mayflies or caddis, do not hesitate to switch to a dry Adams or Caddis. Hook size should probably be close to #14s or 16s.

Directions: Travel east on the Mountain Parkway to Exit 40. Turn right (north) onto KY 15. Drive 0.7 miles. Turn right (north, again) onto KY 715. Follow KY 715 about 6 miles, past Castle Arch parking area, until you get to a very small pull-off and parking area on your right. If you have reached the Red River, you've gone too far.

Eastern Kentucky

- Big Caney Creek
- Cave Run Lake Tailwater
- Greenbo Lake
- Laurel Creek
- Paintsville Lake
- Paintsville Lake Tailwater
- Russell Fork

There are a lot of overlooked trout fisheries in the eastern part of the state.

Russell Fork at Ratliff Hole

Big Caney Creek

Fish a half day in Big Caney, drive 12 minutes, fish the other half in Laurel Creek, and save those long hikes for another time.

Ecosystem: If you feel up to a scenic drive, but are looking for a stream with easy access, Big Caney Creek just might be your ticket to a good day of fishing. In fact, this little outing could net you two streams only a stone's throw from one another. If this piques your interest, be sure to read the section on fishing Laurel Creek before you slide behind the wheel.

Given their close proximity, Big Caney and Laurel creeks offer similar trout habitats. In fact Big Caney could easily be an extension of Laurel Creek, save the slippery limestone slabs that challenge anglers when fishing the Laurel. So pack a lunch and flies for both creeks and you'll be all set.

Driving in on the road to Big Caney, you come upon a bridge under which the stream flows through four culverts. Beyond the bridge and to the right is an unmaintained and trashy roadway—the only sore spot along this stream. This is as good a place to park a vehicle as you'll find. The main gravel road curves left and rises out of the gorge, with the upstream section down and to your left. The stream is wadeable for several miles downstream until it widens and becomes muddy before entering a branch of Grayson Lake.

Residing in a cool gorge, Big Caney stays cold year round, but its flow diminishes to a near trickle in the late, dry summer months as the trout head for deeper pools. Much of the streambed is gravel with occasional patches of silt.  Heavy vegetation lines the banks, including thickets of rhododendron and mountain laurel, hemlocks and some deciduous trees. But the canopy is high enough that casting is no problem if you watch your back cast. Large boulders tucked up against deep pools show the effects of centuries of erosion. Take a minute to examine the undersides of stones, which typically reveal caddis cases and mayfly nymphs.

Stocking and Regulations: Big Caney is stocked with 4,000 rainbows averaging 8-12 inches in length, in the months 4, 5, 6 and 10; and 250 8-inch browns in an undisclosed month (typically March). These are probably released below the bridge with the culverts. Eight trout may be taken per day, but only three of these may be browns, and these must be at least 12 inches in length. A valid fishing license and trout permit are required.

Recommendations: A moderate to heavy rain can put the quietus on fishing the Big Caney, and it is best to let three days pass before venturing out. Once down and clear, the usual dries, such as #14 and #15 Adams and Caddis, and the same size Princes, Pheasant Tails and Hare's Ears nymphs, will do just fine. High stick these along the boulders and root wads. Avoid using an indicator if you can.

Fish the heavy riffles and their tailouts with an olive-colored Woolly Bugger and you might pick up a 14-inch winter holdover. The deeper runs can be fished with nymphs under an indicator. This is a fun stream to fish, and in early summer months the cool air of the gorge is appreciated.

Directions: Drive I-64 to Morehead. Take exit 137 and turn south onto KY 32. Drive 2.5 miles through Morehead and at the "T" turn left. The highway is now both US 60 and KY 32. Continue traveling east for 2 miles and look for the sign indicating a right turn for KY 32. Bear right (south) and drive another 16.1 miles on KY 32. Shortly after passing the Elliot County line you will come upon a sign indicating the Ed Mabry Laurel Gorge Management Area. Another 2.5 miles beyond the county line will be another sign on your right marking Cold Spring Road (also known as Stegal Cold Spring Road on some maps). Drive 0.8 miles past Cold Spring Road. Just past Crum Cemetary Road, turn left (north) on an unmarked gravel road (Binion Ford Road on some maps) and drive for 1.2 miles. You will make a sharp downhill, right-hand turn before entering the gorge. If you don't, you are on the wrong road. This is a gravel road but a front wheel vehicle can manage it with no problem, unless it is snowing. In that case you may want to just sit at home before a warm fire with a good book in hand.

If you have been fishing Laurel Creek, getting to the Big Caney is a snap. Drive back on Cold Spring Road and turn right on KY 32. Drive 0.8 miles and just past Crum Cemetary Road, turn left on an unmarked gravel road. It is 1.2 miles from KY 32 to the creek.

Cave Run Lake Tailwater

This heavily stocked tailwater is less than an hour's drive east of Lexington.

Ecosystem: Cave Run Lake is considered one of the top 10 muskellunge destinations by "In-Fisherman" and "Field and Stream" magazines and is commonly referred to as the "Muskie Capital of the South." The lake is gorgeous with clear blue waters and rolling hills punctuated with the occasional knob. Little development can be found around the lake except for one marina, a few campgrounds and multiple fishing access points.

The 8,270-acre lake reservoir was formed in 1973 by damming the Licking River, and serves as a flood control, water supply, recreation and wildlife habitat project for northeastern Kentucky. Surrounded by the DBNF, Cave Run Lake is endowed with excellent water quality from the Licking River and many of its tributaries. The US Army Corps of Engineers and the US Forest Service jointly manage the lake and its environs. Hiking, mountain biking and horse trails crisscross the region.

Like most tailwaters, the water flowing below the dam remains cool most of the year. While the lake itself averages only 50-60 feet in the large pools, average lake depth is only about 20 feet. In the heat of summer the Corps releases very little water and the tailwater warms quickly. The tailrace is about 75 feet wide for a distance of about 300 yards from the stilling basin.

Confounding fishing at the tailwater is the fall release schedule. In early fall the Corps beings dropping the lake level by drawing off the bottom. As a consequence, with this and the beginning of lake turn over, the water coming out of the stilling basin is laden with dissolved iron oxide, which gives up a reddish cast and hydrogen sulfide, which gives off a sulfur smell. The Corps continues dropping the lake level until the lake completely turns over, typically about mid-October. Anglers may wish to call the Corps office at (606) 784-9709 to find out the current release schedule. The minimum mitigated release is 50 cfs and the maximum is about 5,000 cfs.

Stocking and Regulations: The tailwater is stocked with 6,800 rainbows distributed across the months of 4, 5, 6, 10 and 11. The daily limit is restricted to 8 trout, with no minimum size specified. Some years ago Fish and Wildlife stocked the tailwater with some browns, but this practice was discontinued.

Recommendations: The best time to fish the tailwater of Cave Run is mid-spring or late fall when most of the stockings occur, the water runs cold and most of the winter drawdown has occurred. You may as well skip the summer months and fish elsewhere.

Most bait fisherman can be found along the tailrace at the High Banks Picnic Area (see directions below). The park includes several picnic shelters, bathrooms and a playground. So if you want to keep the kids entertained while you lazily fish, cast a few flies into the large, shady pool along the left bank just below the boat ramp.

Frequently the newly stocked trout will hang out in this pool while they recover. You may see a few rises and if so, something like a small Adams might work. After a few days, the new stockers sufficiently recover and begin to feed further up in the tailrace where the water is more oxygenated and food can be found. A weighted nymph or Woolly Bugger fished below an indicator should work in the tailrace. However, if the release is more than about 200 cfs, fish will not stay up in the tailrace.

A small creek coming out of the Minor E. Clark Hatchery flows into the tailwater on the opposite shore, just below the tailrace. Don't bother trying to fish the small pool above this creek since the sun hits it most of the day. However, there are two ways to reach the water below this pool: cross the tailrace using the steps along the face of the dam, continue down the concrete walkway and down the slope to the point; or drive over the dam to the Minor Clark Fish Hatchery on KY 801 and drive down the hatchery road past the fish races to the end of the road. You may park on the lawn here. There you will see a sign indicating fishing access to the tailwater and the need to leave the area before dusk.

Better fly fishing spots can be had about a mile below the dam. You can either launch a small watercraft and float the river, remembering that there are no public down-river take-out ramps, or hop back into your vehicle and drive a short distance. Coming back out of the picnic area, turn right and continue driving along KY 826 for about 1.2 miles. On your right you will see several gravel pull-offs between the road and the Licking River. Multiple steep paths lead down to the river, but be prepared for a little bushwhacking and sliding if conditions are muddy. The best of these spots is accessed just at the end of the guardrail. An unmanaged trail follows the river until it makes a right turn. This portion of the river can be safely waded only when the water release is less than 150 cfs. Wading at high release rates can be dangerous.

Along this section of the river you'll find multiple riffles and a few root wads. This part of the tailwater is only marginally wadeable in the summer months when you shouldn't be trout fishing here any way. So unless you're floating a boat, bank fishing is your only option. The canopy is close overhead, so roll casts might be your best bet.

After spending a few hours fishing you may want to head over to the Minor E. Clark Fish Hatchery that you passed on KY 801, just north of the dam. Free tours are available. Although trout are not raised here, it's quite an interesting place to poke around if you have some free time.

Then stop by Pop's Southern Style BBQ at the corner of KY 801 and US 60, heading back to the interstate. This little joint is a small mammal taxidermist's delight. Grab a plate of mouth-watering pulled pork and hot, fresh cobbler as squirrels and possums serenade you on miniature banjos.

Directions: On I-64, take exit 133 (Sharkey/Farmers), just west of Morehead, KY. Turn right and drive south on KY 801 for 5.1 miles. Watch for the signs to Cave Run Lake Dam. Turn left (south again) on KY 826 and drive one mile. Shortly after you cross over the dam, turn right into the High Bank Picnic Area. Park close to the boat ramp.

Once you know where to look for the gravel pull-offs, you may want to take exit 123 (Owingsville, Salt Lick) off I-64. Turn right on US 60 East. Drive 9.3 miles. Turn right onto KY 826 (Cave Run Lake Road). Drive another 1.5 miles and start to look for gravel pull-offs on your left. This might save you a few minutes driving time.

Greenbo Lake

Greenbo Lake State Park is the third largest park in Kentucky and considered by many to be one of the most beautiful.

Ecosystem: Greenbo Lake, covering 225 acres, is completely encompassed by the 3,330-acre state park of the same name. The park has 25 miles of hiking and horse-riding trails that meander through wildflower-infused woodlands, over hills and down draws, across creeks, and along the shores of the lake. Pioneer visitors Simon Kenton, Daniel Boone, George Rogers Clark and one of Kentucky's early governors, Christopher Greenup, after whom the county was named, must have forded the nearby Little Sandy River before entering this region.

The lake and park was originally operated by a group of local citizens from Greenup and Boyd counties, known as the Greenbo Recreation Association, until it became a part of the state system in 1955. A fieldstone lodge, named after author and Poet Laureate Jesse Stuart, in part overlooks the lake. The lodge complex boasts catfish dinners served in its Angler's Cove Restaurant and a state of the art conference center. Outdoor features include a full facility campground, swimming pool, tennis court and fishing pier. Swimming in the lake is prohibited; however, permission is granted for licensed scuba divers to explore the depths in designated areas.

A small marina offering rentals of canoes, kayaks, pontoons and paddle-boats is open from April until October. Small horsepower fishing boats may or may not be available. Unfortunately the marina is closed during the trout stocking months of February and October, but the boat ramp remains open for use all year. If you want to fish after the stockings, you'll need to launch your own boat.

Greenbo Lake is best known for its largemouth bass fishing and held the state record at 13 pounds and 8 ounces until 1955. Clay Lick Creek and two of its tributaries, Buffalo Branch and Pruitt Fork, feed the lake. Water depths near the earth-filled dam can exceed 50 feet, allowing for year round cold water and the conditions needed for the over-wintering of its rainbow trout. Fish near the dam and you might bring up a five-pounder that has escaped previous live-bait presentations.

Stocking and Regulations: The lake receives 11,000 rainbows, averaging 8-12 inches in length, distributed in February and October. This level of stocking provides a hefty concentration of 40 trout per acre of water, but most of these fish will find their way to the deeper water near the dam. Standard regulations apply: 8 rainbows per day, with no minimum size limit, and a valid fishing license and trout permit are required.

Recommendations: It's no secret that the best time to catch the stockers is soon after they have been released. During these cooler months the trout have no great need to seek deeper waters and may be found in water no more than 10 feet deep. There are two fishing piers on the lake and a number of lakeside clearings open enough for fly-casting. In early spring and fall, working a streamer in quick six-inch strips may reward you with a few fish.

During the heat of summer, rainbows will drop down to find water below 70°F, and then you must troll minnow imitations like the Clouser at 15-20 feet deep and at about 6 feet per second (4 miles per hour). Late evening is a good time for this. Make no bones about it, the bait fishermen will appear after dark anchored in the deep-water areas with their lanterns and minnows fishing for skillet fries.

Directions: Traveling east on I-64 take Exit 172 near Grayson. Drive north on KY 1 for 15 miles. State route KY 1 twists and turns as it roughly follows the Little Sandy River, passing through a number of small towns with reduced speed limits. Need we say more? Turn left (west) on KY 1711 at the sign pointing the way to Greenbo State Park. Drive an additional 2.5 miles and then veer right (east) on Lodge Road. The marina is 0.3 miles ahead and the lodge 0.8 miles from there.

Laurel Creek

For the price of one trip, you get to fish two streams for both bows and browns in Laurel and Big Caney Creeks.

Ecosystem: Laurel and Big Caney creeks reside on opposite sides of KY 32 with their back-country roads not a half-mile apart. Fishing these two creeks is about as good as it gets for "down in the gorge" trout fishing in Kentucky. Let's talk about Laurel. This cold-water stream lies in the easily accessible Ed Mabry Laurel Gorge Management Area. The gorge, covering 700 acres, is sliced in two by Laurel Creek, forming a chasm scarcely more than 150 yards wide, but 100 feet deep.

The gorge borders both sides of the stream for much of its fishable section and creates an ultra cool summer haven for trout anglers. If it is 80°F topside, it will be 70°F stream level. Apart from the excellent fishing, the multiple waterfalls, rockhouses and moss-covered boulders are all worth exploring. Some of the biggest hemlocks you'll ever rest your eyes on help to keep the stream shaded and cold for the trout.

Access to the stream is not difficult and except after heavy rains wading is easy. However we have a word of caution: The silt-covered slabs of limestone will be slippery and even with felt-soled wading shoes you can easily find yourself sitting in the stream instead of wading it. The stream, no more than 20 feet wide and one to two feet deep in most places, has its share of riffles, slicks, tree falls and deep cold pools. Moving through and around these is not difficult. If you turn over several stones adjacent to the big pools, you are likely to find mayfly nymphs scurrying about and some caddis fly cases. Heavy rains make the stream unfishable and it will take three days to clear out.

187

Stocking and Regulations: Laurel Creek is stocked annually with 3,000 rainbows during the months 4, 5, 6 and 10; and 250 8-inch browns in an undisclosed month (typically March). Although the stream's water remains quite cold through the summer, the decline in flow rate forecloses any stocking during these months. The heavy, cold rains during the autumn bring creek levels back up and the fall stocking allows the trout to overwinter and gain some stamina and weight. This makes the stream a put-grow-take water. The daily creel limit for the stream is 8 trout, of which only 3 may be browns and those must be at least 12 inches in length.

Recommendations: Do not waste your time fishing the creek above the bridge; concentrate on the downstream section. Both dry flies and nymphs have proven successful in this stream. The deep, dark pools next to the boulders seem to hold the greatest concentration of both species. If you see any rises, drift a #14 Adams through the pools as close to the boulders as possible. Don't hesitate to try a Pheasant Tail or Prince Nymph without an indicator. Closely watch the end of your floating fly line for any abrupt movement and be prepared to set the hook. Either a straight or a roll cast of 20 feet is all that is needed.

Fish around the root wads and through the bigger riffles and tailouts. Quickly wade through the shallow slicks, as they will likely hold few trout. But if you feel compelled to fish the slicks, do so with a dry fly, downstream pull cast and feed some extra line for a natural drift.

Unfortunately, the locals hit this stream with their corn and worms soon after the stocking truck's visit and go away with a big share of the fish. But the natural beauty of the gorge makes for a fine day of fishing and rarely do we leave feeling unsatisfied.

Directions: Drive I-64 to Morehead. Take exit 137 and turn south onto KY 32. Drive 2.8 miles through Morehead and at the "T" turn left. The highway is now both US 60 and KY 32. Continue traveling east for 2 miles and look for the sign indicating a right turn for KY 32. Bear right (south) and drive another 15.4 miles on KY 32. Shortly after passing the Elliot County line you will come upon a sign indicating the Ed Mabry Laurel Gorge Management Area. Another 2.5 miles beyond the county line will be another sign on your right marking Cold Spring Road (also known as Stegal Cold Spring Road on some maps). Turn right (south) and drive down this road for 1.7 miles. You will come to a bridge across Laurel Creek. The best place to park is on the right side of the road either before or after crossing the bridge. There is only room for three or four vehicles.

If you have been fishing Big Caney, getting to Laurel Creek is a snap. Drive back up the hill and turn right on KY 32. Drive 0.8 miles and turn left on Cold Spring Road. Drive down this road for 1.7 miles and follow the parking directions above.

Paintsville Lake

Find it hard to get away and fish for a day or two? Bring the family and spend a fun-filled weekend at Paintsville Lake State Park.

Ecosystem: For many anglers, fly fishing provides much-needed solitary time out on the water as we challenge our skills and gaze dreamily at the sky. But it's not always easy finding time away from family and friends. So bring them along! Paintsville Lake State Park offers plenty to keep them busy as you search for the rainbows stocked here.

You and your party can take advantage of the amenities of the state park and adjacent Rocky Knob Recreational Area, including the full-service campground and marina, visitor's center, picnic shelters and playground. The complex is enormous and very nicely laid out. In addition, a 7-mile orienteering course and the 18-mile Dawkins Line Rail Trail are located nearby.

Five years before the completion of the Paintsville Lake dam, 10,000 residents were forced to leave the area below the construction site as an eight-inch rainfall threatened the cofferdam. Today the 100-foot-high earth-filled dam holds back the waters of this 1,150-acre, 29-mile long lake.

The largest and deepest portion of Paintsville Lake, measuring 100 feet deep at the dam, is adjacent to the state park. A large island divides the lake, just north of the dam. Most of the good trout fishing is located between the island and the dam, where the deep waters stay cold year-round. Beyond this the lake takes on a totally different character as the waterway becomes long and narrow, bordered by cliffs and forests. There are three additional boat ramps on the lake, but private developments are prohibited.

Stocking and Regulations: Paintsville is the third largest trout-stocked lake in Kentucky. In February it receives 3,250 rainbows, averaging 8-12 inches in length. No browns are stocked in the lake. Standard regulations apply: 8 rainbows per day, no minimum size limit, and a valid fishing license and trout permit are required.

Recommendations: Brace yourself for the winter winds of late February when trolling a minnow imitation in the section of the lake nearest the dam. During the spring and summer months, you should monitor the lake's temperature and do your trolling in late evening at a depth where the water temperature is below 70°F. Big trout, some weighing up to five pounds each, are taken from this lake each year.

To avoid losing one of these monsters, use clear eight-pound monofilament and a treble swivel. To one swivel attach a Clouser Minnow or similar imitation with a 15-foot piece of mono; to the second swivel attach a bullet-shaped weight with a five-foot piece of mono; and to the third swivel attach your sink tip fly line. Trolling this rig at about 6 feet per second (4 miles per hour) should get it 15-20 feet below the surface. At times you can get a heavy minnow down without using any weight. When the sun begins to set, the bait fishermen will take to the waters with lights hanging over the water and minnows dangling under bobbers. It will be time to call it a day and head in for a hot drink and warm environs.

If you do not own a powerboat or the marina does not have any available, bank fishing may also be an option. In the spring, before the water's temperature rises, stripping a streamer near the shoreline may bring a trout to your offering. Alternately, be sure to read the entry on the "Paintsville Lake Tailwater" for some great bank-fishing opportunities.

As you're reading this you probably have come to an important conclusion. The best time of year to fish Paintsville Lake may not be the best time of year to bring the family. Sacrifices and compromises might have to be made. Of course, that early spring trip taken alone or with a fishing buddy could be written off as reconnaissance work that someone has to do.

Directions: Traveling east on the Bert T. Combs Mountain Parkway (designated KY 9000 down to Campton, and KY 9009 from there to its end near Salyersville), pick up US 460 east at the parkway's end. Drive 16.7 miles on US 460 and then turn left onto KY 40 towards Staffordsville. Drive 1.6 miles and then turn right onto KY 2275. Look for the sign on your right and drive the last mile to the marina. The parking lot has ample spaces for trailers.

Paintsville Lake Tailwater

The tailwater below the 110-foot-high Paintsville Lake Dam is no wider than the creek that flowed here before the dam was built and for locals it has retained the name Paint Creek.

Ecosystem: This tailwater can best be described as an urban fishery since much of the waters flow through housing and business developments in and around the small town of Staffordsville. The tailwater stretches for 3.8 miles as the stream works its way from the dam, before flowing east to the city of Paintsville.

Only 20 feet wide in the upper tailrace section, the tailwater is lined with steep, rocky banks devoid of any vegetation. The waters run cold year-round and wading is out of the question since the bottom is strewn with big boulders. Fishing from the banks is advised and easily accomplished due to recent improvements, including a large paved parking lot, a footbridge across the tailrace, a handicap-fishing pier, restroom facilities and benches. A spur trail loops around the upper section of the tailrace.

About 300 yards below the tailrace, Paint Creek ducks under KY 40 on its way to becoming the Levisa Fork of the Big Sandy River. Below KY 40 the tailwater takes on a different nature. Still only about 20 feet wide, the stream abuts private lands with limited access to fishing. This part of the tailwater is bordered by thick vegetation, making casting very difficult, while silt and gravel make up the creek bed. Along this section the stream has few redeeming features except that it holds some big rainbows.

Stocking and Regulations: The Paintsville Lake tailwater annually receives 20,000 rainbows and 300 browns in a class of 8-12 inches. The rainbows are released near the stilling basin every month from April until November, and the browns are released each year in three locations below the Highway 40 bridge during an undisclosed month (typically April). From the dam down to the first crossing of KY 40, the daily creel limit is 8 trout, of which only three may be browns. In the trophy section running from the KY 40 bridge down to the US 460 bridge, artificial flies and lures are required and only one trout may be taken, which must be 16 inches or longer.

Recommendations: It is best to fish the tailwater between the stilling basin and KY 40 from the banks, although that is easier said than done because as noted above, the banks are very steep and lined with large rocks to eliminate erosion. If you manage your way down to the water's edge on either side of the tailrace, casting is no problem and you probably won't have much competition from other anglers.

If climbing over boulders sounds less than appealing, you have several other choices. You can easily fish from the 50-yard-long handicap-accessible concrete pier that is adjacent to the water or walk down the concrete ramps from the parking lot to the water's edge. The wooden footbridge across the tailwater also provides access to good fishing on the other side.

If you elect to try your luck with a little wading, turn left after crossing the footbridge and walk along the trail until it ends abruptly in a patch of stones. Beyond this you can wade on gravel and fish about 100 yards before you reach the KY 40 bridge. At low to moderate flow rates the tailwater depths average just two to three feet, but these can increase to four or five feet without notice.

The recently stocked rainbows and browns are not picky and weighted #12 or #14 Prince Nymphs, Hare's Ears and Pheasant Tails will suffice. Allow the fly to drift off the bottom below an indicator in or adjacent to the seams in the deeper water. Chances are you will latch onto some 8-to 12-inch bows or even one of the few browns that are stocked. If you catch several in one spot, it is best to move on. Disregard strikes at your indicator, as they are likely chubs.

Fishing the trophy section can be a double-edged challenge and the trout can be fussy. The stream is seldom more than 10-15 feet wide and frequently enclosed with low-hanging vegetation. The bottom can be muddy in some places and gravel in others. While the tailrace water may be running clear, in this section the water may be off color with the bottom so obscured you may not feel like wading. Be cautious!

If you manage to find the rare open area with a few riffles, drift a Woolly Bugger through and into the tailouts. Occasionally you may find a big rainbow holding close to a deep bank. Using short and across downstream casts with a #14 Adams, you might pick up one of these 16-inch trophy rainbows.

Directions: Traveling east on the Bert T. Combs Mountain Parkway (designated KY 9000 down to Campton) and KY 9009 from there to its end near Salyersville, pick up US 460 east at the parkway's end. Drive 16.7 miles on US 460 and then turn left onto KY 40 towards Staffordsville. Drive 1.7 miles and then turn right into a large, paved parking lot. If you have passed over a bridge, you have gone a trifle too far. After parking you will see the tailwater of the lake below and to your left. There are restroom facilities at this site.

Because much of the trophy section of the tailwater between the bridge over KY 40 and the bridge over US 460 borders private land, public access is limited to just a very few locations. As you leave the above tailwater section, turn left back onto KY 40 and drive 1.5 miles. Turn right onto Bridge Street. Here you can pull off the street and enter the waters below the bridge. Next to the tailwater a KDFWR sign is posted indicting that only one fish of 16 inches or more may be kept from this trophy section.   However, you may choose to continue on Bridge Street and, coming to its end, turn right onto E. Dorton Boulevard. At what seems to be its end, the boulevard will make a sharp left turn, but before you cross the tailwater bridge here, pull into the gravel parking area before the turn. You can access the water at this site. A third option is to return to KY 40 and drive back to US 460 and turn right. Drive about 0.1 miles on US 460 and on your right you will see a short road into an unpaved parking area. The tailwater is below and to your left.

If you wish to fish off private land and avoid confrontation with the land-owners, it is best to ask permission first rather than forgiveness later.

Russell Fork River

For many it is a long drive to the Russell Fork that requires an overnight stay, but fishing its waters can be an exhilarating experience.

Ecosystem: About 200 million years ago an inland sea receded along what is now the border between Kentucky and Virginia. A river was left in its wake, carving out the deepest gorge east of the Mississippi River or the "Grand Canyon of the South." That river, the Russell Fork, is a lively tailwater rolling and plunging for 52 miles with a gradient reaching 180 feet per mile through the only break along the towering ridge of Pine Mountain. Locals call the region "The Breaks" because the canyon and its river sever the mountain range and provide an opening for highway travel between the two states.

The cool, clear waters of the Russell Fork originate in the John W. Flannagan Reservoir in Virginia and provide a healthy habitat for the numerous species

of fish and macroinvertebrates found in the river. The width, depth and full character of the river are controlled by the water releases from the reservoir. At places and times the river can vary in width from 50 to more than 150 feet, and in depth from several feet to more than 20 feet.

When the reservoir gates are opened the river becomes a playground for accomplished kayakers, rafters and a few hearty canoeists who set out to challenge the gorge section and its multitude of class IV and V rapids. Tighten down the gates and the river below the gorge becomes a desirable destination for anglers in search of smallmouth and largemouth bass, catfish, carp, and the rainbow trout that are stocked in the spring and fall. If the flora along the river escapes your eye, the impressive rapids, cliffs and boulders are awesome and hard to miss and forget.

In the lower section below the gorge, one side of the river may abut a stunning 150-foot-high cliff and on the opposite side a wide-open shore may be easily accessed for wading or launching human-powered watercraft. Sandstone boulders are sprinkled liberally between long stretches of shallow shoals. For the most part the banks are littered with small stones and leafy vegetation, punctuated by the occasional sandy shore. There are a few muddy banks, but the river clears quickly after a heavy rain.

For fly fishermen, there are four easy access points to the three-mile-downstream section of the river, each of which have long stretches of open shoreline that provide the wading angler ample opportunity to lay out some fly line. The first access point is Ratliff Hole River Access off KY 80 (also known as Potters Ford), close to where the road parallels the river near the state's border before running through Elkhorn City. Ratliff Hole is also the take-out for the nationally renowned gorge section of the Russell Fork that lies upstream. Anglers will frequently encounter whitewater boaters at Ratliff Hole, including commercial vehicles.

The second river access is 1.1 miles downstream of Ratliff Hole at Carson Island, which can easily be reached via Carson Island Road, just off of KY 80 on the eastern side of Elkhorn City. The third access point is another 0.8 miles below Carson Island where KY 80 crosses the Russell Fork very close to Carson Island Road on the eastern side of Elkhorn City. And the last access is 0.6 miles further downstream in Elkhorn City proper, where KY 80 (Center Street) crosses the river yet again.

If you are interested in floating the section of the Russell Fork that runs from Ratliff Hole to Elkhorn City, only do so with extreme caution. Below or downstream of Ratliff Hole the river becomes a class I-II run, with two class III rapids to navigate known colloquially as Meat Grinder and Pinball. From Ratliff Hole to Elkhorn City it is about 2.5 river miles and should only be floated by experienced boatmen at appropriate water levels. A commercial outfitter services this section of the river.

Stocking and Regulations: The KDFWR annually releases 2,250 8- to 12-inch rainbows during the months of 4, 5 and 10 in the Kentucky side of the Russell Fork. These are distributed between Ratliff Hole and sites in downtown Elkhorn City. Anglers may take 8 trout per day and there is no size limit or closed period.

The Virginia Game and Inland Fisheries also stock the Russell Fork with rainbows below Flannagan Dam and undoubtedly some of these find their way downstream into Kentucky. If you decide to fish below Flannagan Dam and upstream of Ratliff Hole, you will be fishing in Virginia waters and will need the proper licenses and permits for that state and other regulations may apply.

Recommendations: Your best opportunities for catching Russell Fork rainbows are after a stocking—other times it will be hit and miss. This is big water and, with an annual stocking of less than 1300 fish per river mile, catching these trout requires a careful read of the water and some special techniques.

Skillful whitewater paddlers and oarsmen can run the 2- to 3-mile river section between the access sites and fish lots of water. However, portaging around the class III waters just below the put-in is a must for most anglers. Another complicating factor is the Flannagan Dam release schedule. For four weekends in October, the Corps of Engineers draws down the reservoir and puts in an additional 800-1,100 cfs of water on top of the 50-100 cfs natural flow. Try running this section of the river in a flat-water boat and you can count on a flip, some nasty bruises and probably a broken fly rod.

But keep in mind that even without a boat, the two access sites still provide over a mile of wadeable, fishable water. The right side of the river provides easy bank access, while most of the cliffs are on the opposite shore. But watch your step—stones in and along the river are covered with slippery slime. Step on one of these and you are likely to end up on your rear end.

The Russell Fork has lots of riffles, back eddies, long runs with foam lines, rapids and deep pools next to boulders. How you fish each of these will determine your success. There is good aquatic life in the river, and fishing nymphs and Wooly Buggers above, through and below the small riffles should bring a jolt to your rod tip. Many of the riffles are wide, so work all sections of these and if they generate back eddies, plunge a nymph deep into them. Avoid the rapids, for neither you, your fly, nor the fish can hang out in these swift waters.

Fish the foam lines with both dries and nymphs, and after the fall stocking drift a hopper or ant along them. In the spring and fall, the mayfly hatches will likely occur in the sunny afternoon in the long runs, particularly those having slow moving water. As dusk settles in so will mayfly spinners, so give an Adams a whirl. Set these adrift in the current with the occasional mend. If the run happens to be deep, say four to five feet, drop a #18 Zebra Midge under the dry and off the bottom and keep an eagle eye for the dry to disappear. Any movement may be a take.

When the stocked rainbows find the deep pools next to the boulders ,they will take up residence there. Most of these pools will require fishing from a water-craft, and getting a nymph down deep will likely bring a hookup.

Directions: From Pikeville to Elkhorn City's access to the Russell Fork River is 21.0 miles. Traveling east out of Pikeville on US 460/KY 80, drive to the town of Belcher where 460 continues straight and 80 veers right. Bear right onto KY 80 and after a short drive of 2.9 miles you will pass the Elkhorn City limits sign on your right. Soon thereafter and immediately after crossing a Russell Fork bridge, turn right onto KY 197 and in about 200 yards, directly across from the Community Trust Bank building, turn right onto a narrow gravel road that leads down to an excellent wading site on the Russell Fork. This is a city park with restroom facilities, picnic tables and abundant parking off the gravel road, which parallels the river for about 400 yards.

The upstream access is located further east off KY 80. From the intersection of KY 80 and KY 197, travel east on KY 80 for 2.3 miles. On your right you will see a sign for "River Access and Recreation Area," marking a right veer onto a paved road that leads down to a day-use recreation park. Here you will find parking, restroom facilities, picnic tables, a covered shelter and lots of fishing holes. The area is open from daybreak to dusk; overnight camping is not permitted.

The nearby Breaks Interstate Park offers excellent accommodations: lodge rooms, cabins and a full-service campground with 138 sites (open seasonally). The lodge is open year-round, but there are days during the fall and winter when the park's restaurant is closed. The 4,600-acre park has miles of hiking trails open all year, but other activities are offered on a variable schedule. The park lodge is 4.7 miles from Ratliff Hole and 7.1 miles from Elkhorn City. There are no accommodations in Elkhorn City, but the mom and pop Gateway Motel and Bridgeview Bar and Grill are located just inside the Virginia state border. Be forewarned: In the "Breaks" hunger has a way of interfering with the fishing, and finding a decent meal can be an unpleasant task.

Appendix 1:

Clubs and Non-Profits, Government Organizations, Local and National Retailers, Web Resources and Guide Services

The following suggestions are for your convenience and are not to be construed as an endorsement of any particular person, company or organization. The information was correct at the time of publication, but we suggest calling or checking the Internet for updates.

Clubs and Non-Profits

Trout Unlimited
Since 1959, Trout Unlimited has worked to conserve, protect and restore North America's cold-water fisheries and their watersheds through grassroots action, professional leadership and partnership support.
Website: TU.org

Trout Unlimited: Bluegrass Chapter
Meetings take place on the first Tuesday of each month, 6:30 p.m. at Columbia's Steakhouse, 201 N. Limestone, Lexington, KY 40507
Email: bluegrasstroutunlimited@gmail.com
Social Media: facebook.com/Bluegrasstu; twitter.com/BluegrassTU

Trout Unlimited: Louisville Chapter
Monthly meetings vary in location and time. See their website for more details.
Address: P.O. Box 6451; Louisville, KY 40206-0451
Website: LouisvilleTU.org

Federation of Fly Fishers
The FFF's goal is to support fisheries' conservation and educational programs for all fish and all waters.
Website: southeastfff.org

Derby City Fly Fishers
Monthly meetings are the third Wednesday of each month,
6:30 p.m. at the Louisville Nature Center.
Fly-tying instruction is the fourth Wednesday of each month, 7-9:00 p.m. at the Louisville Nature Center.
Website: derbycityflyfishers.com
Social media: Facebook at http://tinyurl.com/m4sdwr4

Northern Kentucky Flyfishers
Meetings take place the first Thursday of every month for dinner at the Briarwood
Banquets in Hebron, Ky., except in the summer months when they meet at the
Duck Creek Country Club in Cold Spring, Ky.
Email: nkffwebmaster@gmail.com
Website: nkflyfisher.org

Casting for Recovery
Founded on the principles that the natural world is a healing force and that cancer
survivors deserve one weekend to experience something new and challenging
while enjoying beautiful surroundings within an intimate, safe and nurturing
structure.
Address: P.O. Box 1123, 3738 Main St; Manchester, VT 05254
Phone: (802) 362-9181 or Toll Free: 1 (888) 553-3500
Website: castingforrecovery.org
Social media: facebook.com/castingforrecovery

Project Healing Waters Fly Fishing, Inc.
Dedicated to the physical and emotional rehabilitation of disabled active military
service personnel and disabled veterans through fly fishing and associated activi-
ties including education and outings.
Address: P.O. Box 695; LaPlata, MD 20646
Email: admin@projecthealingwaters.org
Website: projecthealingwaters.org
Social media; facebook.com/ProjectHealingWatersFlyFishing

Reel Recovery
A national non-profit organization that conducts free fly fishing retreats for men
recovering from all forms of cancer.
Address: Reel Recovery, 160 Brookside Rd.; Needham, MA 02492
Phone: (800) 699-4490
Website: reelrecovery.org
Social media: Facebook at http://tinyurl.com/lj5ugv8

Recreation and Boating Fishing Foundation –
Take Me Fishing
A fishing, boating and conservation resource center.
Address: 500 Montgomery St. #300; Alexandria, VA 22314
Phone: (703) 519-0013
Email: info@takemefishing.org
Website: takemefishing.org/state/ky/

Government Organizations

Daniel Boone National Forest
Address: 1700 Bypass Rd., Winchester, KY 40391
Phone: (859) 745-3100
Website: fs.usda.gov/dbnf

4-H Fishing Clubs
National program, with local chapters, run by US Fish and Wildlife Service
Phone: (270) 343-3797
Email: james_gray@fws.gov or kristina_pupak@fws.gov

Kentucky Department of Fish and Wildlife Resources
Address: #1 Sportsman's Lane, Frankfort, KY 40601
Phone: (800) 858-1549 or (502) 564-4336
Website: fw.ky.gov
Licenses Online: fw.ky.gov/avlic.asp
Social media: facebook.com/kdfwr

Nashville Corps Water Management Office
For Wolf Creek Dam release information: (615) 736-5635

Tennessee Valley Authority
Address: 400 West Summit Hill Dr.; Knoxville, TN 37902
Phone: (865) 632-2101
Email: tvainfo@tva.gov
Gauge information for Wolf Creek Dam: tva.gov/lakes/wch_r.htm

US Army Corps of Engineers
Nashville District: (for Cumberland and Laurel Lakes)
Address: PO Box 1070; Nashville, TN 37202
Phone: (615) 736-7161
For Wolf Creek Dam release information: (606) 678-8697
Cumberland River at Burkesville: tinyurl.com/mocpg8h
Cumberland River at Rowena: tinyurl.com/k9csstu

Huntington District: (for Paintsville Lake)
Address: 205 8th St.; Huntington, WV 25701
Phone: (304) 529-5452

Louisville District: (for Cave Run, Nolin and Taylorsville Lakes)
Address: PO Box 59; Louisville, KY 40201-0059
Phone: (502) 582-5736
Lake reports: tinyurl.com/lbacp76

US Geological Survey

Address: 9818 Bluegrass Pkwy.; Jeffersontown, KY 40299
Phone: (502) 493-1900
Website: http://ky.water.usgs.gov/
Gauge Information for Dix River: tinyurl.com/mkpb6w8

Local Retailers

Delamere & Hopkins

Address: Hyde Park Square, 2708 Erie Ave.; Cincinnati, OH 45208
Phone: (513) 871-FISH
Website: bestgear.com/Cincinnati
Social media: Facebook at http://tinyurl.com/k3xauap

Fly and Shot

3516 Dixie Highway; Erlanger, KY 41018
Phone: (859) 342-7700
Website: flyandshot.com

Golden Rule Flyshop

Email: goldenruleflyshop@hotmail.com
Website: goldenruleflyshop.com

The Lexington Angler

Address: 119 Clay Ave.; Lexington, KY 40502
Phone: (859) 389-6552
Website: lexingtonangler.com
Social media: Facebook at http://tinyurl.com/os3p4fv

Smyrna Bait and Tackle

Address: 8205 Smyrna Pkwy.; Louisville, KY 40228
Phone: (502) 964-9213
Email: Tackless@bellsouth.net
Website: smyrnabait.com
Social media: facebook.com/SmyrnaBaitAndTackle

National Retailers

Bass Pro Shops – Cincinnati Area

Address: 300 Cincinnati Mills Dr.; Forest Park, OH 45240
Phone: (513) 826-5200
Website: basspro.com
Social media: facebook.com/bassproshops

Bass Pro Shops – Louisville Area
Address: 951 East Lewis and Clark Pkwy.; Clarksville, IN 47129
Phone: (812) 218-5500
Website: basspro.com
Social media: facebook.com/bassproshops

Cabela's
Address: 5100 Norton Healthcare Blvd.; Louisville, KY 40241
Phone: (502) 365-9020
Website: cabelas.com
Social media: facebook.com/Cabelas

Gander Mountain
Address: 725 Bluegrass Farms Blvd., Suite 1; Bowling Green, KY 42104
Phone: (270) 842-0855
Website: gandermountain.com
Social media: Facebook at http://tinyurl.com/m4g54sj

Orvis – Cincinnati
Address: 77367 Kenwood Rd.; Cincinnati, OH 45236
Phone: (513) 791-2325
Website: orvis.com/kenwood

Orvis – Louisville
Address: 4288 Summit Plaza Dr.; Louisville, KY 40241
Phone: (502) 425-0198
Website: orvis.com/louisville

Sportsman's Warehouse
Address: 2200 War Admiral Way; Lexington, KY 40509
Phone: (859) 263-7000
Website: sportsmanswarehouse.com
Social media: Facebook at http://tinyurl.com/o5ljhzq

Web Resources

Animated Knots
Website: animatedknots.com

Fly Tying Forum
Website: Flytyingforum.com

Southeast Flyfishing Forum
Website: southeastflyfishingforum.com
Social media: facebook.com/SouthEastFlyFishingForum

Troutnut
Photographs of aquatic insects and much more
Website: Troutnut.com

Outfitters: Cumberland Tailwater

Cumberland Drifters Guide Service
Phone: (859) 983-2907 or (859) 492-7906
Website: cumberlanddrifters.com
Social media: Facebook at http://tinyurl.com/ldj7ueq

Cumberland River Fly Fishing
Phone: Louisville (502) 412-7001; Burkesville (270) 433-6007; Cell (502) 432-2727
Email: jnw@bluegrass.net

Double D Outfitters
Phone: (502) 538-8919
Email: ddflyfisher@alltel.com
Website: doubledoutfitters.com

Gone Fishing Professional Guide Service
Phone: (270) 459-1474
Email: bryanbihl@wegonefishing.com

Ken Glenn's Trout Guiding
Phone: (270) 843-3701
Email: kenglenntroutguiding@att.net

Kentucky Trophy Fishing
Phone: (270) 433-6333
Email: kytrophyfish@msn.com
Website: kytrophyfishing.com

Rainbow Guide Service
Phone: (270) 433-7674
Email: rainbowguide@hotmail.com
Website: rainbowguideservice.fghp.com

Southeastern Anglers
Phone: (866) 55-TROUT(87688) or (770) 655-9210
Website: southeasternanglers.com
Social media: Facebook at http://tinyurl.com/n227oau
Stewart's Guide Service
Phone: (502) 330-5267
john@stewartsguideservice.com

Trout-bumz
Phone: (270) 585-4339
Email: capt.joshuaroberts@trout-bumz.com
Website: trout-bumz.blogspot.com

Wolf Creek Outfitters
Phone: (270) 343-2510
Email: wolfcrk@duo-county.com
Website: fishwolfcreek.com

Outfitters: Dix River

Dix River Adventures
Phone: (859) 705-3198
Email: brad@dixriveradventures.com
Website: dixriveradventures.com
Social media: facebook.com/dixriveradventures

Southeastern Anglers
Phone: (866) 55-TROUT(87688) or (770) 655-9210
Website: southeasternanglers.com
Social media: Facebook at http://tinyurl.com/qedyygr

Appendix 2:
Fishable Waters for Select Kentucky Streams, Lakes and Tailwaters

Note: Stream classifications are not applicable for lakes and tailwaters.

Name and Stream Classification	Location	Miles / Acres of Trout Fishing Waters
Bark Camp Creek (II)	Mouth to US Forest Service Road #193	3.9 miles
Big Bone Creek (IV)	Big Bone Lick State Park	2.1 miles
Big Caney Creek (I)	0.5 miles upstream of mouth to 9.2 miles upstream	8.7 miles
Cane Creek (II)	Mouth to 6.6 miles upstream	6.6 miles
Casey Creek (II)	Mouth to 3.6 miles upstream	3.6 miles
Cave Run Lake Tailwater	Dam to 1.2 miles downstream	1.2 miles
Chimneytop Creek (II)	Mouth of creek to 2.3 miles upstream and 1.0 mile up Right Fork	3.3 miles
Herrington Lake (Dix River) Tailwater	Dam to mouth of the Dix River	2.0 miles
Dog Fork (I)	Falls to headwaters	1.0 miles
East Fork of Indian Creek (III)	Mouth of creek to 5.3 miles upstream	5.3 miles
Floyd's Fork (IV)	Multiple access points	19 miles
Greenbo Lake	Not Applicable	181 acres
Hatchery Creek	Wolf Creek National Fish Hatchery to Cumberland River	1.1 miles
Cumberland River Tailwater	Wolf Creek Dam to KY/TN border	75.2 miles
Laurel Creek (II)	0.1 mile above Stegall Cold Springs Rd to 4.1 miles downstream	4.2 miles
Laurel River Lake	Not Applicable	6,060 acres

Lick Creek (II)	Mouth to 6.6 miles upstream	6.6 miles
Lynn Camp Creek (I)	From the mouth of Brushy Creek to 5.1 miles upstream	5.1 miles
Middle Fork of the Red River (IV)	From mouth of Mill Creek Downstream to Hwy 11 bridge	3.8 miles
Mill Creek Lake	Not Applicable	41 acres
Nolin River Tailwater	Dam to 1.5 miles downstream	1.5 miles
Otter Creek (IV)	Mouth to 9.7 miles upstream	9.7 miles
Paintsville Lake	Not Applicable	1,139 acres
Paintsville Lake Tailwater	Dam to upper Hwy 460 bridge	3.8 miles
Parched Corn Creek (I)	From the falls upstream to 2nd tributary on left	1.1 miles
Rock Creek (IV)	From the confluence of White Oak Creek to KY/TN border	18.6 miles
Roundstone Creek (I)	From KY Hwy 1391 bridge downstream 2.5 miles to KY Hwy 1140	2.5 miles
Royal Springs (II)	Mouth to Georgetown Water Treatment Plant	0.7 miles
Russell Fork (III)	Mouth of Elkhorn Creek upstream to VA border	3.0 miles
Sinking Creek (III)	Hwy 60 bridge to Rosetta Corners Rd. bridge	4.5 miles
Sulphur Spring Creek (II)	From 2.7 miles upstream of mouth to CR 1244 bridge	4.2 miles
Swift Camp Creek (IV)	Mouth to 1.8 miles upstream	1.8 miles
Taylorsville Lake Tailwater	Dam to KY Hwy 55	3.1 miles
Trammel Creek (II)	From mouth of little Trammel Creek upstream 4.4 miles	4.4 miles
War Fork Creek (II)	Turkey Foot Recreation Area upstream to Steer Fork	1.1 miles
Wood Creek Lake	Not Applicable	672 acres

Glossary

A

Attractor   An artificial fly that resembles no particular insect but can be effective when other flies seem not to work.

B

Backing   The uniform, braided fishing line first spooled on a reel and the last to be ripped off by a fish.

Barb   A sharp point facing backward on the tip of a hook.

Barbless Hook   A hook without a barb or one with the barb mashed down.

Bend Pool   A deepwater depression along a bank in a river or stream caused by direct wash of water into that bank.

C

Catch-n-Release   Practice of releasing fish immediately.

CDC   Abbreviation for Cul de Canard: the soft wet-proof feathers of ducks.

Culling   Replacing a previously caught fish with another (typically larger) fish, allowing the angler to stay within the creel limit.

D

Delayed Harvest   Practice of releasing fish immediately during a legally imposed period of time.

Desiccant   A fine powder that cleans wetted dry flies and absorbs water from them.

Diptera   Latin name for a group of tiny, two-winged insects including houseflies and midges.

Disc Drag   A small pad inside a reel, adjustable by a button outside the reel that can alter line tension.

Double Taper (DT)   A term describing the identical taper on both ends of a class of fly lines that can be turned around when one end wears out.

Drag   Failure of a fly's speed to match that of the water's.

Dropper   The lowest wet fly attached on a tandem of flies.

Dun   A sexually immature adult mayfly emerging from the larva state: a subimago

E

Emerger   An aquatic insect in transformation from the larva to the adult.

Ephemeroptera   Latin name for a group of aquatic insects including mayflies having very long larva lives and very short adult lives.

208

F

Flex Speed	The slow, moderate or fast action of a fly rod's bending moment imparted by accelerated rod motion.
Floatant	A thin, water repellant oil or paste applied to dry flies to keep them floating.
Fly Rod Weight	The weight of the fly line that the rod is designed to use (and not the actual weight of the rod.)
Foam Line	A thin width of rapidly flowing water carrying air bubbles or bits of debris.
Forceps	Device used to remove fishhooks from fish mouths.

H

Hatch	Emergence of adult aquatic insects above the water.
High Sticking	A continuous down, up and down motion of a rod with a short length of line attached, to present a fly in a natural drift in flowing water.
Hook Keeper	A tiny metal loop of wire attached above the fly rod handle to secure an otherwise dangling fly.

I

Imago	A fully mature insect in the reproductive state.
Imitator	Artificial fly designed to imitate a specific insect.
Indicator	A small oval or elliptical float attached to the leader that jiggles when a fish strikes a wet fly.

L

Leader	A 7- to 15-foot-long tapered, transparent, nylon or fluorocarbon line tied to the end of the fly line.
Level Taper (LT)	Term for the end-to-end uniform diameter and weight of inexpensive fly lines.
Loading	Adding potential energy into a fly rod by accelerating the casting stroke.

M

Mend	Arc-like motion of the rod out and upstream that lifts the belly of the line off the water reducing drag on the line and fly in the water.
Midge	A tiny, two-winged fly in either the larva or adult state.

N

Natural Drift   Term for drag-free movement of fly line and fly.

P

Pawl Drag   A small, spring-loaded, pointed tongue engaging a cogwheel inside a reel, adjustable by a button outside the case, that can alter line tension.

Plecoptera   Latin name for a group of aquatic insects that includes stoneflies.

Plunge Pool   A deepwater depression at the base of a waterfall.

Pocket Water   A relatively still, deep, partially enclosed parcel of water in a stream or river.

Pull Cast   A type of cast where raising then dropping the tip of a fly rod imparts slack in the fly line.

R

Reach   An arc-like motion of the fly rod out and upstream while the fly line is airborne that minimizes drag.

Redd   A fanned out nest in a gravel bed into which a female fish lays her eggs.

Riffle   A stretch of shallow choppy water flowing over gravel or small rocks.

Root Wad   A mass of partially exposed tree or bush roots usually along the bank of a river or stream.

Run   A long, narrow stretch of flowing water in a stream or river.

S

Scour Hole   A deep depression in the floor of a river or stream usually caused by water flowing under an in-stream obstruction.

Seam   The line formed by abutting edges of water moving at different speeds. In fishing, frequently refers to a thin segment of rapidly flowing water adjacent to and beyond a surface obstruction in a river or stream.

Single Haul   Adding length to a basic cast by pulling extra line downward simultaneously with the forward cast and releasing it as the forward loop uncoils.

Sink Tip (ST)   A term describing the short, front section of a class of fly lines that sinks below the surface.

Sipping   Act of fish engulfing insects off the surface without leaving the water.

Slick   A long, smooth pool of water in a stream or river.

Slot Limit   A management tool that increases the number of fish surviving in a specified size range.

Snake Guides	Small wire loops lined up on a fly rod through which the fly line passes during a cast.
Snippets	Small clippers for snipping leaders and tippets and a needle for cleaning out hook eyes.
Spinner	Sexually mature adult mayfly in the reproductive state with transparent wings: an imago.
Strike	Term for fish eating a fly.
Stripping Guide	The small guide closest to the handle of a fly rod.
Stripping	Short, rapid retractions of fly line while fishing wet flies.
Subimago	An immature adult insect, e.g. a dun mayfly.

T

Tailout	Describes the water streaming out of a riffle or pool.
Tailrace	A section of a river immediately below a dam bordered by abutments.
Tailwater	Section of a river below a dam.
Take	Angler's term for a fish taking a fly.
Thermocline	A thin, horizontal zone in a lake separating warm water from cool water, notably during the summer months.
Tip Top	The line guide at the tip of a fly rod.
Tippet	A short, uniform segment of transparent, nylon or fluorocarbon line attached to the end of the leader.
Trichoptera	Latin name for a group of aquatic insects including caddisflies that have swept-back wings.
Turnover	Describes the dipping motion of a fly prior to the line landing on the water.

U

Unloading	Releasing the potential energy from a flexed fly rod into the fly line by an abrupt stop of the casting stroke.

W

Weight Forward (WF)	A term for the greater weight and diameter of the front section of a class of fly lines.

X

X-ratings	Method of designating the diameter and strength of leaders and tippets. (1X to 8X)

Z

Zinger	A spring-loaded string in a small case to which tools can be attached for rapid use and retraction.

Index